SURVIVANGHAI

THE JOURNALS OF
FRED MARCUS 1939–49

Audrey Friedman Marcus/Rena Krasno

With a Foreword by Deborah E. Lipstadt
Diary Translation from German by Rena Krasno

Pacific View Press
Berkeley, California

Text copyright © 2008 Audrey Friedman Marcus and Rena Krasno
Diary translation by Rena Krasno
Cover and interior design by Nancy Ippolito
Cover photo: Fritz and his father Semmy on the balcony of their apartment,
340 Tiendong Road (above the "T" in Tiendong)
ISBN 978-1-881896-29-6

All rights reserved. No part of this book may be used or reproduced,
stored in a retrieval system, or transmitted, in any form or by any means,
electronic, mechanical, photocopying, recording, or otherwise without prior
permission in writing from the publisher. Address inquiries to Pacific View
Press, P.O. Box 2897, Berkeley, CA 94702 or e-mail: pvp2@mindspring.com.
Website: www.pacificviewpress.com

Library of Congress Cataloging-in-Publication Data

Marcus, Fred, d. 2002.
   Survival in Shanghai : the journals of Fred Marcus, 1939-49 / [with com-
mentary by] Audrey Friedman Marcus, Rena Krasno ; with a foreword by Deborah
E. Lipstadt ; diary translation by Rena Krasno.
       p. cm.
   Includes bibliographical references and index.
   ISBN 978-1-881896-29-6
   1. Marcus, Fred, d. 2002--Diaries. 2. Jews, German--China--Shanghai--
Diaries. 3. Refugees, Jewish--China--Shanghai--Diaries. 4. Young men--China--
Shanghai--Diaries. 5. World War, 1939-1945--Refugees. 6. World War, 1939-1945-
-China--Shanghai. 7. Shanghai (China)--Biography. 8. Shanghai (China)--Social
conditions--20th century. 9. Shanghai (China)--History--20th century. 10. Jews,
German--United States--Biography. I. Marcus, Audrey Friedman. II. Krasno,
Rena, 1923- III. Title.
   DS135.C5M37 2008
   940.53'51132092--dc22
   [B]
                                                    2008039703

Printed in the United States of America

Ad Astra Per Aspera.
To the stars, despite adversity.

Dedication

To Rabbi Theodore Alexander and his parents, who saved a bereaved young man from despair, and to his wife, Gertrude Alexander, for her valued friendship and help. And, of course, to Fred, whose wanderings brought him—and a deep and lasting love—into my life.

—Audrey Friedman Marcus

To my beloved parents, David and Aida Rabinovich, and other Shanghai Jews who opened their hearts and homes to European refugees fleeing Hitler.

—Rena Krasno

Contents

PART III:
HOME AT LAST

Foreword

German Jews began to find refuge in Shanghai shortly after the Nazi party came to power in 1933. Initially only a relatively small number of German Jews chose Shanghai as their destination. The number of refugees increased greatly after Kristallnacht (1938), when Jewish homes, places of business, synagogues, and communal institutions were destroyed in a nationwide pogrom. Thousands of Jews were arrested and placed in concentration camps and an undetermined number were actually killed. By 1939 there were approximately 17,000 German and Austrian Jews in Shanghai. Eventually, the German/Austrian refugees would be joined by about 2,000 Polish Jews in the early 1940s.

Shanghai was particularly attractive to these refugees because, at a time when most countries were severely limiting the number of Jews who could settle within their borders, no visa was required to enter there. (In 1939 that would be changed and a landing permit would be necessary.) Ironically, the Japanese, who would become Germany's ally and who took control of major portions of the city in 1937, were instrumental in providing this Jewish sanctuary .

The Jews who found refuge there overwhelmed the far smaller Sephardic community of Jews whose ancestors had come primarily from Iraq in the mid-nineteenth century and Russian Jews who came after the 1917 revolution.

If one compares life in Shanghai for a Jew who fled Europe to the fate of those who did not succeed in escaping, it can be said to have been fairly benign. Life was difficult. Food and material goods were in short supply. Movement was restricted. Nonetheless, some Jews managed to start small businesses and cottage industries. Others worked as doctors, teachers, and other professionals. Those who could not earn enough to survive were able to turn to charitable funds for support. The American Jewish Joint Distribution Committee (the "Joint") provided much of this aid.

The Japanese did not deport Jews nor send them to concentration camps. Most of the Jews who died did so of "natural" causes. Of course, those causes were exacerbated or even created by hunger, lack of medicine, overcrowded conditions, and psychological trauma. Truth be told, the only way in which the conditions in Shanghai can actually be considered benign is if one compares them to the alternative.

Fred Marcus gives us a unique insight into the day-to-day life for a young German Jew in Shanghai. He relates how he manages to find work, food, transportation (getting his bike fixed becomes a major challenge), and friends. He describes the death of his father and his feelings about being left alone in this strange environment.

His diary is not the stuff of high drama. Fred was not, after all, at the center of any major negotiations. He was not a leader of the ghetto. He was a young man on his own, who knew that he had no one to lean on but himself. His loneliness is palpable. But Fred epitomized the notion of "survivor." He does not succumb but manages to overcome the myriad of obstacles facing him. One feels him always trying to find ways to better his situation.

Fred's diary gives one the sense of everyday life in Shanghai. The struggle for survival is intense and Fred's words make that clear. The challenge in front of him is not only physical survival. He must also find friends who will become his "family" during these difficult days. Fred speaks of all this in his diary. In fact, these small details provide readers with a sense of what life was like in Shanghai.

The diary does not end with Japan's defeat, but continues until his arrival in the United States. Readers cannot help but get the feeling that they are making the transition to his new life together with him.

History is written from both the "macro" and "micro" perspective. We must know the "big" picture, but it is the small details which give that picture depth and texture. Fred Marcus's diary together with the commentary and elaboration provided by his wife Audrey and Rena Krasno open a window onto the life of a Jewish refugee in Shanghai during the dreadful years of the *Shoah*.

Deborah E. Lipstadt, Ph.D.
Dorot Professor of Modern Jewish and Holocaust Studies
Emory University

Preface

In March of 1939, Fritz Marcus and his father Samuel traveled overland to Genoa where they set sail for the long journey to Shanghai, a strange and exotic city in the Far East that became a haven for some 20,000 Jews fleeing Nazi Europe. Their lives would be forever changed by that voyage. The boy who had known only the comfortable circumstances of upper middle class life in Berlin was plummeted into an unfamiliar culture in which he had to make his way.

Fritz (later called Fred) became the husband of Audrey Friedman in 1974. She soon learned from him that he had kept diaries in Shanghai, written in German. Intrigued, Audrey suggested time and again that Fred translate the diaries. While he seemed to like the idea, he kept putting it off. He offered many excuses. He was too busy with his work, and when not working, he wanted to be with family, to travel, to study, to teach. He didn't have the right kind of tape recorder. He would do it when he retired.

In 2002, Fred died without having done the translation.

What, Audrey wondered, could the diaries reveal about Fred's life as a young man in a strange land? What were the enormous challenges and difficulties he and the other refugees had to face? How did he make enough money to survive? Who were his friends, his confidants? What did he do for fun? What was Jewish life like in Shanghai? What were his wartime experiences? What did he do after the war? Why did he remain in Shanghai until 1949, leaving just ahead of the Communist takeover? And, perhaps most puzzling, why did he resist translating the diaries? Would the recollections have been too painful? Were there things in the diaries he did not want others to know?

It was indeed a great mystery, and one Audrey wanted very much to unravel. She felt that the diaries, which were written by Fred solely for himself, would be the key to his past, about which he had spoken only in general terms. Further, it would be one of the very few day-to-day records of refugee life in Shanghai during the 1940s and therefore a true historical record of those tumultuous times. She decided to seek a translator.

The translation of the diaries, however, presented innumerable problems. The task required someone who had a broad knowledge of history in general and of the wartime years in particular, a person who was compassionate and able to envision the translation as both a contribution to family history and refugee Shanghai lore. These qualifications eliminated commercial translation services. Moreover, the translator would have to be someone with infinite patience and skill, as Fred's handwriting was extremely difficult to read, particularly in the first diary, which deals with the trauma of the war years and the segregation of European Jewish refugees by the Japanese occupying forces. Furthermore, the quality of the wartime ink was poor, resulting in somewhat faded writing in the diaries.

In January of 2003, Audrey saw a notice in her local Jewish newspaper that a woman named Rena Krasno was giving a talk at Congregation Emanuel in Denver. Some years before, Audrey had read and enjoyed Rena's book, *Strangers Always: A Jewish Family in Wartime China.* Audrey decided to attend the talk. As she listened intently to the captivating stories and facts about growing up a Russian Jewish girl in Shanghai from 1923 to the end of the 1940s, she was impressed with Rena's energy and intelligence. In the course of her lecture, Rena mentioned that she spoke six languages, among which was . . . German. She also revealed that she had done simultaneous translations for a number of international organizations. What could be more perfect, thought Audrey; here before her was her translator.

Shortly after that, Audrey wrote to Rena about the diaries and about Fred, his early life, and later accomplishments. The idea of reading and translating a young man's diary that contained daily short notes on the events through which both of them had lived fascinated Rena. After examining several sample pages, it was clear that she could read (most of) what Fred had written!

And thus began their long collaboration, which blossomed over several years into a beautiful friendship and resulted in this book based on the Shanghai diaries of Fred Marcus.

Although a number of memoirs have been written about Shanghai, none reflect in such precise detail daily events or indicate how historic developments changed the lives of refugees in subtle and sometimes brutal ways. The authors have carried out rigorous research on the facts contained in the diaries, adding historic background and little-known information regarding events Fred wrote about that influenced life in Shanghai directly or indirectly. Yet, while it is historically accurate, this book is not meant to be an academic tome. The pertinent references are cited in the bibliography, but there are no footnotes or endnotes to interrupt the flow of the story. *Survival in Shanghai* is a poignant coming-of-age story of a young man forced by Nazi horror and world war to overcome desperate circumstances.

Fred Marcus's diaries were written solely for himself. With rare exceptions, he wrote without emotion about the events through which he lived, reporting in a matter-of-fact manner an account of each day's happenings. Because these diaries were written at the time rather than many years after the events took place, they form a remarkable historic document. They also demonstrate the human capacity to adapt to difficult and unfamiliar circumstances. Through it all, Fred never lost his courage, never complained, and, in spite of increasing pressures, injustice, and cruelty, ploughed forward, attempting to maintain intellectual and moral standards.

The authors wish to thank the following individuals whose invaluable help furthered this project: Gertrude and Ted Alexander, Fred's dearest friends, whose unflagging help, excellent advice, and patient response to numerous questions, as well as readings of several versions of the book, clarified details of Fred's years in Shanghai; Dr. Deborah E. Lipstadt, who graciously offered to write the Foreword; Renae Levin and Rabbi Raymond A. Zwerin, readers who were generous with their time and honest in their appraisal; David Marcus, who offered much encouragement as we wrote about the Shanghai experiences of his father as a young man; Erich Call-mann, a walking encyclopedia about refugee life in Shanghai, who was a constant source of information and help, and who responded speedily to every query and was kind enough to loan some of his photographs; Sonja Mühlberger of Berlin, who devoted many years to research on refugees in Shanghai, and was always willing to share her knowledge; Dorothy Fleischner (Thea), for her help and her friendship; and Margit Diamond, for her reminiscences of her aunt, Lucie Hartwich, the headmistress of the Kadoorie School in Shanghai.

Special thanks are also due to Helene DeGroodt-Belt, for her photos and vivid memories of Fred and of the months she and her husband, Capt. Frank DeGroodt, spent in Shanghai after World War II, and especially for sharing the remarkable columns she wrote for *The Enquirer and News* in Battle Creek, Michigan; Vadym Kavsan, who meticulously researched the correct spelling of cities mentioned by Fred as he followed, regardless of Japanese censorship, Russia's military campaign against Germany and the Normandy invasion; Tess Johnston, a loyal friend and longtime resident of China, who replied in detail to requests for information; Dr. Warren Capell, who sought information from his colleagues on the medicines doctors prescribed for Fred; Miriam Gross, for the loan of her superb unpublished thesis, "An Oral History of the Shanghai Jewish Community"; Robert Nevitt, former USIS/USIA Director for East Asia and the Pacific, for his sleuthing abilities; the Dorot Jewish Division of the New York Public Library, for their assistance with research; Audrey's writers group: Joyce Fine, Dyana Furmansky, Rebecca Reynolds, and Rachel Pollack, for listening intently and providing sage advice; Hanan Krasno and Wes Blomster for their attempts at deciphering almost illegible passages; Gabby Korn and June Morrall, Fred's cousins, both of whom are mentioned in his diaries, for their help in sorting out Fred's family relationships; Ed Diner for his insights and memories of his military service in China after World War II; Jack Cain for sharing his stories; Leah Mehler for information on the Mirrer Yeshiva; Faith Goldman, who offered continued encouragement and generously shared the fruits of her own research; and especially Nancy Ippolito, Bob Schildgen, and Pam Zumwalt of Pacific View Press for their caring support and expert advice throughout the publishing process.

A particular debt of gratitude is owed to Dr. David Kranzler for his pioneering and comprehensive work, *Japanese, Nazis & Jews: The Jewish Refugee Community of Shanghai 1938–1945*, the first scholarly account of this experience, and for his painstaking read of and detailed comments on this manuscript. Sadly, Dr. Kranzler passed away in December 2007.

Special mention must be made of Shanghailanders not cited above who willingly submitted to interviews and related their past life experiences in an open and candid manner: Gerda Alexander Abramchik, Ruth Callmann, Marion Elliot, the late Morris Feder, Arthur Feiner, Daisy Flynn, Steffi Gelb, Marion Goldstein, Gertrude Gruenberg, Horst "Peter" Eisfelder, Trude Kutner, Margot Luftman, Klaus Marcus, Ruth Marcus, Gary Matzdorff, Henry Meyer, Inna Mink, Eva Perkal, Evelyn Pike Rubin, Armando Salinas, Herta Shriner, Judy and Ernie Urman, and Trixie and Frank Wachsner. Their help is deeply appreciated. Sincere apologies to anyone who has been inadvertently left out.

Names of former refugees used in this book are the actual names of individuals. All monies are quoted in local currency (marks or Shanghai dollars) unless otherwise noted.

PART I:

ESCAPE FROM EVIL

Prologue

Berlin, November 10, 1938, from the Writings of Fritz Marcus: I'll always remember the morning after Kristallnacht. Since I had started going to the Jewish school, I had to take the elevated S-Bahn, the electric train, about five stops to the Hackescher Markt station with my school friend, Herbert Giesen. Herbert boarded the train three or four stops before me. We were in the habit of riding together and then walking from the station the three and a half blocks to the school. On this particular morning, I got on the train, carrying my briefcase. I found Herbert standing in our regular car. I tossed my briefcase across the breadth of the train car so that it landed with a big bang at Herbert's feet. This caused consternation among the proper adults on the train. Standing next to Herbert, I greeted him, then noticed that he was as pale as a sheet.

I said, "What's the matter, are you sick?" He only mumbled.

"What is the matter with you?" I persisted. Again, Herbert wouldn't say, which I found very annoying.

"For God's sake," I said, "I'm your friend! Tell me what's wrong." Still no response. I was really becoming angry. Finally, we came to our school station and got off. When we were out in the open, he looked over his shoulder and said, "You know near the station Zoologischer Garten, where the train passes the synagogue on the Fasanenstrasse?"

"Yes," I replied. "I know the train goes by there and you can see the synagogue from the train."

Herbert continued, "Well, the synagogue was on fire."

"On fire?" I exclaimed.

"Yes! It was burning. The fire department was there but, as far as I could tell, they weren't doing much."

This surprised me and, when we got to school, every student who had passed a synagogue reported seeing that synagogue on fire.

The last five years, since Hitler came to power, had been a period of political upheaval and rising Nazism, leading to increasing anguish and uncertainty for Jews in Germany. For Samuel "Semmy" Marcus and his 14-year-old son, Fritz, it was also a time of deep personal grief. Semmy's beloved wife, Gertrud, had succumbed to heart disease in May of 1938 after a long illness, and the widower, devastated by his loss, was unable to concentrate on plans to escape from the menace of Fascism. Fritz, still a teenager, was far too young to focus on the dangers that lay ahead. Deprived of a mother's love, he felt confused and alone. Days of mourning and inaction followed for father and son. *[See Figure 1 for a photo of Gertrud's grave. According to the custom in Germany, she was cremated.]*

With the advent of Kristallnacht on the night of November 9–10, 1938, every hope that the situation for Jews in Germany would improve was shattered, along with the broken glass. That night, and into the next morning, Nazi gangs smashed the windows of Jewish stores throughout Germany and then looted the shops. Virtually every synagogue was destroyed or damaged, including the Levetzowstrasse Synagoge, where Semmy and his family attended services. According to *The Holocaust Encyclopedia,* 20,000 to 30,000 Jews were arrested, many of whom were sent to concentration camps; 7,500 stores were looted, and 91 Jews were killed. This event, later called "Night of Broken Glass," was the culmination of the Nuremberg Laws and other ordinances aimed at removing Jews from the economy. The provocation for the Nazi leadership to launch the massive and well organized pogrom was provided by the shooting by a young Jew, Herschel Grynszpan, of Third Secretary Ernst vom Rath in Paris. Grynszpan was distraught over his parents' desperate situation when, deported by the Nazis with other Jews who held Polish passports, they were driven over the border into Poland.

Now that there could no longer be any doubt that urgent action was imperative, father and son finally began to speak about leaving Germany. They proceeded as many other families did: they made numerous inquiries and spent hours sitting on the floor together studying maps, with geography books and bulky encyclopedias spread out before them. They also read about the principal products of various countries, what grains, fruit, and vegetables grew there, the climate and average rainfall, almost in the manner that one prepares for a pleasure trip. The world lay before them, but at that late date, where could they go? What country would accept them? Bolivia? Peru? Argentina? Madagascar? China?

Thoughts surely rushed in a mad jumble through Semmy's mind as he and Fritz pursued their research. Semmy and his brother Martin were successful manufacturers of men's ties. Germany was their homeland, their *"Heimat,"* where the Marcus family had lived for generations. In World War I, Semmy had served in Germany's armed forces and was awarded the Iron Cross. *[See Figure 2 for photo of Semmy in uniform.]* He was now 64 years old. At this stage of his life, how could he start over in a strange environment and support himself and his son? Would his health hold up in a tropical climate?

By the end of the year, a decision was made. Semmy purchased tickets for March 29, 1939 out of Genoa on the flagship of the Lloyd Triestino line, the *Conte Biancamano.* The destination? Shanghai, an open port that required no visa or proof of capital, and which—until the doors closed—became a haven for many refugees from Nazism.

Semmy set about liquidating the tie business, as well as G. Marcus Shirt Materials, a small business owned by his wife that had supplied shirt fabric to the many fine custom shirt makers in Berlin. (Fritz's after-school job had been to deliver the fabric by subway all over Berlin.)

While Fritz's childhood was marred by the illness of his mother and the rise of Nazism, it had also been characterized by many happy times. He felt very close to his parents and extended family, lived in comfortable surroundings, and was immersed in the richness of German culture. Now, preparing to leave behind all that he had ever known, the boy couldn't help but look back at the memorable people and events, both pleasant and harsh, that were part of his first years.

His paternal grandfather Sally (a derivative of Salomon or Solomon) was a short man with a white pointed, neatly trimmed beard, of the type the Germans called a *Spitzbart*. Grandmother Doris, a tiny, white-haired lady, always wore high necked black taffeta dresses with a little touch of white lace at the neck and sleeves. Friday evenings were spent at the grandparents' apartment. Before the Sabbath dinner, Fritz and his cousins Gert and Klaus received the traditional blessing of the children from their grandfather.

Fritz's maternal grandparents were Fritz and Berta Kowalewski, Protestants, who died before he was born. (Fritz's mother converted to Judaism when she married his father.) His maternal aunts played a significant role in his childhood, particularly Tante Ella, who was like a second mother to him. Because she was unmarried and had sufficient time, she took it upon herself to assist Fritz's mother, who suffered from chronic heart disease. Tante Ella was a "schoolmistress" type who adored Fritzchen (little Fritz), and taught him good manners and perfect High German.

Semmy, Fritz's father, was a dapper, if not to say, elegant gentleman.

He was often photographed with a cigar in his hand at a resort on the Baltic Sea where the family spent summer vacations, informally dressed in shirtsleeves, but wearing flannel pants and a tie. *[See Figure 3 for photo of Semmy and Fritz on the beach.]* He met Gertrud at an outdoor concert in the Berlin Zoo, and married her when he was nearly 50 years old. *[See Figure 4 for photo of Gertrud.]* She was a sweet, good-hearted woman, who dressed her Fritz in stylish, expensive clothes that caused him to complain that he felt like a *Zierpuppe,* (a doll with a delicate porcelain face and a black beauty spot). Semmy, who traveled during the week for his business, took on the responsibiity of teaching and amusing Fritz on weekends. Little Fritz adored both his parents, especially his dad, and on their birthdays wrote them sweet notes and occasional poems. The family took wonderful trips together to the North Sea, the Harz Mountains, and Marienbad in Czechoslovakia.

Fritz began school in 1930 at V. Tietzenthaler, a private school near his home. Photos of that first day reveal a shy, well dressed child with the largest possible *"Schultüte,"* the horn filled with sweets given to each German child on the first day of school. *[See Figure 5.]* He completed his first four years of school in three years and immediately transferred in 1933 into the fifth grade at the Friederich Weldershe Gymnasium, an all-boys school with large classes of 35 to 40 students.

It was in the gymnasium that Fritz had his first experience with anti-Semitism. No longer did teachers say good morning when they entered the classroom; instead they called out "Heil Hitler," and gave the Nazi salute. During recess, the Nazi children threw water bombs, some containing rocks, at the Jewish students. In music class, if students were well behaved, they were rewarded with choosing the closing song. Invariably, the Nazi boys selected the "Horst Wessel Song," so closely identified with the Nazi movement that it had become a second German national anthem. (Horst Wessel was a Nazi Storm Trooper who was stabbed to death in unclear circumstances. Seizing the occasion, Joseph Goebbels, the Nazi propaganda chief, asserted that he was stabbed and killed by Communists in a brawl. The conniving Nazis made him into a martyr of their movement and glorified him in song.)

Another song favored by Fritz's schoolmates was the Nazi marching song in which appeared the infamous words, *"Und wenn das Judenblut vom Messer spritzt dann geht's nochmal so gut"* (When the blood of the Jews spurts from the knife, then everything is going even better). Twice a week, week after week, Fritz's classmates chose these songs, adding to the misery of the Jewish students who steadfastly refused to join in the singing.

Fritz would say later about these school experiences that they marked the end of his "sunny childhood."

During the Nazi era, theatres, restaurants, and other venues posted signs that said "Jews not wanted." However, the director of the Berlin Zoo, Dr. Heck, maintained that during World War I it was the Jews of Berlin who kept the animals alive by bringing them food, and he refused to put up such a sign. Thus, in Fritz's early teens, visiting the Berlin Zoo on his own became one of his sole outlets for fun. He especially liked *Das Grosse Raubtierhaus*, the Large Predator House, which housed lions, tigers, leopards, cheetahs, and jaguars. He became known to the caretakers, and after a time they let him help to feed and care for the animals. In the morning, he would even be allowed to hose out the cages. Once, as a reward, they took out the cheetah, whose name was Pardi, and put him on a park bench. With Fritz's camera, they photographed Fritz with his arm around the cheetah *[see Figure 6]*. It was because of these experiences at the zoo that Fritz aspired to become a zoologist, a goal that was never realized.

Anti-Semitism was on the rise, and the political situation was beginning to change. The infamous newspaper *Der Stürmer (The Stormtrooper)*, published by Julius Streicher, which was posted by the Nazis in wooden reading cases on street corners throughout Berlin, exposed Fritz to cartoons of Jews with huge noses and thick lips, and articles that described in exaggerated detail disgusting acts purportedly required by Jewish law. These denigrating newspaper stories affected Fritz's Jewish self-image in a very negative way, and he often felt ashamed to be a Jew.

Fritz saw Hitler on two occasions. The first time, he was on his way to the zoo, crossing the boulevard in the heart of the Tiergarten, the beautiful park near his home. People had lined the sidewalks, four and five deep on either side. Several open limousines drove by and Fritz caught sight of Hitler sitting erect in one of the cars. The women around him lifted up their children in adulation, hysterically sobbing and crying.

The second time, in another part of town, the crowds again thronged the sidewalks, waiting for Hitler to come by in a parade. Policemen stood shoulder to shoulder along the curbs in front of spectators craning their necks. The narrow space between the houses and the mob of people became the only place to walk. Fritz tried in vain to pass through, but was unable to squeeze by the throngs who pushed and pulled from all sides. Caught up in this human mass, he became frantic, until finally someone yelled, "There's a child in here, there's a child in here!" To his immense relief, Fritz was at last shoved free.

As a result of the changing political situation, Fritz's parents enrolled him in a Jewish school, the Jüdische Schule Grosse Hamburgerstrasse. In the *aula*, or auditorium, pictures of Leopold Zunz and Abraham Geiger and other great liberal Jews of the nineteenth century looked down solemnly upon the assembled students. A nearby park contained Berlin's oldest Jewish cemetery, and the tombstone of the great philosopher and Jewish leader, Moses Mendelssohn. The experience in the co-ed Jewish school was a happy one for Fritz, and he felt a sense of belonging that he had not felt in the *Gymnasium*. He received excellent academic training in secular subjects and a thorough Jewish education that included Hebrew and biblical history. After Kristallnacht, more practical subjects such as metalworking and cooking were introduced, which were geared to helping students to survive. One after the other, however, students (and teachers) emigrated or were sent away, leaving behind fellow students who were saddened, bewildered, and often depressed. By the end of 1938, only a handful of students remained, and these were placed in one classroom. The school, like all Jewish schools, was closed by the Nazis in 1942.

One of Fritz's friends in Berlin was Theo Rolf Alexander, a boy four years older than he. The Alexanders lived on the Flensburgerstrasse around the corner from the Marcus apartment on the Lessingstrasse. Theo Rolf's father, Hugo, worked on a part-time basis for the Jewish community. He sold High Holy Day tickets for the Levetzowstrasse Synagogue, and knew Fritz's parents quite well. Hugo, a salesman of hotel linens, realized in 1932 that he would lose his job and, with his wife, opened a stationery store. Fritz acted as an outside salesman for the Alexander family, and sold school supplies to his friends.

Fritz's mother died on July 17, 1938. In December, Fritz and Semmy made a solemn ceremony of disposing of his mother's bedside pills and barbiturates, flushing them down the toilet, as an affirmation of life. The furniture was sold and smaller items, such as fine china and lead crystal, Fritz's extensive Bar Mitzvah gifts (mostly expensive art books with color plates of famous paintings and sculptures) were packed in large cases called "lifts" and shipped to Shanghai.

Father and son then rented a room from a Jewish family on the Motzstrasse, where they lived until they left Germany. Their time was spent obtaining all the permits and clearances that were needed in order to be allowed to leave. They were required, for example, to have a clearance from the German equivalent of the U.S. Internal Revenue Service to show that no taxes were owed. And all valuable jewelry had to be sold at the state pawnshop, where it was purchased solely for the price of its weight in gold.

Still reeling from the shock of the recent loss of their wife and mother, Semmy and Fritz set out in March of 1939. Uncle Martin and his two sons were unable to obtain passage on the same ship. So Semmy and Fritz sailed ahead with cousin Gert, and Martin followed on May 31 with Klaus, also on the *Conte Biancamano*. In an unpublished autobiography, Fritz described the trip:

> After one night in Munich, we boarded the express train across the Brenner Pass, down through Italy, to Genoa. I was very surprised that I couldn't read any of the signs there, even the one for "Exit" from the railroad station.
>
> In Genoa, the hotel must have been paid for, because we left Germany with ten marks apiece in cash in our pockets, the equivalent of about US $2.50. (One could take only that much currency out of the country. The only thing we could do was prepay board money, as it was called, to be spent on board the ship for incidental expenses.)
>
> Dad and I carried German passports that were stamped with a large "J" for Jew. These passports expired 30 days from the date we left Germany. This meant that from that time on, we became stateless refugees who had no protection or rights.
>
> The next day, we were taken down to the ship and boarded the very elegant Conte Biancamano for a 29-day voyage from Genoa, Italy to Shanghai, China.

The luxury ship with four classes for passengers stopped in Naples, headed further south along the coast of Italy through the straits of Messina, then across the Mediterranean to Port Said and the Suez Canal into the Red Sea, stopping at Aden. From Aden, it sailed across the Indian Ocean to Bombay, where the passengers were not allowed to go ashore. From Bombay, it continued to Colombo, Ceylon (now Sri Lanka), Manila, Hong Kong, and finally Shanghai. For Fritz, the exotic ports, the Italian cuisine, exploring the ship, and making friends with the crew represented the greatest adventure of his young life. *[Fritz took many pictures on this trip, but in Shanghai he lacked the money to have them developed.]*

> The ship was most luxurious, and although we traveled in third class, the food was wonderful. There were three forks and three knives, two spoons, and a water glass set beside two wine glasses. I remember a lot of card playing aboard the ship and a few shore excursions, notably in Colombo and Singapore, where hawkers traded us a pineapple or a tropical pith helmet (which I aspired to acquire) in exchange for small personal items.

The strangest thing about the trip was that, during it, I never gave any real thought to what was in store for us. We had left Genoa on March 29, 1939, and arrived at Shanghai pier on April 25, 1939.

I

The Shock of Shanghai

The arrival of Semmy and Fritz in Shanghai after a journey of 7,000 miles was a momentous event in Fritz's life, one that remained deeply imprinted in his memory.

Although the name Shanghai means "on the sea," the city actually lies within the delta of the Yangtze, some miles up the Whangpoo River. When the British won the Opium War against the Chinese in 1842, one of their prizes was the fishing village, Shanghai. They called it "Muddy Flats." To control the strength of the river, the British reinforced its embankment. This process was called "bunding," hence the name "Bund," which was attributed to the wide thoroughfare along the Whangpoo.

By 1939, Shanghai had become the fifth largest city in the world, enjoying a very favorable geographic position: open to the Pacific and the navigable Whangpoo River, thus ensuring an easy flow of merchandise to and from the interior of China.

When Semmy and Fritz and the European passengers in their homburgs, double-breasted suits, and fur coats stepped onto the soil of Shanghai, they were totally unprepared for what greeted them. A cacophony of sounds assailed their ears: the honking of cars, ringing of bicycle bells, the chant of workmen carrying heavy burdens, the piercing shrieks of foot peddlers, the sharp whistles of Sikh traffic policemen, the warning cries of rickshaw men winding dangerously in and out of vehicles. Sometimes, a superstitious Chinese would rush in front of an oncoming car, thinking that the invisible devil chasing him would be crushed.

Along the Bund, smells of garbage and fish wafted from the brownish waters of the Whangpoo, mixed with those of sweat, gasoline, foods, and occasional whiffs of opium. Incongruously, also along the Bund, stood imposing buildings with marble halls and stone columns that reflected the colonial power of Great Britain. The British had imported immense Oregon pines to strengthen the foundations of the majestic stone buildings in Muddy Flats in order to prevent them from sinking in the mud.

Thus, on the Bund, destitution and wealth intermingled. *[See Figure 7 for photo of the Bund.]*

> Awaiting us ashore was a flatbed truck with wooden siding. We sat in the open, expressing concern for our baggage and were assured that it would follow us. We were driven into the district of Hongkew, which was then technically under Japanese rule. I saw Japanese sentries standing on the bridge.

Two years earlier in 1937 during the Sino-Japanese wars, the Japanese had conquered the surrounding countryside of China. Shanghai, however, remained an outpost of western administration and civilization in a part of China totally dominated by the Japanese.

The truck carried the newly arrived refugees into Hongkew—a romantic name meaning the "Mouth of the Rainbow." But there was nothing romantic about the area. Only one street, Broadway, had street lights; the rest were in total darkness. Foreign Shanghailanders called the area "The Badlands." According to Fritz:

> The fighting between the Chinese and invading Japanese had created an area resembling a bombed-out war zone. Only the shells of buildings remain standing, and with the exception of the jail and the occasional brick police station or school building, everything had been destroyed. What had not been burned out had been burned down. Anything left standing had been looted.
>
> A red brick school house was converted into a refugee shelter. Known as the Ward Road Heim *[literally "home," but actually "camp"]*, this became our first domicile since leaving the luxury ship. We were put into a large classroom, Room 17 on the second floor. Here, some 58 people were housed in double-decker bunk beds. The only private storage available was under the bed.

After a brief discussion with his father, Fritz chose the top bed for himself. The new arrivals were then told to go to the dining hall for a snack. Fritz later wrote about the initial shock that came over him:

> I recall a bare table of deeply scarred, unfinished wood. Someone passed down an open piece of white bread with two sardines on margarine, and I vividly remember a chipped enamel mug of tepid, pre-sweetened tea. The tears ran down my cheeks and mingled with the thin tea as I was absolutely and suddenly overwhelmed by my situation. At that moment, the fact of my refugee status became a reality to me. *[See Figure 8 for photo of the Ward Road Heim.]*

Conditions in the Heim were grim. Many refugees had to part with their possessions in order to survive. Some had been daring and had the foresight to hide jewelry in the linings of their coats and jackets and the hems of their skirts and dresses. They bartered these pieces, as well as embroidered tablecloths, wedding rings, silver cutlery, and fine porcelain for sardines, medications, candles, and razor blades. Some had precious antique jewelry to sell, and hence were able to set money aside to open small businesses.

To supplement the poor diet and pay for little necessities, Semmy also began to sell some personal belongings. His first sale: a beautiful lead crystal fruit bowl on a tall pedestal.

Semmy desperately wanted to leave the Heim with his son. As a result of the sale of the crystal bowl, he had enough money to rent a room in a restored bombed-out house. Here, at least, he and Fritz obtained some privacy. With the passing of time, Semmy was even able to start a business selling woolen suit fabric by the yard to the many tailors in Hongkew. He also began to import mother-of-pearl buttons from Japan, and functioned as an agent. Eventually, he and Fritz managed to move out of Hongkew and into a rented room in a refugee doctor's house at the west end of Bubbling Well Road in the International Settlement. Their third apartment, slightly larger, was at 340 Tiendong Road.

The Shanghainese (as Shanghai Chinese were called, while foreigners were referred to as Shanghailanders) were puzzled to see destitute Europeans streaming into their city. They gazed in amazement at a young Austrian boy who suddenly appeared daily on the Bund selling newspapers. Despite creeping Japanese encroachment, the British and Americans still controlled the International Settlement, and the French the French Concession. Each of these two foreign-ruled sections had its own tax system, police, armed forces, and courts of justice. To the average Shanghainese, Shanghailanders represented might and money.

The influx into Shanghai of thousands of refugees from Nazism did not surprise the Jewish Shanghailanders already living there, who were well aware of the anti-Semitic cruelties perpetrated by Hitler and his followers. There were two Jewish communities living in the city: the Middle Eastern Sephardi Jews (primarily from Iraq, which was British at the time, making them British subjects) and the West European Ashkenazi Jews, who were mainly from Russia. Initially, the Sephardi community, with the help of the American Jewish Joint Distribution Committee, played the most important role in helping the refugees. Sir Victor Sassoon (see p. 130) provided stipends to hundreds of refugees to enable them to start businesses. Jewish relief committees were speedily organized. The Ward Road Heim, where Semmy and Fritz were accommodated, was the result of such efforts. The Russians helped individually, inviting families to their homes and befriending them, and later joined forces with the Sephardi community to provide aid. Their efforts increased greatly after the Sephardis with British passports or British colonial passports were interned by the Japanese.

Still, Sephardi and Russian Jews worried about refugee children living in slum-like conditions. Hoping to give better opportunities to refugee youngsters, some offered to adopt them. However, parents generally refused to part with their offspring. In fact, there is only one registered case of a Russian Jewish family adopting a German baby boy.

As for Fritz, an offer to adopt him came from Ellis Hayim, a Sephardi Jewish tycoon and Vice President of the Executive Committee of the CFA (Committee for Assistance of European Jews in Shanghai).

> As Dad developed business contacts, I came within a hair's breadth of being adopted by one of Shanghai's patrician families. Ellis Hayim was a philanthropist and a man of great standing, who met with my father and me. In the course of our talks, he offered to give me an education and to send me to one of the fine British schools of Shanghai. I recall leaving my father and being invited to tiffin (the term used for lunch in Shanghai), at the Hayim's luxurious villa. I was ushered into the large dining room where a family of some 20 people sat around a huge, long, formal table and were being served a five- or six-course luncheon. I was introduced to each one of them in turn, and after lunch was taken by limousine to Ellis Hayim's richly appointed office. A secretary brought in all sorts of clothes for me: shorts and shirts, hats, socks, and shoes. I thanked Mr. Hayim and told him I was going to see my father, from whom I hated to be separated, out in the Hongkew district. Mr. Hayim, without great formality, expected me to show up again.
>
> I think, in hindsight, that between my father, who hated to be abandoned, and my own feelings of not wanting to be parted from him, I deliberately misunderstood the arrangements and let this offer go for nought.

Like thousands of other European refugees in Shanghai, Semmy and Fritz were confronted with a serious problem: how to stay healthy. Old-timers in Shanghai were familiar with all the precautions that had to be taken in a city where infectious diseases were rampant. Newcomers, however, were unaccustomed to the necessary safety measures in matters of food and hygiene.

Fruit and vegetables could not be eaten raw unless they were first washed in boiling water or a solution of potassium permanganate. To be really safe, thin-skinned fruit, such as berries, apricots, and peaches had to be cooked. Drinking water always had to be boiled. Shellfish was generally avoided completely. The advice of the Public Health Department was: Don't consume foodstuffs that are not fresh, and that have not been recently cooked, boiled, or otherwise sterilized.

Temperatures in the summer hovered between 90 and 100 degrees, with a high average humidity. As a result of endemic diseases, yearly small-pox vaccinations and cholera and typhoid inoculations were compulsory. Even with all these precautions, refugees became victims of frequent bouts of debilitating illness. Semmy and Fritz were no exception.

Indeed, life in Shanghai, especially for destitute refugees, was quite different from the comfortable and clean surroundings they were used to in Europe. Surely, in Berlin, father and son could not have imagined sitting in a rickshaw, a dilapidated two-wheeled cart, pulled by an undernourished man running as fast as he was able. This was one of the most common ways of getting about in Shanghai.

An American missionary in Japan is credited with having invented the rickshaw. In 1869, he converted a baby carriage into a vehicle to transport his invalid wife. It was to become the "jinricksha" (jin, meaning "man" in Japanese; riki, "power"; and sha, "vehicle"). This type of vehicle soon reached Shanghai, where it was simply called "rickshaw." Some Shang-hailanders had the luxury of private rickshaws hired on a monthly basis, but Semmy and Fritz hailed rickshaws on the street, as one would a taxi in Berlin. The charge was about 16 cents a mile. How much to pay a rick-shaw puller was a problem for newcomers, who were usually overcharged. If one paid too much, one was mocked for being an easy prey. If one bargained, the rickshaw man responded with loud accusations in unintel-ligible Chinese. A crowd would gather and embarrass the foreigner with shouts, laughter, and taunts. Old-timers in Shanghai well knew that the best solution was simply to pay what one thought was fair at the end of the ride, and walk away in dignified silence.

In spite of all the difficulties Fritz encountered, he adapted to his new surroundings and treasured the freedom from Nazi mind control. Yet, momentous events were soon to sweep over him and all the beleagured refugees.

While Semmy and Fritz struggled to survive and to create a semblance of normalcy, the clouds of war were gathering over Shanghai. On September 1, 1939, just five months after their arrival, World War II broke out in Europe. Jewish refugees now observed an exodus of foreign nationals from China, many of whom left reluctantly, certain that international immunity would be granted Shanghai, as it had been during World War I. Their governments, however, were more pessimistic. The U.S. Consulate ordered the evacuation of all American women and children. Many companies transferred members of the staff to Hong Kong and Manila. The British government, too, advised all their nationals to leave Shanghai immediately. Uncertainty settled over the city. Tensions increased and new fears gripped the refugees who had viewed their sojourn in China as temporary and suddenly felt trapped.

On November 27, 1941, the *North China Daily News*, Shanghai's venerable English-language paper that had been founded in 1864, carried a shocking headline: "American Marines Will Depart Shanghai."

Some years after China's defeat in the Opium War and the ratification of the Treaty of Nanking (1842), the International Settlement was founded in Shanghai. It was a British and American enclave. Great Britain and the U.S.A. had acquired special "extraterritorial" rights, which included trade, administration, justice, and defense. Among the most popular foreign troops in Shanghai were the U.S. 4th Marines, who had arrived in 1927. Now, 14 years later, they were ordered by the U.S. government to withdraw. The British Fusiliers had left several months before to defend Singapore and Hong Kong. The two greatest foreign powers in Shanghai were abandoning the city.

Two American ships, the *President Madison* and the *President Harrison* were waiting for the marines at the Customs Jetty. On that cloudy and rainy November day, 350 men were transported in double-decker buses to the *President Madison*.

On November 28, 1941, the rest of the 400 marines, led by the Fourth Marine Band (called the Last China Band), marched snappily down Bubbling Well Road and Nanking Road to board the *President Harrison*. All along the way, crowds of Chinese, old China hands, and a scattering of Jewish refugees lined the sidewalks to see them off. A French group burst into an emotional rendition of the "Marseillaise" as the marines strode by. In front of the Race Course, 50 Mongolian ponies stood in line. Their riders held high U.S. flags, which they dipped respectfully when the Marine Color Guards passed. Dignitaries from the Shanghai Municipal Council, civic organizations, diplomatic representatives, and commanders of military units, including the Japanese, were all on hand.

One Fox Newsreel cameraman filmed the departure of the marines from the Cathay Hotel roof garden, and another shot photos of them as they arrived at the Customs jetty. Shanghai was not to see these films because one week later, Japan attacked Pearl Harbor. The Pacific War began, and Japanese troops overran Shanghai.

These same 4th Marines were to fight bravely in the battle of Corregidor. They surrendered to the Japanese on May 6, 1942 and were taken as prisoners of war. After the attack on Pearl Harbor on December 7, 1941, Japanese troops armed with bayonets marched through the streets of Shanghai and rode in speeding military trucks, shouting at frightened civilians. Shanghai was no longer to be the legendary city of glamour and excitement and sin; instead, it was occupied by a tough, uncompromising enemy. Fritz recalled that significant day:

> The night of Pearl Harbor was a time I won't forget. The Whangpoo River makes a wide bend before it flows in a straight line in front of the Bund, and the Western military presence was simply made known. Three or four river gunboats were anchored in the middle of the Whangpoo River, proudly flying their respective French, Italian, British, and American flags. Around the wide bend, at one of the Hongkew district wharves ruled by the Japanese, was anchored an enormous World War I battleship. It was owned by the Japanese and dated back to the Russo-Japanese War (1904–1905). There was speculation as to whether it would ever be able to move again.
>
> On what turned out to be the night of Pearl Harbor, much of Shanghai was awakened by gunfire emanating from the Japanese battleship. It trained its guns on tiny river gunboats of the Western powers lying in the harbor. The Italians, of course, being partners of the Axis, were not threatened. The Japanese aboard the battleship had devoted months and months to training and measuring their distances. When they opened fire with their cannons on the anchored boats, it was an unfair contest. The gunboats were sitting ducks.

The American gunboat was captured by the Japanese and its small crew taken prisoner. The British, however, as Fritz described it, "allowed their ship (the *Peterel*) to be sunk with flag flying."

After Pearl Harbor, the Japanese put up notices on all Allied property stating that it was now under their control. They took over local radio stations and confiscated all shortwave radios. XMHA, Shanghai's popular American radio station, an affiliate of NBC, was also taken over. Favorite announcers Caroll Alcott and Horst Levin had made the station a mainstay in keeping up the morale of the refugees.

Carroll Alcott, an American journalist, joined XMHA in 1938. He prepared, announced, and commented on news several times a day, seven days a week. The Japanese tried to terrorize him into silence, and even attempted to blow up XMHA. However, Alcott remained undaunted, although he did go around in a bulletproof vest. Shortly before Pearl Harbor, Alcott left China, hoping to establish a powerful radio station in Manila, but the Pacific War broke out and he was unable to return to Shanghai.

Around the same time, Horst (later Howard) Levin, who had never been in front of a microphone before, initiated a very popular two-hour program that broadcast in German and English Monday through Saturday on XMHA. Later, a Yiddish segment was added. Those who didn't have radios listened in restaurants and cafés, and even in Chinese shops that tuned in to the show. In addition to reporting the news, which he got off the wires, Levin played selections from the huge collection of 40,000 RCA records owned by the station, and also brought in live musicians and actors, as well as other speakers and entertainers.

In an interview for National Public Radio in 1990, Levin stated the underlying philosophy of his program: to give the people something they were used to from home, to tell them they had a future, and to give them hope. He was clearly pro-Western, and expressed certainty that the Allies would win. His program was a lifeline for the refugees during difficult times. After Pearl Harbor, Levin was interrogated by the Japanese for his anti-Nazi philosphy. While some other correspondents were sent to the Bridge House, where typhoid ran rampant and death was certain, Levin was miraculously released.

The Nazi German radio station XGRS rose in stature, broadcasting not only locally in Shanghai, but to all parts of the world. The press was no longer free. *The Shanghai Times* became the official English language, anti-Ally, pro-German Japanese mouthpiece. American, British, and Dutch citizens were forced to wear red "enemy" armbands with the letters "A" for the Americans, "B" for the British, and "N" (Netherlands) for the Dutch. Eventually, the Japanese interned nearly all of these foreign nationals in camps for the duration of the war.

With the advent of Pearl Harbor, the emigration of Jews from Europe to Shanghai began to slow. It stopped completely after war broke out between Germany and the Soviet Union. In 1940, the Shanghai Municipal Council had already written to the authorities in Germany and Austria, begging them to stem the tide of Jewish immigration, as the infrastructure was unable to absorb the many immigrants who were arriving. They also instituted stricter requirements, including the insistence on at least $400 (per person) in order to land.

According to statistics released in Shanghai in 1942, approximately 19,500 to 20,000 refugees entered prior to that time, with 1,374 arriving in 1938; 12,089 in 1939; 1,988 in 1940, and an estimated 4,000 in 1941.

2

Isolated by the Japanese

The fragments of news stories that filtered to the refugees discouraged them in the extreme. The defeats in Singapore, Bataan, and the Philippines in the early months of 1942 led to a pervasive sense of despair and hopelessness that persisted through the year. Perhaps this explains why few refugees, Fritz included, wrote in detail about the months that followed upon the shock of Pearl Harbor.

Then, on February 18, 1943, the unexpected occurred. The commander-in-chief of the Imperial Japanese Army and the commander-in-chief of the Imperial Japanese Navy in the Shanghai Area issued a Proclamation directed at all stateless refugees, ordering them to move into a Designated Area, consisting of a 2.5-square-kilometer area of Hongkew (about one square mile) where approximately 100,000 Chinese were already living. (Many historians assert that this step was the result of extreme pressure from Japan's German allies.) The Japanese called this area *shitei chiku,* and it was later referred to by many refugees as the "ghetto." Japanese soldiers posted the Proclamation on the walls of important buildings, and foreign language newspapers published its contents.

The word "Jew" was not mentioned in the Proclamation; it said instead "stateless refugees," which referred specifically to Central Europeans without passports who had arrived after 1937, all of whom were Jews. (Russian Jews, who were also stateless, "White Russians," but had arrived before 1937, were excluded.) A very small number of Central European Jews were able to avoid internment. For example, Marion Elliot's mother had rented a room in Berlin to Mamoru Shigemitsu, then an official at the Japanese foreign ministry, and the family became quite friendly with their lodger. Shigemitsu, in 1943 the Japanese ambassador to China, provided permission for Marion and her husband to remain in their apartment in the French Concession. Remarkably, the couple was able to have this permission renewed every three months in the offices of the Bureau of Stateless Refugees Affairs. (Later, after Japan capitulated, Shigemitsu was one of the signers of the surrender on the USS *Missouri*. He was tried as a war criminal in Tokyo and imprisoned.)

A small number of others received extensions, or even exemptions, from moving into the Designated Area, including some administrators and medical staff employed in the French Concession Rue Pichon Jewish Hospital. This small hospital was founded by Russian Jews in the French Concession on land rented from Jesuits. It provided the best care available in spite of very limited wartime resources.

Several days after the Proclamation, the Japanese initiated the formation of the Shanghai Ashkenazi Collaborating Relief Communal Association (SACRA) to aid stateless refugees who had arrived after 1937 to comply with the order to relocate. The Russian Jews supported the organization with obligatory contributions assigned on a sliding scale.

The entire Mirrer Yeshiva, a famous institute of learning from Mir in Poland where students studied sacred texts, primarily the Talmud, was initially given the YMCA building for their living quarters. However, they refused to remain in these accommodations because of undesirable individuals who also lodged there. Additionally, they did not want to risk destruction of their entire group that might have occurred if they were all under one roof. Angry young students revolted, furiously flinging furniture out of the windows. Later, their battle proved fortuitous: the YMCA building suffered an accidental direct hit by American bombs and no member of the Yeshiva perished.

At first, the other Polish refugees refused to relocate at all, claiming that since there was a Polish government in exile in London, they were not stateless. Their pleas to the Japanese and to the International Red Cross went unheeded, and in 1944 they were forced to join the Central Europeans in Hongkew. Fritz later described the shock of that fateful pronouncement:

> Like a bolt from the blue, the Japanese issued a Proclamation, one that established the infamous Shanghai Designated Area. They ordered the refugees to move by May 18, 1943 to a specific area, bordered by certain major streets, as was described in the newspapers. They did not need to establish any fences or walls to keep us prisoners, because it was very simple to recognize that every Caucasian leaving the area was a refugee. (The Chinese in the area could come and go as they pleased). All the Japanese had to do was to place signs at the intersections leading out of the Designated Area with the words: "Stateless Refugees Are Prohibited to Pass Here Without Permission." It was a rather fiendish scheme on the part of the Japanese that they did not put us in a camp. They simply restricted our freedom, our liberty, and our mobility

without assuming responsibility for feeding or clothing us, or for providing us with medical care. We were on our own.

Fritz told of obtaining housing for himself and his father and described the living conditions in the Designated Area:

For refugees who were living outside the established ghetto area, as we had been, the matter of finding housing was critical and difficult. We eventually found housing in what is called the SACRA on Muirhead Road. There the community had taken a large, five-story Chinese Middle School and erected separating walls. This created a large number of individual rooms and a central corridor. The dividing walls were not terribly strong, but Dad and I were fortunate to get a private room of our own, which had enough room for the small amount of furniture that we had accumulated. *[There were actually two facilities provided to SACRA by the Japanese to house displaced refugees. The other one had been a Salvation Army compound. Both buildings required significant repairs.]*

Because the SACRA where we had been promised housing was not finished, we needed an extension of time. I headed for the famous Wayside Police Station and joined a long line of refugees who were also there to ask for more time. I was used to taking care of errands for my father, because he did not speak English very well. Whatever the transaction was, it was my task to be his interpreter. This matter was not deemed to be of sufficient importance for him to come with me, so I went alone. After standing in line for about a half an hour, I ended up at the desk of Mr. Kubota (who was in charge of the Bureau of Stateless Refugees Affairs). I don't know whether it was my youth, or maybe my attitude, but as he granted my request for an extension, he suddenly reached out and hit me in the face. This embarrassed me and injured my pride, especially since I had to pass a long line of people waiting as I came out. A whisper went down the line, "That's the one who got slapped." *[It is possible that Fritz was actually hit by Okura and not Kubota. Okura was Kubota's subordinate and the more sadistic of the two. According to former refugees, Kubota was not known to hit people.]*

The biggest drawback of living in the SACRA was that there were only two bathrooms on each floor. Seventy or 80 people had to share these two bathrooms, resulting in a terrible overloading of the available toilet system and a horrible mess. In addition, the higher one went in the building, the weaker the water pressure, because the building was not designed to be a dwelling. We had a modicum of privacy, and that was important to us.

Depending on our financial situation, we brought our meals home from the soup kitchens or, if we were able to splurge, [we ate] in a restaurant. To obtain hot water, we had to go around the corner to one of the Chinese hot water shops where they boiled hot water in huge copper cauldrons. Refugees and Chinese alike stood in line with their various thermos bottles and containers. The price was one "cash" per ladle. A cash was one third of a Chinese cent. Since, originally, the copper in a coin was worth much more than its face value, we paid them something like ten cents in paper currency and received change in little bamboo sticks carved with the initials of the hot water shop. The next time we went for hot water, we paid with one of the sticks.

The other way of cooking was to buy what we called a "flower pot," a little earthenware stove into which we put charcoal. The grill itself was also made of clay. It was always breaking, and then we had to buy a new flower pot. I had to make a fire using newspaper, then a few sticks of kindling, and then a few pieces of coal briquets. Once I had that glowing, with the aid of a large Chinese palm leaf fan, I cooked some rice, then took it off the fire and wrapped it in newspaper. Then the pot of rice was placed among the bed pillows until it was of the desired consistency. Even living as we did in the simplest of circumstances, we still counted ourselves fortunate.

Although Fritz and many other refugees were taken completely by surprise by the Japanese Proclamation, a number of Shanghai Jewish leaders were not. The refugees, as well as most Shanghailanders, were unaware of secret negotiations between this courageous group and the Japanese authorities. The goal of these Jewish leaders was to ease the anti-refugee measures that Nazi Germany was pushing the Japanese to undertake. Doubtless, these desperate efforts involved personal danger for all participating Shanghai Jews. Certainly, Fritz would have been gratified to learn that the man who had wanted to adopt him, Ellis Hayim, was an important participant in this bold endeavor.

Details of these negotiations came to light only after the war. D. B. Rabinovich, Honorary Secretary of SAJCA, the Shanghai Ashkenazi Jewish Communal Association (and father of author Rena Krasno), wrote in his report dated January 2, 1968 to Moshe Shiloh, Director of Israel's Military Archives:

Mr. Shibota—Japanese Vice-Consul in Shanghai

Risking his career, and perhaps his life, in August 1942, Mr. Shibota called a meeting of leaders of Shanghai Jewish communities in the private residence of Mr. Speelman *[Michel Speelman, a Dutch businessman, the head of the Committee for Assistance of European Jews in Shanghai]*, and confidentially advised them that the Japanese authorities under pressure from the Germans were contemplating segregation and isolation of German Jewish refugees on an island at the mouth of the Yangtze river and suggested Jewish communities organize themselves and take steps to prevent, or at least soften, the pending order.

The leak of information before an official announcement led to the postponement of the restriction order till February 1943 and enabled the Jewish communities in China to intervene and make the necessary representations. Dr. Abraham Kaufman proceeded to Tokyo, and managed to meet there with the highest Japanese authorities. *[Dr. Kaufman was the esteemed president of the Harbin Jewish Community. All the Jewish communities in China agreed to single him out for this delicate and dangerous mission.]* As a result of all this, some important changes were introduced in the original orders. The most important of these changes was that the Designated Area was to be established within the city limits of Shanghai, thus making it possible for those in other parts of the city to maintain contact with their fellow Jews and give them every possible assistance.

All those who attended the above meeting—Mr. Ellis Hayim, Mr. Michel Speelman, Mr. Boris Topas, and Mr. Joseph Bitker, as well as Mr. Shibota, were arrested within 24 hours by the Japanese Gendarmerie. Mr. Shibota was dismissed from his post and sent back to Japan. His fate is unknown to me. Though I was acting as Honorary Secretary of the Shanghai Jewish Communal Association—Ashkenazi—for some reason, I could not attend the meeting *[it is probable that he had the flu.]*.

Mr. Boris Topas, President of the Ashkenazi Jewish Community, was tortured for more than ten months and remained broken in body and mind for the rest of his life.

Mr. Shibota was located after the war by the Jewish community in Tokyo. During Passover 1976, he was honored publicly by the Jews in Japan. He died the following year.

The winter of 1943 was a difficult one for the refugees whose lives were drastically changed by the Proclamation. Their freedom restricted, they bcame dependent on handouts. Coal was difficult, if not impossible, to obtain and was extremely expensive. Electricity was rationed, and food was in short supply. Only one free meal a day was provided by the soup kitchens. Poor nutrition caused diseases and near starvation in the Heime. Because of the crowded living conditions and difficulty earning a living, people became contentious. Arguments among families and between neighbors were frequent. The divorce rate soared, and there were reports of suicides. Of necessity, some women became prostitutes in order to feed their families. A small number of refugee girls dated Japanese soldiers because of the extra food and other help their families might receive. Many refugees were undernourished, and diseases proliferated. It was indeed a very bleak time, with no letup in sight.

3

A Tragic Loss

The introductory page of Fritz Marcus's first extant diary *[see Figures 9 and 10]*, was begun in Berlin on May 8, 1937, shortly after his Bar Mitzvah, and recommenced in Shanghai on May 5, 1944. What happened to the diary pages from these missing seven years? Perhaps they were, as Fred asserted, "destroyed." Indeed, it is obvious that a number of pages had been torn out. It is possible that another diary was lost or misplaced in one of the moves in Shanghai—first to the Heim, then to the different flats and, finally, back into Hongkew when it became the Designated Area in 1943.

Fritz often related that one day in a fit of rage he had torn up his German passport. Longing for the comfortable life he had known, discouraged by life in strange surroundings, enraged at the lack of prospects for the future, and overcome at that point by a sense of futility, he may have destroyed both the passport and the diary pages simultaneously. The immediate impetus for his action may have been the declaration by Germany in November 1941 that Jews living abroad were no longer citizens, and that their assets belonged to the Third Reich.

The events that began on May 1, 1944, which were reconstructed in his diary beginning on May 5, revealed a watershed occurrence in his life. He wrote in detail about this traumatic happening.

> **May 5, 1944**—Pappi *[Dad]* does not feel well at the beginning of April. He has a temperature of 101.3 *[temperatures have been converted from centigrade to Fahrenheit throughout]*, is coughing and goes to bed. He thinks it is a cold and that he can manage without calling a doctor. On Sunday, his temperature rises suddenly to over 102.2 and we decide immediately to call Dr. Streimer. At first, he determines it is a light bronchitis and a slightly swollen bladder. He prescribes cough medicine, heart and circulation medication.
>
> Without any apparent reason, Pappi's condition deteriorates.

We call in Dr. Kneucker for a consultation. On Thursday, April 20th, both doctors have a consultation and decide to send him to the Ward Road Hospital, since he requires good care. At first, I resist, but eventually they convince me to agree.

Toward evening Pappi is driven to the hospital in an ambulance. In the morning my temperature is 100.4 degrees. But since I urgently need to go to town, I pull myself together and drag myself to the hospital to Pappi. He needs various things, such as coffee, pajamas, etc. So I set out once again to do all the errands.

On Saturday Dr. Streimer determines that I have pneumonia in my right lung. During the next 8–10 days, I lay with a fever of between 100.4 to 104 degrees and could not possibly leave my bed. I hear about Pappi's condition only from Dr. Streimer, my Uncle Martin, and the Alexanders.

In the meantime, my financial situation becomes critical. Missie Gerendasi [a friend of the family and the wife of Seppi, their dentist] therefore goes to Mr. Scheininger of the Kitchen Fund to start the necessary arrangements [for aid]. [The Kitchen Fund (KF) was established in 1942. The daily meal and loaf of bread the KF supplied to the refugees was in large part responsible for their survival. Funds were derived from the minimal cost refugees paid for food tickets and contributions by wealthier refugees, the Joint Distribution Committee, and an organization called CENTROJEWCOM, founded by Russian Jews.]

A series of visitors came to see Fritz, including a member of the Chevra Kadisha [the Burial Society]. While he was perplexed by this visit, the real reason for it seems not to have occurred to him. Following that, his cousin Klaus reported that Semmy's condition was very critical. Neither Klaus nor the next visitor, Missie Gerendasi, was able to tell Fritz the awful truth until the next morning when Hugo Alexander, the father of Fred's friend Theo Rolf, appeared.

After a few trivial exchanges, Mr. Alexander tells me that he has the sad duty to inform me that my father passed away in the hospital on Monday, May 1, 1944, at 3:00. A horrible pain goes through me, but I can weep no tears.

The room seems to turn around me. I have to close my eyes in order to grasp fully the meaning of the news. A feeling of complete helplessness overcomes me. I don't know what will become of me. I cannot place myself at all in this new situation. I feel only one thing: loneliness.

My Pappi, with whom I had shared every thought, from whom I had no secrets, who was the backbone of my entire life, I would never see him again. From now on, I have only myself, myself alone, on whom I can depend. This demands from me a strong moral stand. But, I believe that the way I was raised does give me this strength.

It was Fritz's father's wish that he be cremated, but after a call to the International Funeral Directors, it was discovered that the cheapest cremation cost $10,000. Despite his desire to carry out his father's request, Fritz was forced to abandon this idea.

On Wednesday, May 3, 1944, the funeral took place at the Columbia Road Cemetery. Unfortunately, I could not leave my bed and know only from others that it was very solemn. My friend Cantor Lewkowitz sang, and Rabbi Dr. Kantorowski made a speech.

Following his father's death, a number of friends visited Fritz, and a *minyan [prayer quorum of ten adult Jewish males]* was held on Wednesday and Thursday evenings.

From then on I say my *Kaddish [mourner's prayer]* alone mornings and evenings. It is a very solemn prayer for me. I have daily visits from Missie, Theo Rolf, Uncle Martin, and Klaus. This calms me, and slowly I am adjusting to my new situation. I look through a box and find some of Pappi's poems. *[Around this time, a roommate, Günther Looser, moved into Fritz's room. Slightly older, and educated as an attorney in Germany, Looser treated Fritz "as a brother," and they became good friends.]*

Monday, May 8, 1944—In the morning: 97.5 temperature. Get up for breakfast. Look through my summer suits. All Pappi's things are too small for me, especially the jackets. Still don't know what I will do. Somewhat worried because still no answer to a telegram I sent to Japan in regard to the import of buttons. No reply about the application to Kitchen Fund for food and glucose injections. In the afternoon Missie visits me. In the evening informed by KF to come the next morning from 9:00–11:00 to see Dr. Cohn. *[Dr. A. J. Cohn was a functionary of SACRA. Because he was educated in Japan and spoke the language, he was chosen by the Russian community to represent them to the Japanese.]* No fever.

Tuesday, May 9, 1944—In the morning Dr. Streimer comes to see me. No post-pneumonia complications. But still coughing.

Suggests a blood and sputum test. At 11 o'clock to the KF Alcock
Heim. Very shaky on my feet. Use an umbrella for support. KF
gives me lunch tickets and I also get some bread.

Get farewell evening meal from Rosauer *[presumably because his meals
would now come from the Kitchen Fund]*: snacks and dessert. Rest 2 hours at
home. Then on to the Heim for my meal, to Uncle Martin, and to Dr.
Streimer. Also get Pappi's death certificate. Must go tomorrow to the
Police *[probably to notify them of Semmy's death]*. Temperature: 98.6 degrees,
or normal.

>   **Wednesday, May 10, 1944**—[To] Alcock Heim regarding med-
>   ical care. I belong to the Chaoufoong Rd. Heim. *[The Chaoufoong
>   Rd. Heim dispensed relief to very needy refugees.]* Lunch—Heim: tongue
>   and porridge. Get a one-day pass from Ghoya *[see pp. 31–32]* so
>   that I can get documents from James W. *[James Wong was the owner
>   of a shirt factory to whom Fritz's father sold buttons he imported from Japan
>   and with whom Fritz continued to do business after his father's death. On
>   the basis of a letter from Wong, Fritz was able to obtain a pass to leave the
>   Designated Area.]* Return home. In the evening go with Looser to
>   Theo Rolf's Cultural Club. Silberstein lectures: "Thoughts about
>   the Origins of the Modern State." After that, discussion. Go to
>   bed at 1:00 a.m. No fever.

When refugees first came ashore in Shanghai, they were housed in the
Embankment House on Whashing Road. (Built by Sir Victor Sassoon, this
was Shanghai's largest apartment building. It fronted Soochow Creek for
a quarter of a mile, and featured 194 apartments, and a swimming pool.)
As the mass immigration overwhelmed those facilities in the fall of 1939,
the community leased former warehouses, school buildings, and barracks
at a reasonable rent from the Shanghai Municipal Council. The first of
these, the Ward Road Heim, opened in early 1939, and there were soon
to be five others: the Chaoufoong Road Heim, the Alcock Road Heim,
the Wayside Heim, the Kinchow Road Heim, and the Aerocrete Camp on
Pingliang Road. The latter, which was used primarily for bachelors, closed
in 1941, and was replaced by the Seward Road Heim.

Approximately 20 percent of the refugees lived in the Heime *[plural
of Heim; camps]*, where conditions left a lot to be desired. In an interview,
one former refugee, Jutta Lübschütz (now Judy Urman), recalled the conditions in the Heim where she lived for six and a half years. Many couples
resided together in one room, with sheets or blankets dividing the tiny
living areas in order to provide a modicum of privacy. Young people lived

in dormitory rooms with others of their sex. The rooms were intolerably hot in summer and freezing cold in the winter. Clothes hung on bamboo sticks between the double-decker beds. Lice and bedbugs "walked over" on the sticks. Diseases were rampant.

In the beginning, three meals a day were provided to those living in the Heime. One statistic indicates that in July 1940, slightly over 8,000 meals were served daily from the public kitchens. Funds for these meals came mainly from the American Jewish Joint Distribution Committee (JDC), with some help from local donors. After May 21, 1942, the Joint had to honor restrictions imposed by the Anglo-American Trading with the Enemy Act, which prohibited sending money and communications to enemy countries. It was therefore necessary for them to break off contact with their representatives and with the refugees in Shanghai until December 1943. The local JDC representatives, Laura Margolis and Manuel Siegel, had to raise money through loans, which they pledged to repay in American dollars (all monies were subsequently repaid). Margolis gave her personal guarantee for these loans against the order of the Joint. She and Siegel also set up a local JDC organization and arranged for money to be channeled to it through the International Red Cross via Switzerland. Despite these efforts, the situation in Hongkew remained very severe during this time. Russian Jews helped out by providing one meal a day for adults and two for children. The Mirrer Yeshiva continued to receive money illegally through Uruguay.

According to Urman, the adolescents in the Heime had fun despite the difficult conditions. Strolling together in Wayside Park, they were fascinated by the Japanese in their kimonos and enjoyed watching little children with typical Japanese haircuts. *[Today this park is called Huo Shan Park, and there is a plaque in Chinese, English, and Hebrew dedicated to the Jewish refugee experience.]*

Dancing was also a popular activity, as was listening to refugee musicians play and perform. Cards and chess were favored games, as were visits to second-hand shops, which sold merchandise brought by the refugees. They also went to the movies when they could afford it. They congregated at the Roy Roof Garden (the roof of Café Roy), an "in" gathering place to relax and enjoy delicious treats. This spot was also a favorite of Fritz's.

Among the refugees, there was a subtle class structure (referred to by one of them as a "caste system"). Those not living in the Heime looked down on those who did. One refugee, who lived in the Chaoufoong Road Heim for six and a half years, stated that when she was married, her husband "rescued me from the Heim." Fritz was fortunate to have spent only his first few days in Shanghai residing in a Heim.

It was necessary for refugees to obtain a pass to leave the Designated Area. The frustrating endeavor of renewing one's pass was accomplished at the offices of the Bureau of Stateless Refugees Affairs, which was located in the Wayside Police Station in the Designated Area. A blue pass, which was in force for six weeks to three months, allowed the bearer to go to those locations that were stamped on a map on the back of the pass. The refugees were permitted to take only the most direct route to their destination, and within hours specified on the pass. A pink pass was issued for one day up to four to six weeks, and allowed the holder to go only to a specific location. Children attending school outside of the Designated Area also needed a pass, but these were readily provided. The bearers of passes were required to wear a badge on their left lapel, visible at all times, that was the same color as the pass. All passes had to be renewed, usually 15 days before they expired. If the renewal was granted before the pass expired, the expiration date was crossed out and a new one stamped on the pass. Refugees had to replace lost badges, and were charged for this service.

Sergeant Kano Ghoya, a sadistic Japanese government official who was much feared by the refugees, was responsible for granting the long-term passes. Another official, Okura, issued the daily and short-term passes. Reportedly, he sometimes sent pass applicants at whim to the Ward Road Jail, where lice infected them with typhus, which was frequently fatal. Ruth Callmann, a German refugee who was the office assistant, typed each long-term (three months or one month) pass after it was issued. Then Tsutoma Kubota, Ghoya's superior, stamped it. According to Ruth Callmann, Kubota was a "nice older man who acted like a gentleman."

Ghoya was a short, moody, and rude man in his forties or fifties (some say he was only four feet tall, others barely five feet), who liked to call himself "King of the Jews." Because of his diminutive size, he would often jump on his desk or a chair when dealing with applicants. He was as likely to scream at or slap applicants as to douse them with a bucket of water. Nervous refugees had to stand in line for hours, and when they finally reached his post, were often ordered to come back the next day. *[See Figure 11 for a photo of refugees waiting in line for passes. Ghoya is in the center in a dark jacket.]* Often, refugees would ask in Yiddish before joining the line, *"Petscht er heute?"* (Is he hitting today?) If the answer was yes, they would leave and return when it was rumored that Ghoya was in a better mood. According to former refugee Gary Matzdorff, some young people never obtained a pass, feeling the effort to do so was too demeaning. They simply sneaked out and back under cover of darkness.

It is interesting that, according to Ruth Callmann, Ghoya was not feared by his office employees, whom he treated decently. In fact, he used the money collected for the replacement of lost badges to provide the several employees of the Bureau of Stateless Refugees Affairs with coffee and cake on Saturdays.

Ghoya became a legendary figure in the course of the segregation in the Designated Area, and remained so afterward in the memory of the refugees. Despite the fact that he played the violin and sometimes joined families for musical evenings, that he was friendly to children and attended cultural and sports events in the Designated Area, he was widely despised by the refugees who seem to have projected onto him their hatred of Hitler. After the Japanese capitulated, there were numerous reports that Ghoya was beaten by at least one group of young refugees. He was repatriated to Japan, along with the other Japanese in China. His later fate is unclear.

Thursday, May 11, 1944—For the first time *[since his father's death]* go to the city. *[Although Hongkew was part of Shanghai, most refugees considered it almost another world. Thus they referred to other parts of Shanghai as "the city."]* Again to James W., who receives me in a very warm manner. He is very shocked by Pappi's death. Gives me a letter so that I can extend my pass. Then to the library. Send a telegram. No news for me from Japan. Strange! Lunch: vegetable soup and one boiled egg. Good. Muirhead Rd: get a pass *[from Ghoya at the Bureau of Stateless Refugees Affairs]* till 12/6. To Alexanders. Drink coffee there. In the evening at home. Look through the library of Will.Y. Tonn. *[Tonn, from Berlin, was an expert on Sinology who, without the permission of the Japanese, founded the Asia Seminar where he taught adult classes in the Designated Area. He later emigrated to Israel with his wife.]* Then read. We again have light in the house.

4

Fight For Survival

Little by little, Fritz learned to live with his sorrow. Lonely, without education, job, family, and nationality, he often referred to this period as the nadir of his life. Fortunately, the Alexander family all but adopted him. He spent most of his free time with them, and Theo Rolf became like an older brother. According to Fritz, Hugo Alexander, Theo Rolf's father, was a "very strong and wonderful person," whom Fritz deeply respected. From the Alexanders, Fritz learned the joys of Jewish observance and grew closer to Judaism, which later led him to a professional life in Jewish education.

Fritz's main concern was to scratch out a living. Despite problems communicating with Japan, he attempted to maintain the button business his father had begun. To pay for food, he sold his Bar Mitzvah presents one by one. Gradually, he began to see his friends and to return to an active life.

He recovered from pneumonia, but was plagued with various ailments, including a bout with malaria, and recurring problems with his teeth. He described several series of shots he was given, including vitamins, tonifos, panfos, arsol, and strychnine drops. The origin of these medicines is unclear. It is probable that tonifos and panfos in particular were German drugs. Possibly they were phosphate tonics, at the time called "chemical foods," which were prescribed for patients as a restorative after prolonged dysentery to aid them in absorbing nutrients. These remedies are no longer used.

Prior to Pearl Harbor, it was still possible to import drugs from Europe. After 1941, these supplies dwindled and the scarcity caused a sharp rise in prices. Some of the medicines used to treat refugees might have been left from small stocks brought over by refugee doctors. Refugees also started several pharmaceutical companies, among which was one that used snake venom "to strengthen people," one that produced vitamin shots, and another that specialized in medicines for stomach and intestinal illnesses, as well as dermatological and gynecological medicines.

Doctors who attempted to learn about Chinese herbal medicines were often stymied because many Chinese doctors refused to teach Westerners about their methods.

Numerous refugees suffered from a variety of very unpleasant ailments. Head lice was a common complaint, as were chilblains, a painful inflammation on the hands and fingers caused by exposure to cold. Even worse, despite mandatory inoculations, many suffered (and some died) from diphtheria, typhoid fever, and cholera. Scarlet fever, beriberi, and malaria were also prevalent, as was tuberculosis. Yet, even without many essentials, dedicated doctors were able to prevent a major epidemic.

Soon after the Japanese took control of Shanghai, they requisitioned all stocks of gasoline and kerosene. This measure affected Jewish refugees, many of whom used cheap kerosene stoves for heating and cooking. Restriction after restriction followed. Headlines in local papers glorified Japanese victories and never mentioned defeats. Shanghai residents learned that Japan now occupied strategically important islands in the North and South Pacific, but neither radio broadcasters nor news agencies ever announced Japan's disaster in Midway (1942). A heavy cloud of gloom enveloped Shanghai.

In the fall of 1942, even before the Proclamation and the creation of a Jewish Designated Area in Hongkew, the Japanese had established the Foreign Pao Chia *[PC]*, a voluntary self-policing police system, based on one that had operated in East Asia for hundreds of years. *[Pao Chia means "protection of the community born from the community."]* Beginning in October, about 2,000 males between the ages of 20 to 45, including Fritz Marcus, were required to stand guard for a three-hour shift twice a week, helping to maintain peace and order in Hongkew. Each member received an armband, a rope, and a whistle. Later, after the Proclamation, their duties expanded to include watching over points of entry and exit, checking passes, enforcing the curfew and other regulations, performing air raid drills, as well as providing first aid in conjunction with refugee doctors. By the middle of 1944, there were 3,600 men in the Foreign Pao Chia. According to an August 1944 article in the *Jüdisches Gemeindeblatt*, 1,186 cases were handled by the Foreign Pao Chia during 387,803 hours of duty. The official director of the Refugee Pao Chia was Dr. Felix Kardegg, who was also President of the Jüdische Gemeinde *[the Jewish Community]*. However, true power was concentrated in the hands of the Japanese authorities. Fritz was very conscientious about his Pao Chia duties, and rose in the ranks to be Assistant Chief in his district.

The Jüdische Gemeinde, which was founded in 1939 on the European model, had departments that handled statistics for births, deaths, and B'nai

Mitzvah, and administered the cemeteries. At first, the German Jews used the existing Russian Jewish cemetery on Baikal Road, founded in 1917, paying for each plot and depending on the services of the Ashkenazi *Chevra Kadisha*. In late 1940, however, they formed their own *Chevra Kadisha* and purchased the Columbia Road Cemetery. A second cemetery on Point Road was acquired the following year. Beginning in 1958, the graves in these cemeteries, as well as in the Mohawk Road Cemetery, which had been founded in 1862, were transferred to a new location outside of the city limit. All the Jewish graves and, in fact, all foreign graves were trashed and built over during the Cultural Revolution from 1966 to 1976. Today, Jewish gravestones continue to be found in the suburbs of Shanghai, being used as floors, tables, stairs, bridges, and foundations.

After a time, the Gemeinde also sponsored lectures and cultural events, and began a women's association. The distribution of bread, food products, and medications was also under their jurisdiction, and they ran the ambulance service.

Several organizations with the goal of settling and aiding the refugees preceded the Gemeinde. The first of these, the Hilfsfond, was begun in 1934 by early German refugees. When in 1938 it could no longer cope alone with the enormous influx of refugees, the International Committee for Granting Relief to European Refugees was formed. Known as the IC, or Komor Committee after Paul Komor, a Hungarian, the secretary and administrator, the IC functioned on monies raised by subscription and worked with the Hilsfond to provide room and board and assistance in getting a job or establishing a business. The IC also furnished milk to children and established an Arbitration Board staffed with several judges who settled problems that arose between stateless refugees. (The Chinese court system functioned only in Chinese and was avoided if at all possible. American, British, French, and other foreign nationals settled their differences with the help of their consulates.)

Later that same year, another organization, the Committee for the Assistance of European Jews in Shanghai, was organized. It was referred to as the CFA, or Speelman Committee, after Michel Speelman, a Dutch businessman and the first treasurer, and operated through seven subcommittees, each with a different responsibility. After the founding of the CFA, the IC still issued passes to enable travel to other parts of China, provided banking services, and ran an extensive thrift shop on Nanking Road near the Bund and the big hotels where refugees could sell possessions when money was needed. (Possibly the crystal fruit bowl Fritz and his father brought from Germany was sold in this shop to enable them to move out of the Ward Road Heim.)

All German and other Jewish European refugees were obliged at all times to carry a Resident Card with a yellow stripe printed on the top. The Nazis used yellow to identify Jews, and now the Japanese adopted a similar custom. The effect was chilling. (All non-Chinese were issued IDs with green stripes, and Allied nationals—before their internment—held cards with a red stripe.)

Despite the turmoil and the death of his father, Fritz remained active in the community.

> **Friday, May 12, 1944**—Lunch—Heim:. Noodle soup. Good. Chaoufoong Rd. for outpatient treatment. Dr. Harry Salomon prescribes medication for me. Rested at home. Will go tomorrow with a bottle to the Ward Rd. Heim drugstore to get the medication. To the police to get back the death certificate, for which the Pao Chia had given me a form. Speak with Dr. Kardegg about establishing a district volunteer firefighters group. Kardegg insists that I give him a list of 40 people willing to volunteer. Will push this forward. *[Although Fritz managed to mobilize the required number of volunteers, this project never came to fruition.]* Receive bill from the Gemeinde for $2,500 for Pappi's funeral.)

> **Saturday, May 13, 1944**—In the morning Radio Office. Apply for a new certificate.

Fritz was at this office because strict controls on radios remained in place, forbidding radios with more than seven tubes or capable of receiving anything outside frequencies between 550 and 1500 kilocycles or able to be altered for transmitting purposes. Those who needed such equipment for official duties or "urgent necessity" were required to obtain permits.

In Shanghai, all Japanese proclamations were signed only by their military and not by representatives of the Japanese Foreign Office. This was a result of a decision by Premier General Tojo to strip the Foreign Office of power. In November 1942, Tojo had created a new department, the Ministry of Greater Asiatic Affairs, thus removing control by the diplomatic corps in occupied territories.

> **Saturday, May 13, 1944 (continued)**—100.4 degrees fever. Get Dr. Salomon. Finds that *[I]* just have a cold. Pick up Braun from the office. Go together by truck to the Western District. Buy baskets $150. Make a commission. Then to Alexanders.

> **Sunday, May 14, 1944**—This was a very nice day. Lunch: Heim. Bean soup. Very good. In the afternoon pick up the medicine from the Ward Road Heim pharmacy. Toward evening with

Braun to Marcuses *[see below]*. Present are the whole family and the Hoffmans. We talk and suddenly have an idea. With Martin and Kay and Gerhardt and Pueppi, go to Gruenfeld, Liaoyung Rd. *[a little bar they frequented where they most often ordered small bottles of vodka which they drank from little glasses]*. Looser has the flu.

This Samuel Marcus, called Sammy, was a relative of Fritz's father, though the exact connection is unclear. Although Fritz sometimes called him Uncle Sammy, it is likely that he was a first or second cousin. Sammy and his wife Lieschen had two children, Charles and Edith. Charles was married to Catharine, also known as Kay. Edith (fondly called Pueppi, or Doll) and her husband, Gerhardt Abraham, lived with Sammy and Lieschen and were the parents of little Gaby, on whom Fritz especially doted. Gerhardt and Joseph Hoffman, also mentioned above, had an aunt in common with the Marcuses, and the couple was often included in family gatherings. Soon after they arrived in Shanghai, Charles and Edith and their parents started a small storefront business called Elite Fashion, manufacturing silk blouses as they had in Berlin. The family employed both refugees and Chinese as sewing machine operators.

Monday, May 15, 1944—In the morning *[run]* errands for Looser, who already feels better. Lunch in Heim: millet with mushroom sauce. Nothing special. After lunch to the city with Braun for a haircut. In the evening with Theo Rolf and Lewkowitz to lecture of the Loewenberg group *[at the]* Jüdische Gemeinde). *[There were a number of other cultural groups like Theo Rolf's.]* Subject: "The Structure and Legality of Criticism." Scientific. Graphic. At 11:00 o'clock we finally go to Gruenfeld. We agree to Theo Rolf's wish to wait till midnight when people congratulate me warmly *[on his twentieth birthday]*. At 1:30 we return, caught in a downpour of rain. After a short discussion we go to Alexander's house. Theo Rolf prepares makeshift beds for us. And so I fall asleep on the floor on my birthday.

Tuesday, May 16, 1944—Wake up at Alexanders. Again people congratulate me. Must stay for breakfast. After that go home. Looser feels better. Almost no fever. Go to the Race Course to pick up bread coupons. From there go to 57 Great Western Rd., to the Bank. Heim to eat: vegetable soup, one egg. Good. Then I ride alone to Great Western Rd. Return Pappi's unused *[food]* tickets. Get receipt. Get new tickets for myself for June and July. Then to Braun's office. Then to Hongkew Modern Candy Factory, *[where we each get]* 1 slice Sacher Torte. With B. *[Braun]* to Alexanders, for whom B. takes along 10 petits fours to eat when we drink coffee. Around 7:00 o'clock to Uncle Martin.

Thursday, May 18, 1944—Early morning to the city to take inventory at Braun's godown. *[The word "godown," (warehouse), originates in the Malaysian word "gedong," which means "space." The British East India Company carried the nomenclature to the various places in the Far East where they traded. The Malays, who were themselves great traders, may have borrowed the term originally from southern India. Braun used his godown as his office and storeroom. On this day, he offered Fritz a much needed opportunity to earn a few dollars taking inventory.]* Lunch with Braun in his office. Get $40.00 from him. Heim: rice with stewed fruit. 1 egg. Prima *[popular expression for "great"]*. Make Pao Chia duty list. In the afternoon to Pao Chia Headquarters.

Sunday, May 21, 1944—Get up early in the morning. With Klaus, *[Cantor]* Lewkowitz, and another couple of people get a group pass to Columbia Road Cemetery. Visit Pappi's grave.

Wednesday, May 24, 1944—Lunch: vegetable soup. Dessert. Chaoufoong Heim. Outpatient. Dr. Salomon charming. Need blood test, and will meet chief doctor. Ward Rd. Heim. Blood test appointment for next Wednesday.

Thursday, May 25, 1944—In the morning go to the Committee to get cards for next month. Get bread. Gratis! *[Refugees received one small loaf of bread daily.]* Lunch—Heim: millet with stewed fruit. With Looser to Alexander's. Arthur Kornick lecture: "Greek History." Very nice.

Friday, May 26, 1944—Get a letter from Japan. Merchandise promised. Yuhang Rd. worship services. With Looser to District meeting in Pao Chia Headquarters. Between 26.7–31.7.44 *[July 26–31, 1944]* there will be 2 days of anti-air raid drills *[against U.S. bombings]*.

All Shanghai newspapers published the following information regarding air raid signals and light regulations:

AIR RAID SIGNALS

1. Sirens

Precautionary period: one 2-minute blast

Air raid: 7 five-second blasts

All clear: 2 fifteen-second blasts

2. Flags and lamps

Precautionary period: 2 green flags or 2 green lamps
Air-raid: 2 red flags or 2 red lamps
All Clear: 2 yellow flags or 2 yellow lamps

New Light Regulations: All shops must be closed by 2:00. For cinemas, cafes, hotels, night clubs, the closing time is 10:00 p.m. Should they violate the regulations, businesses will receive a warning, a second offense is to result in the cutting of power supply and a fine, a third will be punished by a ten-day business suspension and a fourth by withdrawal of business license.

The Japanese had also ordered that all windows be covered with thick curtains at sunset so that no lights could be seen by enemy planes. This order was strictly enforced. On more than one occasion, Japanese soldiers would shoot at improperly darkened windows.

Sunday, May 28, 1944—First day of Shavuos *[Jewish holiday signifying the end of the grain harvest and the giving of the Torah]*. In the morning to Chaoufoong Rd. Heim to Dr. Salomon. Chief Dr. *[Theodore]* Friedrichs present. Measures and weighs me. Height: 1.75 meters *[just under 5'7"]*. Weight: 55 kgs *[120–125 pounds]*. Doctor checks me and writes a note. Get no further information. Lunch—Heim: fish goulash with potatoes. Evening with entire Alexander family to services: Cantor Warschauer. Then with supper to Uncle Martin. Then together with Theo Rolf to Uschi Sachs *[a friend of both young men]*. We rehearse an original play—a parody of "St. Joan" by Shaw.

Monday, May 29, 1944—2nd day of Shavuos. In the morning 5:30 preparatory air raid alarm. Awakened by a courier. Fire fighting overalls. Pao Chia compound. On duty till 9:00 without anything happening. Get properly dressed because I want to go at 9:00 o'clock to prayer services. Am dressed and ready to go when at 9:30 the air raid alarm sounds. I whistle the alarm on my police whistle and change my clothes again. All troops report. At 10:15 I decide to take off, but on the way I meet a group of neighborhood Pao Chia Chiefs who order me and Looser to go to the Japanese District Pao Chia Point Road Headquarters. Said and done. Spend a long hour there discussing air defense exercises planned together. No results. Hurry to the Eastern Theatre barely in time for Yizkor services *[Memorial Service]*. Then go to the Main Post Office. Mail a letter to Japan. *[After Pearl Harbor, when the Japanese took full control of the Post Office, and instituted severe censorship,* *all regular communication from Shanghai to the rest of the world, as well as within China proper, was disrupted or completely eliminated.]*

Just as I leave the Post Office an air raid alarm. Then on foot to Chusan Rd. Pao Chia Headquarters, and then home. Had just let my people go, when a Japanese from the Point Rd. Pao Chia arrives and wants to start an exercise. I whistle for all to gather again. Then I take command, in spite of the presence of Pao Chia Chief (Looser), and Deputy Chief (Bromberger) and Chief Inspector (former Captain) Weinberger. Japanese seems satisfied. Theo Rolf comes over. Finish work on "St. Joan" and I type the play. In the evening in spite of an alarm, manage to get to Uschi and we go through the play three times.

Tuesday, May 30, 1944—At 6:00 a.m. air raid alarm. Dog tired, I jump out of bed. Have a small fire alarm practice. At 7:30 all clear. At 11:30 again an alarm. At 11:45 again all clear. Between 3:00–5:00, again an alarm. Carry out traffic stopping and traffic regulation duty both times, and traffic duty on the street. At 6:45 anti-air raid exercise. Air Defense Engineer Stricks appears in person. He criticizes my people during the exercise, without giving instructions: "We will still talk about this," *[he says]*. I don't care. Looser supports me in everything. In the evening, in spite of the alarm, go to Uschi. We go twice through "St. Joan." Goes badly. By rickshaw home. Eat noodles from the noodle man.

Wednesday, May 31, 1944—In the morning to the city. Yokahama Specie Bank. No documents from Japan. To Braun's office. Have lunch together. He pays me on account till 18.7 1944 *[July 18, 1944]*. Ward Rd. Heim Laboratory. Blood test. To Marlene Sweetshop. Get present for Gerda Alexander for her birthday. Then home. Put on Pappi's evening suit. Go with Looser to birthday party. Table: tea, sandwiches, and cakes. Clear table. Dance. Then with Theo Rolf and Uschi present "St. Joan." Great success. Egg liqueur, dancing, games. "Hanschen piep einmal" *[a game, "Johnnie Make a Peep"]*. Then presentation by me: poems, prose. Then "Spin the Bottle," etc. Vodka and the previously mentioned drinks. Wonderful party since all the people get along so well. To bed at 3:15 a.m.

Saturday, June 3, 1944—In the morning Theo Rolf asks me to accompany him to help interpret housing negotiations with Japanese. 2 o'clock at Muirhead Rd. *[The headquarters of the Bureau* *of Stateless Refugees Affairs was located in the Wayside Police Station at 70 Muirhead Rd. in the Designated Area.]*

Tuesday, June 6, 1944—In the morning by truck with Braun and Cohen to load coal. After lunch the same. Weather heavenly beautiful. Warm. Blue sky. Rome fell. The invasion has begun. The Americans and British have landed in Normandy and are in the area of the Seine estuary. Le Havre under Anglo-Americans. Waiting tensely for latest news.

The invasion of Normandy, which began on June 6, 1944, was a great achievement for Allied planners, military leaders, and fighting forces. By the evening of the first day, all five Allied divisions (about 150,000 men), were ashore in Normandy and in contact with airborne units. The refugees and most Shanghai residents greeted this news with joy, relief, and hope. At the same time, with the end of the war possibly nearing, the refugees' exhilaration was accompanied by fear that they would not survive until liberation. Everyone assumed it was inevitable that U.S. bombings would pound the city and that the Japanese occupying forces would react with bitter fury against the local population.

After his father's death, Fritz attempted to fill every moment of every day with activities. His days were packed with Pao Chia duty, religious observances, cultural events, and social gatherings. No doubt this frenetic schedule provided an escape from his sad circumstances, as well as from his uncomfortable housing situation.

The following diary segments are examples of typical days.

Saturday, June 9, 1944—6th Air Defense Day. *[Air Defense Day appears to have taken place at least once a month from from June 1944 until the end of the war. On these days, the Pao Chia explained air raid procedures to the public and provided training in how to respond.]* Get up early in the morning. Weather fine. Type Pao Chia Duty List. Morning Shanghai. To Wong. Letter for pass extension. Get application without a problem. Bureau of Stateless Refugees Affairs. Do not get my turn. Again to Ghoya. Again do not get my turn. Lunch: Heim. 4:00 o'clock with all the group to big Air Defense exercise. Around 3:45 Precautionary *[air raid signal]* ends at 5:00 o'clock. Then with the entire group and Engineer Stricks to Yunan, Kungpin, Muirhead Rds. *[This section was entirely rebuilt and became part of the hub of "Little Vienna," given this name because of the many European stores and coffee shops]*. Work with Special District Representative. Authorities satisfied. Go home at 6:00 p.m. Change clothes quickly. To prayer services. Supper at home. 9:00–10:30 lights control duty (blackout). *[The Pao Chia helped the Japanese enforce the regulation to keep windows covered.]* Invasion: Bayeux taken by the Allies.

Sunday, June 10, 1944—Morning: Bureau of Stateless Refugees Affairs. Extend pass. Invited to Uschi Sachs. The following guests are there: Uschi Sachs and *[her sister]* Inge, Theo Rolf Alexander and *[his sister]* Gerda, Fritz Juliusburger *[a close friend]*, Eli Ruckenstein *[a well-known boxer whose nickname was "Kid Ruckenstein"]*, and I. Radio. Dance. Games. Horror stories in the dark. During horror stories lay next to Uschi on the couch, but very decent. Tip top. Party ends at 3:00 in the morning. 4:00 in bed. Summer weather continues.

Sunday, June 11, 1944—Go to the Chaoufoong Rd. Outpatient department. Checked by Dr. Salomon. Prescribes 1 ampoule glucose, vitamin. At 3:45 Theo Rolf and Gerda come over. Go together to the sports ground, which is reopening today. *[The sports ground, which was next to the Chaoufoong Heim, was a popular gathering place for young refugees who came on Sunday afternoons to watch the soccer games.]* Speeches by Kubota, Dr. Cohn. Then fun. Ball games. Till 6:30. Then for a quick visit to Uschi. Pick up the card with a poem that I had received last night and forgot to take. Uschi writes a dedication on the back. Weather nice but very warm.

Uschi's note read as follows: "This is just for you to remember an evening which I hope you too enjoyed." On the back she wrote the following charming poem, which provides some insight into the character and personality of the youthful Fritz:

> Jumping up and down—you see
> Just like the silvery mercury
> he wants to be the party's life
> he never feels all business strife
> he's never happy when he sits—
> it's "cigarette-holder-sucking"—Fritz.

Fritz and his contemporaries seem to have adapted better to the unusual circumstances of their lives than did the older generation. They enjoyed planning elaborate parties for birthdays and holidays, during which dancing, silly games, and drinks played a large role. They attended operettas, concerts, plays, comedy performances, and sporting events. They also rehearsed and put on their own plays and skits to entertain each other, and attended Theo Rolf's cultural club, which met in his home on a regular basis. Fritz and the other participants took turns giving lectures on various subjects, some historical, some quite esoteric.

Although his family had not been particularly observant in Berlin, Fritz continued to be immersed in the Jewish life of the Alexander family, attending Sabbath worship services with them on most Friday evenings and also sharing in their holiday observances. Theo Rolf's father, Hugo, brought a Torah scroll with him, and in his early years in Shanghai, had acted as rabbi for the Heime and conducted worship services at each of them. Later, he organized the first liberal services [*similar to American Conservative Jewish services*], which took place at the Broadway Theatre. Many traditional Jews were shocked at the inclusion of a mixed choir and organ in these services. In fact, one of the newspapers issued a tirade against such practices. Nonetheless, these were the most popular services. Dr. E. Silberstein was the first liberal rabbi, followed by Rabbi Georg Kantorowski. Max Warschauer was the Chief Cantor. Rabbi Willy Teichner, who died at an early age in 1942, founded a competing liberal congregation. Fritz spoke frequently of these religious leaders in his diaries.

Many other Jewish religious groups functioned in Shanghai. The Sephardi Jews had founded two synagogues, Beth Aharon (built by Silas Aaron Hardoon in 1927) and Ohel Rachel (endowed by Sir Jacob Elias Sassoon in memory of his wife, and consecrated in 1920). The Russian community established Ohel Moshe in 1907. They later moved to a larger rented space on Ward Road. Architect Gabriel Rabinovich (uncle of author Rena Krasno) designed its interior. In 1926, the Rabinovich family convinced Rabbi Meir Ashkenazi to come to Shanghai from Vladivostock. He served as spiritual leader of Ohel Moshe from 1926 to 1949 and was the Chief Rabbi of Shanghai. Orthodox Jewish German refugees with Eastern European origins felt most comfortable at Ohel Moshe. Eventually, refugees held their own worship services, either at the Broadway Theatre, the Eastern Theatre, or the Shanghai Jewish Youth Association School (see p. 67). Still other services were conducted in the *Heime* and in people's homes.

In 1941, the entire Mirrer Yeshiva, rabbis and students, arrived from Kobe, and was allowed to establish its house of study in the Beth Aharon Synagogue, where they also had their meals.

5

Conflagrations

After the Americans landed in Saipan, the largest of the Mariana Islands, in June 1944, U.S. Superfortress B-29s began to bomb Japan proper. As a result of these initial raids, the industrial complex in northern Kyushu was badly damaged. In spite of strict censorship, this forbidden news filtered into Shanghai, and the repercussions from Japanese reverses were felt throughout the city. Visibly tense Japanese occupation troops began acting more aggressively. All Shanghai residents awaited further developments with some trepidation. Would they bear the brunt of mounting Japanese frustration?

The majority of Shanghai's refugees—like the other Shanghailanders—did not know that even as the official propaganda machine kept on announcing continuous victories, most Japanese were now aware that they were losing the war. However, it seems that many in the Japanese government had come to believe their own falsehoods about the invincibility of their country.

Fritz described an increasing number of American air raids over Shanghai. From June 12, 1949 on, he listed 86 such raids by number in his diaries. There were actually many more than 86, since Fritz sometimes neglected to specify at the beginning of entries the number of the raid or raids he mentioned for that day.

Monday, June 12, 1944—REAL ALARM NO.1

At night, at 2:45 *[a.m.]* we are suddenly awakened by our group leader Rotholz. There is an air raid alarm. While Looser is still lying down, I jump out of bed. Still in pajamas rush out. Rubber boots. Briefcase. Money. Identity papers. Armband. Steel helmet hanging on my back. Below, in the courtyard, many people have already gathered. Announcement from Chaoufoong Rd. Heim: We should not wait for any instructions from the Headquarters because the Heim telephone is not working.

I send an orderly by bicycle to the Wayside Rd. Police Station and go myself to the Chaoufoong Rd. Heim. The gate is locked.

I knock. They let me in, then lock the gate again. I find myself surrounded by a half circle of policemen armed with batons. In the background: fire bell ringing and police whistles blowing. The Pao Chia Chief greets me. We decide on an identification system. I return home. Suddenly we hear the sirens again. Acute alarm. I meet the orderly who has returned from the police. Announcement *[from the]* Wayside Police Station: Situation serious. Everything to be done as prescribed. I inform Looser. Then sound the alarm with whistles.

People are gathered in the courtyard. I say to them: "Ladies and gentlemen! You are gathered here not only because of the siren alarms, but upon direct orders of the Wayside Police Station. This is not an exercise. This is serious. Turn and go as quickly as possible up the steps to the left, through the corridor to your rooms, pick up your valuables and identity papers, and return as quickly as possible. Mothers keep close to your children. The sick must not be left alone." General applause and movement.

Send Melch back to the Police Station. Looser and Deputy Chief Braun appear. All squads are here. Fire fighting squad is put up in "Middle Godown," first aid squad in the entrance of Building I, alarm squad in the entrance of Building II. Security squad divided. Almost everyone has appeared. The atmosphere is tense. No sounds of motors. Dep. District Chief Hendl comes. Orders: Everyone prepare. Fill the buckets *[i.e., with water; photographs of the time show people in Hongkew lined up with buckets of water during fires]*. I announce: Already done. New order: Dress the children.

I stay a while, then go on a tour of the neighborhood. The streets are empty. No people. Just here and there a Chinese Pao Chia man. Before I reach home I hear the all clear siren. Weather: hot.

Tuesday, June 13, 1944—Library. Borrow a copy of the map of France for the 3rd time *[in order to follow the progress of the invasion]*. In the evening listen to radio: From the World of the Opera. Wonderful. Lonely. A little too much Wehmut *[melancholy]*.

Wednesday, June 14, 1944—ALARM NO. 2

At night, at 2:00 o'clock *[a.m.]* we are awakened by the watchman. Preparatory alarm. I grab my uniform again. Ten minutes later acute alarm. All the people awakened and told to get dressed. Otherwise, take no other steps. At 3:30 all clear. Precautionary alarm status remains. All go to bed. I remain awhile downstairs. Suddenly I hear the familiar command in English outside, "Shut your light." I go out on the street. There are two men on bicycles. Police. It is Okura from the Bureau of Stateless Refugees Affairs. He asks me: *[in English]* "How many Pao Chia men do you have on duty?" "Ten men, sir." "Ten mens. Good!" Then he gives the order to enforce the blackout operation. I wake up Looser, Bromberger, and the squad leader. Continue my duty till 4:30. Then Bromberger, Looser, and I take turns. But since the all clear sounds at 6:10 I don't stand in line any more. I hear Looser go out at 5:15 and I fall asleep. At 7:30 the washman *[laundryman]* comes. I give him the laundry and go back to bed to sleep a bit more. *[Later]* pick up Pappi's summer suit that has been altered from tailor.

There were many refugee tailors in Hongkew. Some brought their skills from Europe; others learned this trade in classes offered by ORT, the Russian acronym for Organization for Rehabilitation through Training. This remarkable organization was founded by Jews in Russia in 1880, and later extended to many parts of the world, including China. In 1941, Shanghai refugees established a branch in Hongkew that offered training in various fields, including sewing, locksmithing, carpentry, driving, and bookbinding.

Many refugees could not afford to order custom-made clothing from tailors, and instead, paid them for turning old clothing inside out. Toward the end of the war, some residents of the Heime had worn out all their clothes, forcing them to wear pants made out of flour or potato sacks, a very demeaning experience.

Thursday, June 15, 1944—ALARM NO. 3

Evening: with Looser to Alexander's culture group. Lecture: Theo Rolf on Beethoven. I am the chairman. Very good lecture. Then a gemuetlich *[cozy]* get-together. Then suddenly at 11:30 preliminary air raid alarms. Looser and I return home as quickly as possible. The streets are very dark and the sky is cloudy. We are very relieved to find that everything at home is well prepared to keep lights out.

Saturday, June 17, 1944—ALARM NO. 4

In the morning to prayer services with Theo Rolf. Bar Mitzvah. In the evening Theo Rolf picks me up to go to Roy Roof Garden. Just as we enter, the manager rushes in: "Girls! Rake in the money!" And as the waitresses don't move fast enough, he shouts: "Quick! Quick!" I glance at Theo Rolf, stretch out my hand and drag him with me down the totally dark staircase, since I suspect a raid *[air raid]*. It is only a precautionary alarm. Very early *[for a raid]*, since it is only 9:30 *[p.m.]*. We rush home. At 11:45 all clear. The first alarms were apparently for American reconnaissance planes. On June 15 there were American planes over Nanking [Nanjing]. Yesterday Kyushu (Japan) bombed.

Sunday, June 18, 1944—ALARM NO. 5

Before lunch: to Klaus, whose birthday it is. Congratulate him. Suddenly at 11:50 *[a.m.]* acute air raid alarm. Immediately return home. Pao Chia muster. Supper at home. Pick up Theo Rolf to go to Roy's. Ice coffee, Baumkuchen. $70. Frivolity. Inv.: St. Sauveur le Vicomte taken. Germans use new secret weapon: planes without pilots. *[Probably V-1s; missiles were still fired by the Germans in mid-June 1944.]*

Monday, June 19, 1944—Jüdische Gemeinde, cemetery office. Mr. D. Asks me about payment *[for Semmy's funeral]*. Whatever sum possible *[would be acceptable]*. I promise to pay as soon as I can. Inv.: Cotentin Peninsula near Barneville. Contrary to expectations, no air raid alarm.

Tuesday, June 20, 1944—PCHQ *[Pao Chia Headquarters]*. Then pick up and make payment at the Radio Office for people who have no pass *[to leave the Designated Area]*. Earned $68.50. *[Fritz earned money by renewing such licenses for other refugees.]* Go home. Listen to first part of *Walküre*. Great music. Inv.: *[Invasion]*: Bonneville, Tartinet taken.

Wednesday, June 21, 1944—Morning: Chaoufoong Rd. Outpatient. Ampoules already prepared for me. Shanghai Bubbling Well Rd. to Dr. Gordon (sell coal ticket for $35.00). *[Fritz probably sold his coal-ration ticket to bring in a little cash.]* Concert: excerpts from *Aida*.

Thursday, June 22, 1944—PCHQ. Work on the Disraeli lecture. *[He was to give a lecture for the cultural club on Disraeli, Britain's historic prime minister, who was born a Jew and converted to Christianity.]* In the evening go with Looser to meet the Alexander cultural group in the Corso Garden *[a popular garden café in the Designated Area]*. Very pleasant get-together.

Friday, June 23, 1944—Morning: Chaoufoong Rd. Outpatient dept. Get first Tonifos injection, intramuscular. Work on Disraeli lecture. Lunch: Heim. Take bus #7 to the city. Radio Office. Back with #7. See a streetcar surrounded by military guards. Inv.: 2 kms from Cherbourg.

Saturday, June 24, 1944—Streetcar strike. To Wong. Receive payment *[for the buttons he had sold to him]*. Rickshaw to Post Office, $20.00. Pick up my shoes. Soles. (Had *[them made in]* leather, $260.)

Monday, June 26, 1944—Sell 1 pair of Pappi's shoes: $96! Do gymnastics at the Betar *[Brith Trumpeldor, youth affiliate of the New Zionist Organization, or Revisionists]* courtyard, led by sports teacher Leo Meyer *[Leo Meyer was a beloved gym teacher at the Kadoorie School]*. Inv.: the Americans entered Cherbourg.

Tuesday, June 27, 1944—In the morning 3rd injection. Have trouble at Radio Office: have to buy cigarettes for the employees. *[Probably the cigarettes were "squeeze," a bribe given in order to smooth the way to obtaining the certificates.]* Weather: very hot. Library. Make $91 *[from work for Borchardt]*. Sit on the roof garden till 12:00. *[When the heat was extreme, people went to the roof of their buildings to attempt to cool down. Often, they brought their bedding and slept there as well. It was so humid that their blankets were soaked through by morning.]* Streetcars working again. Inv.: Cherbourg taken. Russ. *[Russians]*: Vitebsk, Zhlobin taken. *[The Russians had opened a massive offensive in the central front.]*

Air raids resulted in fires in the Designated Area, which Fritz often helped to put out as part of his Pao Chia responsibilities. He was experienced at fighting fires due to his service as a member of the elite 100-man volunteer auxiliary of the Shanghai Fire Brigade (SFB) prior to Pearl Harbor. *[See Figure 12 for a photo of Fritz in Shanghai Fire Brigade Volunteer Auxiliary.]* That reserve was made up entirely of Westerners, some 90 of whom were British (the noncommissioned officers were all Chinese), and its purpose was to protect the International Settlement in the event the Chinese firemen were to go on strike. Fritz was recommended by his good friend and dentist, Dr. Joseph Gerendasi, who was a member of the reserves. After rigorous training that included rolling out hoses, pulling up ladders, and jumping into a safety net, Fritz attained the rank of lieutenant.

The minute details about fires in the diary demonstrate Fritz's life-long fascination with firefighting. As a young boy, he had learned that his Grandfather Marcus had been a volunteer fireman in Magdeburg, where he had a shop before moving to Berlin. Perhaps that was what triggered Fritz's interest. Even as he described devastating fires, Fritz wrote excitedly about the awesome sight it was to see the fire engines and firemen in action. Acting on this passion, he often chased fires, both in Shanghai and later in life. Looking back, he laughingly said that during his 12 to 24 hours of duty once a month, he mostly sat in the clubhouse learning to drink Scotch and hoping there would be a major alarm. (There never was while he was on duty, but he did use his skills when fires occurred under Japanese occupation.) Nonetheless, his time in the Shanghai Fire Brigade remained for Fritz one of his happiest memories of his years in Shanghai.

When the Japanese occupied Shanghai, they disbanded the Shanghai Fire Brigade, incarcerated "enemy national" firemen, and hired inexperienced Chinese. The result was disastrous.

Thursday, June 29, 1944—Just as I finish eating I meet Dr. Lavritz who said: "We must call the fire station." He rushes past me up the stairs to the roof garden. From below I hear the voices of many people. The women living there take up the cry: "Fire!" I yell in a loud voice: "Nothing is burning!" The women become slightly calmer. However, the children are still crying. Still, the panic has been stopped. I hurry to the roof and take a look.

A huge sea of flames can be seen. They are a golden yellow color. A fantastic sight. I don't wait and run back to my room where I tell Looser what is going on, put on overalls, boots, and leave the house, taking a baton and a pocket lamp. I hurry along Point Rd. The whole width of the road is taken up with people fleeing the fire. Three soldiers in uniform are carrying a long bamboo pole at the end of which is attached a huge lantern. A candle is burning in it. Japanese writing says: Imperial Japanese Navy Fire Defense. A Nissan fire engine arrives sounding its siren.

At hydrant (1), Navy Firemen are unsuccessfully trying to get water. They give up. Nissan Motors is burning and they are dragging out cars. I help. Since dull explosions can be constantly heard, I move back a little. The fire keeps getting bigger. I discover a hydrant that is blocked by a Navy truck.

After a couple of minutes, I decide to go to Tongshan Rd. In the left cross corner the flames have overpowered a godown. This is the storage house of family Th. Schneider & Co., 1007 Tongshan Rd. Left, on Dalny Rd. I see a big group of fire officers. A large number of hoses are lying in this direction. Many cables are lying around or are hanging on pylons. I now cross the corner to Tongshan Rd., to Ward Rd. No more hoses have been laid. I hurry back to the corner and bring along two firemen with a 2½ inch hose and nozzle, have the hose laid out. Get water from the garrison. At least here the greatest danger has been avoided.

Engineer Stricks comes running, calling for Foreign Pao Chia. He calls me by name, so I have to follow his order. He sends me with two other people to bring back the defense ladders from 818 Lane. We run there and get the defense ladders. I grab the first one, put it over my shoulder, followed by the other two carrying another couple [*of ladders*], and we get out of the Lane to Dong-sha Rd. A huge number of people are standing there filling the entire street. I yell like a stuck bull and order, "Run! Run! Run!" Shocked, the people move to the side. We run as fast as possible. Once we are out of the crowd, I let the people continue walking. Shortly before reaching the fire I start running again.

Attempting to stop the fire in a godown from spreading, Fritz used a special fire quenching method he knew, moving the hose from up downwards to create a solid cover of water, which acted like ten buckets at a time drenching the flames. After a wall collapsed endangering 300 kongs [*earthenware jars*] of sulphuric acid stored below, Fritz was ordered to find a messenger. He borrowed a bicycle from a man named Jokl and set off. However, the bicycle broke down, and he left it with a repairman to be fixed the following day. After going back to inspect the fire, he hitched a ride home in a Ford inspection car from the Hongkew Station. As he got off, he underestimated how fast the car was going and jumped off too soon, landing head over heels and injuring his little finger. By the time he got home, it was early Friday morning.

Friday, June 30, 1944—In the morning ask to be awakened early. To Dr. Salomon. Small finger swollen and in 2 places there is bleeding. Must carry my arm in a sling. Then have to go to the Chinese bicycle man. The repairs cost $200. Must bite the sour apple! In one hour get the bicycle back. It is not fixed. Everything inside is supposedly broken. Proceed to Jokl and he sends me to Mercur, his bicycle man, where repairs costs $20. The man takes the bike apart and shows me that the fork and steering controls are broken and must be soldered. Around $200. I say: OK. PCHQ. [*Look for and find my name*] on the list of those who were recruited to help during the fire. Then I return to the bicycle man once again. Jokl excited. Nervous. The bicycle man needs new replacement parts. Around $2500. Home. Theo Rolf and Looser there. Consult with them. Go to Dr. Kardegg. Pao Chia can't pay me *[for the bicycle repairs]*.

The matter of the bicycle repair was to plague Fritz for the next several weeks. His financial situation was already desperate, and the cost to fix the bicycle was well beyond his means. He was clearly very worried, and pursued a variety of business opportunities with varying degrees of success. He performed odd jobs, some of which were sent his way by his friend Herbert Braun, and he continued to import and sell buttons. No job was refused and nothing too menial to take on. Sometimes he was forced to sell his ration card. During this period, he also took time to visit family and friends, many of whom, like everyone in the Designated Area, were suffering from poor health. Amidst all of this, he battled his own continual health problems.

Like all the refugees, Fritz avidly followed the progress of the Normandy invasion and the Russian front. He often listed the battles and victories in his daily diary entries, and plotted the daily progress of the Allies with pins on a map. His spelling was sometimes erratic, no doubt because, due to the Japanese news blackout, he never saw these place names in writing, but heard them only from friends or on the Russian radio station, XRVN. The broadcasts on this station were not censored as a result of the Russo-Japanese Neutrality Pact signed in Moscow on April 13, 1941. While Fritz and his friends did not understand Russian, they were able to discern the names of cities that the Soviets reconquered. And all were thrilled by the words in English that concluded every program: "Eternal glory to the heroes who died defending their country."

6

Deteriorating Conditions

The early days of July 1944 were marked by constant air raids. With German precision, Fritz detailed the type of siren and the exact time for each. Japanese propaganda trumpeted Japanese victories while emphasizing the bumbling and stupidity of the Americans, with reports like the following in an English language newspaper:

U.S. Gunners Shoot Their Own Planes

American inefficiency is becoming clearer every day. Sergeant Fosie stated that U.S. gunners shot down 20 of their own planes. He explained that the incident is due to inexperience.

Although the refugees didn't completely believe reports like this, they were nonetheless discouraged by the constant trickle of bad news.

Even though five million Japanese troops were stationed in China, the occupation failed to have the military's hoped-for results. Forces were concentrated in the main cities, while the Chinese still held the countryside, seriously draining Japan's resources.

The following diary entries exemplify the frenetic life of a young refugee in the Designated Area, as he struggled to make ends meet, to stay healthy, and to enjoy a normal social life.

Saturday, July 1, 1944—To Dr. Salomon in Chaoufoong *[Heim]* Outpatient department. To Jokl *[about the bicycle]*. Get letter. PCHQ. Meeting with Captain Weinberger, who sends me to bicycle man Neumann. Then back to the fire. Everything quiet. Leylands withdrawn 20:15. Two jets from hydrant working. *[Altogether, Fritz spent 84 hours at the fire.]*

Monday, July 3, 1944—Outpatient: 5th injection. To Wayside Police Station. Hand in my old residence certificate. Take bicycle to Liaojung Rd. Repair of left handlebar $28.00. Order the work to be done. For other repairs I offer $200, which Jokl rejects. 20:20–21:30 and 22:15 air raid alarms.

Thursday, July 6, 1944—ALARM NO. 8

0:30 air raid alarm again. 2:00 all clear. Letter to Jokl in
which I set my terms which I wrote with the help of Looser
[who had a law degree from Germany]. Jokl refuses to accept the
terms of the letter. 6:00–7:00: precautionary air raid alarms.
Evening with Alex's *[Alexander's]* group on the Roy Roof Garden. Just as we are about to go home, at 22:55 precautionary
alarm. At 24:00 the alarm wails again.

Friday, July 7, 1944—ALARM NO. 9

In the morning Outpatient. 7th injection. Uncle Martin sick visit.
Meeting of troop leaders. I lay out general planning of duties
in case of an alarm. At 22:50 precautionary. Prepare everything.
24:00 acute alarm. After an hour and 20 minutes, all clear. Am
relieved of duty. Take Looser's folding bed to the roof garden.
Fall asleep. Suddenly bombs and shots, but no sound of engines.
Shortly after that acute alarm. Relieve Looser and Bromberger
and take over the watch. Sit with the watch team in full moonlight.
Wonderful. 1:25 all clear. To bed. Russ.: Kovel.

Sunday, July 9, 1944—Air Defense Day. Outpatient. 8th
injection. 10–10:30 In charge of preparations. Carry out streets
supervision duty. 15–15:30 precautionary alarm. Wear overalls. In
spite of the great heat only the helmet is permitted to be worn
on the head, but did my duty wearing my SFB cap. *[The heat can be
ferocious in Shanghai, and wearing a steel helmet undoubtedly felt like being
in an oven. Fritz solved the problem by wearing his Shanghai Fire Brigade
cap, defying the regulations.]* Home 21:00–22:30. Precautionary alarm.
Klaus goes on duty with me with Japanese on our roof for blackout control. Sleep on the roof garden. Russians: Baranow.

Monday, July 10, 1944—Summons about the Jokl matter from
the PCHQ. Dr. Kardegg: still no decision. To Yoshikiu. *[Yoshikiu
Choseingo, a Japanese man with whom Fritz did business related to his button
imports, is frequently mentioned in the diaries. Sometimes referred to as Y. or
Yosh., he had two offices, one on North Szechuan Road and one on Peking
Road. Fritz generally noted which of the offices he visited.]* Get the address
of the Customs brokerage company. Inv.: Caen. Russians: Lida.

Tuesday, July 11, 1944—ALARM NO. 10

Outpatient. 9th injection. To the Gemeinde in reply to an ad for
an office assistant. 13:37: preliminary alarm. 14:50: all clear. To
Ghoya to apply for a monthly pass. Evening: Theo Rolf comes
over to play chess.

Thursday, July 13, 1944—Outpatient: 10th injection (last one). Receive prescription from Dr. Salomon. Alcock Heim: get new medical card. Shower. Meet Neumann. Pay $280 for steering repair. In the afternoon go to a button store on Foochow Road to buy a fireman's badge which I wear in my buttonhole. Evening with Alexander group on the Roy Roof Garden. As usual, sleep on the roof garden. Russ.: Idritsa.

Friday, July 14, 1944—Wake up at 3 o'clock because I feel rain on my head. I jump up, grab my couch, and try to drag it to the staircase. Can't get through and I am stuck in the entrance, since others manage to get in before me and are blocking the way. Behind me, more people are trying to get in. Suddenly there is a downpour followed by general chaos. It takes half an hour until I finally am back with my things in my room and get to sleep. At 5:20 someone knocks. I don't answer but Looser calls: "Who is there?" "Here is Gruno"—our night watchman. "Is Mr. Marcus there? I think the fire has started again." I leap out of bed and rush to the roof garden. Luckily it is dry again outside. Find out that the fire is not in the District. So, this is no longer of main concern to me. This is already the third godown fire, and I suspect that these fires are acts of terror, since Japanese goods or buildings are always damaged. *[Although most Shanghai residents were unaware of their existence, there were some groups of Chinese resistance fighters. Naturally, their activities were never publicized by the Japanese.]* Russians: Vilna.

Monday, July 17, 1944—Meshuggener *[Yiddish for "crazy"]* day. Yoshikiu. Merchandise there, but the necessary papers are not. Outpatient. Hand in my Arsol prescription. Rockbottom financial situation. $6. in the pocket.

Tuesday, July 18, 1944—Get up at 6 o'clock. Braun has an order from Nademstein (who works for the Kitchen Fund) to pick up flour. The flour is in a mill 20 minutes ride away from our lane, through which no truck can drive. Therefore, the flour has to be transported in a hand pushcart through the street. I have been employed to supervise the transfer of the flour from the factory and sit there from 9:30 to 4:30, in the glaring sun in a rickety watchman hut, without food or drink. Then go with the truck to Hongkew. Nademstein pays $200. At the Heim no supper for me. So I eat a hamburger with potatoes and sauce for $29 *[probably at the Seward Rd. canteen]*.

Thursday, July 20, 1944—With Looser go for Braun to Robert Lee Godown to pack bottles of rum. Doesn't work out, so we get only 50% of our agreed payment, namely $15 per nose *[i.e., per person]*. Great Western Rd. to get a bread card for August–September. Russ.: breakthrough in Ostrov.

Friday, July 21, 1944—Evening visit Theo Rolf then to Uschi. Prima. Attempt to assassinate Hitler.

Most Shanghailanders were unaware of this bungled attempt on Hitler's life. Claus Philipp Maria Schenk von Stauffenberg belonged to an influential Catholic family of noble origin. On July 1, 1944, Hitler promoted him to the rank of Reserve Commanding Officer. However, by then von Stauffenberg had reached the conclusion that to save humanity, the Führer had to be assassinated.

At a July 20th meeting presided over by Adolf Hitler at the Wolf's Lair, his military headquarters in Rastenburg, in East Prussia, von Stauffenberg placed his briefcase containing a bomb close to Hitler under the map table, then excused himself on the pretext of an urgent phone call. When the bomb exploded, Hitler was injured, but not killed, protected by the heavy oak table or because one of the officers had inadvertently moved the briefcase. In the meantime, von Stauffenberg, believing the assassination attempt had been successful, fled to Berlin. He was caught, arrested, and executed by a firing squad. His wife—who was pregnant—and his four children were imprisoned, and his fifth child was born in jail. The widow and the five children were freed by the Allies.

The other conspirators were rounded up, summarily tried, and hanged on hooks in Plötzensee, a prison for political prisoners. After the war, this site, including the execution shed, became a memorial to the victims of Nazism. (On a trip to Germany in 1976, Plötzensee was the first place Fritz took his family. At a later date, he visited the memorial in the courtyard of the Benderblock, the former army headquarters where von Stauffenberg was shot.)

Sunday, July 23, 1944—Morning at Jokl's place with the balance of $200. Pay for the bicycle repair. Keep Theo Rolf company while he is on Pao Chia duty.

Tuesday, July 25, 1944—ALARM NO. 11
Morning home. Diarrhea. Go to Uncle Martin *[who has bronchitis]*. Klaus is also sick. Angina. 22:40: Precautionary. 24:00: all clear. Russ.: Lublin.

Thursday, July 27, 1944—Have been running around with Braun for the past 3 days. We get a job to drive people and guide them. We *[also]* drive with 6 trucks to the French Bund, and load sugar. We take the sugar to the North Station, where we load it in a freight car. Since Braun's company has only 2 trucks at its disposal, we have to order 4 trucks from a Chinese firm. It is my job to prepare the order, including a commission of 10% for us. The Chinese agree. We actually get $1,500, which we divide 50/50.

Sunday, July 30, 1944—Outpatient. Arsol first injection. Dr. Salomon finds me OK.

Monday, July 31, 1944—Ward Rd. Heim Laboratorium *[laboratory]*. Give a stool sample. Sell flour card for $15.

7

Striving for a Normal Life

In spite of the suffocating August heat, Fritz forged ahead, never complaining, never expressing a hint of self-pity. Nothing discouraged him, not the air raids, not his poor health, not poverty. Despite the many difficulties, he managed to maintain his cultural interests and develop close friendships that gave him both support and joy.

As a child in Berlin, Fritz had been exposed to literature, theatre, and classical music. Now and then his Aunt Ella took him to hear an opera. In a little red book, he kept a record of every opera performance he attended, listing the date, the venue, the names of the singers, and his comments. (As a child, he also listened to operas on the radio with the libretto open before him. However, he knew only the first and second acts of many operas, because he had to go to bed before the third.)

In Shanghai, these varied interests continued. Fritz listened to classical music, made frequent visits to the library, attended and gave lectures, and went to the theater whenever possible. *[There were scores of opportunities to see plays in Hongkew. In fact, over 60 German plays were produced by refugees, in addition to many operettas.]*

> **Tuesday, August 1, 1944**—Outpatient. 2nd injection. Get letter from Japan. To Yoshikiu, Peking Rd. Can pick up a case of merchandise. To Theo Rolf. Bathed Teddy *[Theo Rolf's dog]*. Russ.: Mariampol, Seydelitz *[now Minsk]*.
>
> **Wednesday, August 2, 1944**—Phone Foo (Standard). He wants the merchandise. To Yoshikiu on North Szechuen Rd. Check the merchandise. Eat ice cream. Visit Heinz Krebs who had a malaria attack. Introduced to Gerti Langer.

When the boys first met Gerti Langer, both were very interested in her. In fact, when she "accidentally" left her handkerchief behind, they argued over who was to return it. Fritz got the handkerchief, but Theo Rolf got the girl.

Thursday, August 3, 1944—Outpatient. 3rd injection. To Foo. Refuses merchandise due to size. After lunch to Wong. Takes the merchandise. $25,000 in cash—deposit by check. In the evening with Looser to Theo Rolf. ½ year existence of the culture club.

Sunday, August 6, 1944—Outpatient. 4th injection. Settle with G. *[It appears that Seppi Gerendasi has loaned money to Fritz to tide him over.]* Go for a ride until 6 o'clock. I learn to drive on a difficult road. Take along Theo Rolf and Uschi for part of ride. Already drive quite well. Today, at 4 p.m. a bomb explodes in the former Navy YMCA. Inv.: Louchac, St. Nazaire. Bretagne cut off.

Tuesday, August 8, 1944—ALARM NO. 13
All clear. Sleep on the roof. Suddenly awakened by a horrible rumble of engines. I sit up in bed and see an enormous plane coming out of the clouds over the Bund. Several dull explosions follow. Then antiaircraft fire starts. The plane disappears again. Acute alarm. It is 5:00 a.m.. At 5:30: precautionary, at 5:45: all clear. Cannot go back to sleep. What intrigues me is that the plane is of a very unusual type, and must have very special engines. In fact, during the day, we find out that early this morning an American B-24 attacked the Whangpoo area (Conte Verde). Russ.: Sambor, Baranow. 22:45: precautionary. 23:15: acute alarm.

The *Conte Verde*, an Italian ship that had carried many refugees to Shanghai, had been anchored in Shanghai harbor in 1943. As long as Italy was a member of the Axis powers, the Japanese did not take possession of the ship. However, on September 13, 1943, when Mussolini was deposed and Italy signed an armistice with the Allies, the *Conte Verde* crew scuttled their ship to avoid a Japanese takeover. The Japanese eventually salvaged and repaired the vessel, converting it for military use and renaming it the *Kotobuki Maru*. In his diary entry of August 8, 1944, Fritz went on to describe the unsuccessful attempt by the U.S. on that day to bomb the ship while it was docked in Shanghai. The "Axis Nightmare" (possibly the first radar-equipped plane in World War II, whose valiant crew destroyed many enemy aircraft) finally bombed and sank the *Conte Verde* in the Sea of Japan in 1945.

Wednesday, August 9, 1944—2:00: precautionary. 2:15: all clear. Air Defense Day. 9:30: precautionary. 10:30: acute. 11:30: precautionary. 12:00: all clear. Get money from bank. Meet Missie Gerendasi and return part of the loan. Watch big anti-air raid exercise, followed by address by Ghoya. G. takes into consideration people's stress caused by the numerous night alarms. Meet Borchardt. Together to Cafe Falbaum. 8:30 p.m–9:30 p.m.: acute alarm. 21:30 to 22:30: precautionary. All clear.

Thusday, August 10, 1944—ALARM NO. 14

Outpatient. To silver wedding anniversary of Hugo and Kaethe Alexander. Had ordered a cream cake from Cafe Louis inscribed with the number *[of the anniversary]* and asked that it be delivered. *[Café Louis, a popular café known for its continental style cakes and handmade chocolates, was owned by the Eisfelder family. Opened originally in 1939 in Bubbling Well Road, the family reopened in Ward Road Lane 24 in Hongkew after the Proclamation. When they left Shanghai in 1947, the café was sold to a Chinese businessman.]* Big reception. Prominent representatives of various Jewish religious organizations. Religious celebration. Chief Cantor Wartenberger, Chief Rabbi Silberstein, and four other speakers. Stay till 12:30. Get application for extension of pass. Buy margarine in Wing On *[big Chinese department store with fixed prices on Nanking Road]*. To Yoshikiu. Bring along shipping sample. Then invited for dinner to Alexanders. Dreadful rain. Shoes in my briefcase. Rubber boots over freshly cleaned suit. That's how I go in a rickshaw! When I arrive I fix myself up. Menu: Vodka. Stuffed tomatoes. Vodka. Noodle soup. Brisket of beef with potatoes and beets. Stewed peaches. Apple Strudel. Cream cake. The rain stops. Around 22:15: precautionary, 2:45: acute.

Friday, August 11, 1944—0:30 acute. 1:00: precautionary. We don't let it bother us at all. The festivities continue in the dark. Sometimes by candlelight. The party ends around 2:45 *[a.m.]*. I stay behind to help clean up. They convince me to sleep over. As we finally go to bed, a third acute alarm sounds. It is 3:00 o'clock. Lucky I did not return home, because I would have had to be on duty again. So, I just turn over and sleep till the morning. Precautionary: 5:30. All clear: 6:15. Americans have bombed Japan. Have breakfast at Alexanders. Clean and make order. Home.

When the Americans started bombing Japan, they dropped leaflets over cities and villages. Citizens would turn the propaganda over to the police, usually refusing to read it. But later, as the bombings intensified and the people realized Japan's situation was deteriorating, the Japanese began reading the content of the leaflets.

Saturday, August 12, 1944—Get sugar from Domberg. *[It is likely that to earn a little money Fritz was selling the sugar he obtained from*

Domberg to other refugees.] It's pouring. To Theo Rolf for supper. My cake *[from Café Louis]* is cut. Fritz Juliusburger comes over. I teach them both poker. We play till 2:00 a.m.

On August 13, the following life-changing notice appeared in the English language newspapers:

Registration of All Stateless Persons

In order to obtain a census and statistics of all Stateless persons residing in the Shanghai area, all those falling under the following categories are hereby ordered to register without fail:

1) Stateless persons of German, Austrian, Hungarian, Polish, Czechoslovakian, Latvian, Lithuanian and Estonian origin, who arrived in Shanghai before the year 1937 and were not subject to the Proclamation of February 18th, 1943, issued by the Commanders-in-Chief of the Imperial Japanese Army and Navy of the Shanghai area.

2) Stateless persons of above mentioned origin who arrived in Shanghai on or after 1937 but were given extensions to live outside the Designated Area, or exemptions from the above mentioned Proclamation.

Place of registration:

Bureau of Stateless Refugees Affairs

70 Haimen Rd. (Muirhead Rd.)

Period of Registration

August 14th to 31st, 1944 (with the exception of Sundays)

Time of Registration:

 9 a.m. to noon

Application forms to be filled in will be given applicants at the above mentioned address.

August 13th, 1944

By order

T. Kubota

Director General

Bureau of Stateless Refugees Affairs

This sudden order caused a great deal of consternation to all refugees both inside and outside the Designated Area. What were the Japanese planning to do? What was the reason behind this new development? Diverse rumors flew throughout the area.

At the same time, in the French Concession, the cultural Russian Jewish weekly *Our Life* (*Nasha Jhizn* in Russian, *Unser Leben* in Yiddish) published another notice, without a doubt upon Japanese instructions, stating:

> By order of Mr. T. Kubota, Director-General of the Bureau of Stateless Refugees Affairs. In order to take a census and statistics, all Stateless persons of Jewish origin residing in the Shanghai Area, who were not subject to the Proclamation of February 18, 1943, are hereby requested to register without fail with the Association, regardless of whether they are members of the Association or not.
>
> Place of registration:
> 132 Rue Tenant de la Tour
> or
> 137 Peking Rd., 2nd floor
> Date and time of registration:
> August 14 to 31, 1944, 9 a.m. to 1 p.m.
> Shanghai Ashkenazi Jewish Communal
> Association

This second notice was even more shocking to all Jews in Shanghai. It was the first time that persons of "Jewish origin" were specifically mentioned, a designation the Japanese had previously carefully avoided. Did the words "of Jewish origin" indicate increasing anti-Semitism resulting from pressure by Japan's Nazi allies?

Just as frightening was the fact that a Japanese official named Harada employed three teenage Jewish refugee girls in the Designated Area "to transcribe demographic data relating to the Hongkew refugee population from handwritten papers." The purpose: "For census taking." Seventeen-year-old Sonja Golombek (now Poizner) and Eva Mannheim, (now Zunterstein), age 15, were best friends. They and the third young typist (whose identity is unknown) had little typing experience and were understandably nervous about their task. They worried about the reason for the new order. Would it be harmful to Jewish refugees? Hesitant about the objective of their work, they typed slowly on antiquated typewriters, in spite of being constantly prodded by the Japanese to complete the task quickly. Then, abruptly, and for no given reason, the teenagers' assignment was stopped before completion. Still, they had typed a list of 14,784 names, most of whom were persons living in and around the Designated Area. Years later, this list surfaced in Vienna, made its way to Berlin, and is now included on a CD in the publication *Exil Shanghai* (see Bibliography).

Monday, August 14, 1944—In the afternoon go with Theo
Rolf and our friend Kornick to the editor of the *Jüdisches Nachrichtenblatt.* We want to put together a youth section. *[Arthur Kornick
was an older friend who had newspaper experience as an editor in Germany.]*

The newspaper the boys approached with their idea for a youth page
was a weekly evening paper published by the Gemeinde. Philip Kohn, the
editor, must have been impressed with their enterprising spirt, as their
proposal was accepted and their column appeared regularly for about six
months. The *Jüdisches Nachrichtenblatt* also continued after the Japanese
occupation, and was available to refugees in a free reading room set up
by the publishers. After the war, it was renamed *The Jewish Voice.*

In the years before Pearl Harbor, there were many newspapers, both
dailies and weeklies, published by refugees. A list found in the papers of
David Rabinovich enumerated 22 such publications. However, after December 1941, the Japanese halted publication of all but the *Shanghai Jewish
Chronicle*, which allegedly received financing from the Joint Distribution
Committee. After the war, the editor, Ossie Lewin, changed the paper's
name to *The Shanghai Echo*, and the paper survived until 1949.

The German language *Die Gelbe Post* (The Yellow Post) was considered
one of the best cultural newspapers in Shanghai, if not in all of Asia. Its
editor and publisher was Dr. A. J. Storfer, a close friend of Dr. Sigmund
Freud, whom he had hoped to follow to London. However, Dr. Storfer's
efforts to escape from Nazi Germany were unsuccessful and, in 1939, he
finally decided to leave for Shanghai where he soon founded the refugee
newspaper. It was so successful that in 1940 it became a daily paper.

Sunday, August 20, 1944—Crazy day. Morning at home.
Lunch: Heim. With Theo Rolf to Kornick. Discuss the next
Youth Page. Home. 15:00: acute alarm. Street duty. 16:00: Pre-
cautionary. Get dressed. Go to Theo Rolf. Work on the editing.
Around 6:30 a bomb is dropped on the Hongkong and Shanghai
Wharf. 19:15: acute alarm. Carry out Pao Chia duty together with
Theo Rolf. 21:00: precautionary. 21:10: all clear. Fritz J. comes
over. At 22:15 we start to play poker till 22:45 when there is a pre-
cautionary alarm. Leave and go back on duty. 23:00 acute alarm.
About midnight there are two frightening explosions. We run out.
It's pitch dark. We hear that before the second explosion, the sky
had turned dark red for a moment. Apparently, these were bombs
placed by terrorists. After a long walk to get ourselves under control, we continue to play poker.

Monday, August 21, 1944—ALARM NO. 17

We break up at 3:00. I win $26. Since the party included vodka, I have $4 left. Go home and take over the watch with two newly recruited men. 4:30: acute alarm. Wake up another team. 5:30: precautionary. 5:45: all clear. Drop into bed. *[During the morning]* visit Missie who is in the Ward Rd. Hospital with a light angina. 16:50: precautionary. 16:55: acute. 17:35: precautionary. 17:45: all clear. Pick up new food tickets for September from Alcock Rd. Heim. Hand in the article on the fire station. *[This article, one of two that has survived, describes a visit to a fire station, with detail about the tower, the watchroom, the engines, storerooms, etc.]*

Fritz remained close to Seppi and Missy Gerendasi, both of whom suffered from chronic health problems. Whenever they were ill or hospitalized, he always made it a point to go and see them, performing the *mitzvah* (commandment) of *Bikur Cholim*, visiting the sick. According to Theo Rolf Alexander, Fritz was very much loved by all his friends. Besides Theo Rolf and Gerti and the sisters Uschi and Inge Sachs, his close group of friends at the time included his roommate, Günther Looser, as well as Herbert Braun, Fritz Juliusburger, Alec Borchardt, Walter Wartenberger, and Arthur Kornick. He also got together often with his first cousin Klaus Marcus.

Wednesday, August 23, 1944—Outpatient. 9th injection. At home find an urgent message from Missie. Hurry over. Her husband, Dr. Gerendasi, is lying seriously ill in the Rue Pichon Jewish Hospital. Go on bicycle to get the written forms to apply for a monthly pass. Work on a poem. Pick up Uschi in the evening. Go together to Alexander's cultural group. Set the September-November winter program. I am to give the first lecture on September 6th on Disraeli.

Thursday,. August 24, 1944—To Yoshikiu. He has the documents on hand for the new merchandise and had sent people to the Customs Broker. Bank. Library. Evening: chess at my place. Inv.: Paris on the point of being taken. *[Supported by U.S. 4th Infantry Division, Free French General Leclerc entered Paris. Charles De Gaulle followed the next day.]* Americans take Grenoble. Allies pushing into Marseille. New landing near Bordeaux.

Friday, August 25, 1944—Outpatient. 10th injection. Go on bike to get papers for Missie G's transfer from the Ward Rd. Hospital to Country Hospital *[before the Japanese occupation, a fine, very well equipped British hospital in the International Settlement]*. Services.

Supper: Uncle Martin. Pick up Theo Rolf. Go together to Uschi.
Very loving. Russ.: Kishinev *[King Michael of Romania declared war on
Germany on this date]*. Inv.: Lyons taken by partisans.

Saturday, August 26, 1944—ALARM NO. 18
13:00: Precautionary. 13:30: acute. 14:00: precautionary. 14:13: all
clear. 23:00: precautionary. Evening: with Theo Rolf and Fritz J.
to Uschi. Acute air raid alarm. Hear explosions of falling bombs
and sounds of antiaircraft guns nearby. We press ourselves against
a wall and see searchlights directed to the sky. After a few minutes
the noise stops.

Sunday, August 27, 1944—At 0:05 *[a.m.]*: precautionary. To
everyone's surprise at 0:55 already all clear. Meet Theo Rolf at
Jüdisches Nachrichtenblatt. Hand in our article for next week. *The
Shanghai Times* publishes an article about yesterday's bombing in
the area between Shanghai and Woosung. The Japanese report
that the planes were chased away by Japanese antiaircraft guns and
the damage was minimal.

Tuesday, August 29, 1944—ALARM NO. 20
KF. Pick up coupons. 22:45: precautionary. Quickly on bike to
Juliusburger's Lane. Then further on by foot. At home take over
the entire Pao Chia. Send Looser to sleep. 23:15: acute alarm. Try
to have the courtyard completely evacuated but do not succeed.
Allow people to remain outside leaning on the building walls. Dull
bomb explosions can be heard. On the horizon, lights of antiaircraft fire. Finally get the courtyard vacated. The people fairly well
disciplined. Those on duty take cover behind benches. Antiaircraft
fire stops and it is quiet again.

Wednesday, August 30, 1944—Duty in steel helmet. 0:35:
again some explosions followed by a frightful hit. All conversation
stopped. But nothing else happens. 1:45: precautionary. 1:55: all
clear. Evening with Looser to Alexander's cultural group.

8

A Time of Transition

Fritz conscientiously discharged his responsibilities as Assistant Chief of his Pao Chia, and strove for a promotion to Inspector. His many social and cultural get-togethers gave him relief from this oppressive routine, as did his service as a member of the volunteer choir at Alexanders' services. He saw his friends very often, and seemed to be quite smitten with Uschi Sachs.

>   **Saturday, September 2, 1944**—Afternoon and evening work on my Disraeli lecture for next Wednesday.
>   **Sunday, September 3, 1944**—ALARM NO. 22
> Since Friday, PC *[Pao Chia]* Inspector Schranz *[the second highest official in the Ordnungsdienst, the Designated Area police]* has disappeared. He had an accident with his bicycle and a Japanese military truck. Since his bicycle was completely destroyed, he rode in the truck. As of today, he has still not reappeared. *[My Pao]* gets **an order** from the police to search all immigrants' apartments. *[Many refugees suspected that the Japanese, angry about Schranz's collision with their truck, arrested or even killed him.]* After the search, take my report to the HQ. There, I remain on duty with Fritz J. until 7 o'clock. 22:20: precautionary. Home. 23:40: acute. Observation from our roof together with Japanese.

At a later date, Fritz wrote in his autobiography more details about Shranz's disappearance:

> Shranz was on a bicycle inspection tour when he was hit by a Japanese army truck. People witnessed the incident. He was unhurt, but his bicycle was badly damaged and, using sign language, he discussed this with the Japanese soldiers. He made the mistake of arguing with them, asking restitution for his damaged bicycle while witnesses looked on. The result of the argument was that he put his bike onto their truck and climbed aboard in order to let them drive him to their military post where he could report

the incident to an officer. This was the last that was ever seen
of this man. We knew about the incident only because, after he
disappeared, the whole Designated Area passed the news through
the grapevine. Two days later, Shranz's body was found floating
in a canal into which he had been thrown by the two soldiers.
Rather than lose face or be reprimanded by their officers, they
just decided to dump him there in the canal. What they had not
counted on was the watchful nature of the Jews in the Designated
Area. The head of the Jewish community lodged a formal protest
with the Japanese authorities. Eventually, the Japanese authorities
acknowledged what everyone knew by then. They said that the
two soldiers had been apprehended and would be appropriately
punished, although we had no idea what this meant.

Every Japanese in uniform considered himself a representative of
the Emperor, a god to whom complete submission was demanded. For
this reason, almost all Shanghailanders and Shanghainese knew never to
argue with the Japanese military, nor to react when hit or slapped, because
this would almost certainly result in their death. Whenever a pedestrian
passed a Japanese soldier, he or she was required to bow. Even passengers on trams crossing the Garden Bridge over Soochow Creek had to
face the sentinels and bow. Disregarding this protocol could have grave
consequences.

Wednesday, September 6, 1944—Evening: Alexander cultural
group. Give my lecture on Disraeli. Inv.: Brussels, Antwerp.

Thursday, September 7, 1944—Looser hands in his resignation *[as Chief]* to the PCHQ *[nonetheless, he would still have to carry out
his assigned duty as a member]*. Inv.: Ghent. Italy: Lucca.

Saturday, September 9, 1944—Air Defense Day. Since Looser
is on holiday and Bromberger does not bother too much, I have
to do the main Pao Chia work. 4 o'clock: big Air Defense exercise.
Messrs. Inouye and Shimisu from SFB *[Shanghai Fire Brigade]* present. Greeted Inouye *[Fritz undoubtedly knew him because of his service
as a volunteer in the Brigade before the Proclamation]*. After the exercise
to Theo Rolf for supper. In the evening pick up Gerti Langer. All
four of us go over to Uschi. Spend a very pleasant and tender evening. One of the loveliest evenings of my life! Inv.: Liege. Bulgaria
declares war on Germany.

In the first of the diary entries that follow, Fritz reported attending a
wedding at the Kadoorie School. Later in the month, on September 30,

he went to a concert there, and over the years, also attended many other events at the school.

When he left Germany, Fritz received a diploma from Bobby Stern, the principal of his Jewish school, even though he was somewhat short of graduation. In Shanghai, though, he never attended school because he had no family to support him. Young refugees who did attend school in Shanghai recall fondly their years at the Shanghai Jewish Youth Association School (known as the Kadoorie School).

Lucie Hartwich, who became the headmistress of the Kadoorie, had been a public school teacher in Berlin until Jews could no longer teach in such schools. She continued teaching Jewish children in her home and later founded the Lucie Hartwich School, which was housed in the Prinz-regenten Strasse Synagogue. When she sailed to Shanghai, Ms. Hartwich gave English classes on the ship. The wealthy Sephardi philanthropist, Horace Kadoorie, who was traveling on the same ship, was impressed by Ms. Hartwich, and conveyed to her his intention to start a school for refugees in Shanghai with her as headmistress.

The school was established in 1939 in a building adjoining the Kin-chow Road Heim. Eventually, the school served 600 students, providing them with English and French instruction, music classes, a nurturing environment, an excellent lunch, and many sports, social, and cultural programs. The girls received cooking lessons, and all students learned good manners. Jewish worship services were held as part of their Jewish education. In 1942, again with the help of Horace Kadoorie, the school relocated to a new, modern building on East Yuhang Road.

Margit Diamond, the niece of Lucie Hartwich, described an unusual occurrence at the Kadoorie School. It seems that Ghoya (see pp. 31–32) would now and then stop by and visit the school. On one such occasion, during the holiday of Purim, the children were putting on a play about the heroic Queen Esther and the wicked Haman, who wanted to destroy the Jews. Suddenly, Ghoya, thinking Haman was meant as a representation of him, stopped the performance and arrested Lucie Hartwich. It was only at the subsequent behest of Horace Kadoorie that she was released.

Many Jewish children, including Russian, Sephardi, and European refugees (before the formation of the Designated Area) attended the Shanghai Jewish School, also called the Seymour Road School. That school was built in 1931 by another rich Sephardi Jew, M. Perry, who left money in his will for its construction, and a second Sephardi Jew, Elly Kadoorie, donated enough to complete the project. Later, as refugee children began pouring into the school, additional funds were raised by both Sephardi and Russian Jews. No refugee child was refused schooling. The school system was based on British educational standards. Children graduated after passing the Cambridge Matriculation, recognized in England as well as in some other countries. In addition to the British curriculum, students were also given classes in Judaism.

Sunday, September 10, 1944—With Theo Rolf. to Kadoorie School for wedding of Fritz Sello. Then worked on the youth page. Supper: Played poker with Theo Rolf and Fritz J. till 11 o'clock.

Tuesday, September 12, 1944—Bubbling Well Rd. *[to see]* Dr. Gordon. *[He]* did not buy coal tickets. Library. In the evening: Alexander cultural group. Lecture: Walter Silberstein: "Man and Economics." Allied troops 5 miles from German territory. Inv.: Luxembourg occupied.

Wednesday, September 13, 1944—Morning: To Social Welfare Department: housing matter. Get form for renewal of pass from Wong. Library. Post Office. Yoshikiu: North Szechuen Rd. Crates 8-9-10 still at customs. Papers arrive for 11. PCHQ. Evening to B.N.Z. for performance: "Mitn Shtrom" (With the Stream). *[The B.N.Z. was Brith Noar Zioni, an active Zionist youth group. "Mitn Shtrom," written in 1904, was the first play by the world renowned Yiddish author Sholem Asch.]*

In the next few days, Fritz had to stand in line for Ghoya three days in a row, twice a day for two of those days, before he was finally able to obtain the pass he needed to leave the Designated Area. This frustrating effort was repeated later in the month.

Thursday, September 14, 1944—Go early to stand in line for Ghoya. Then sell Pappi's old glasses. In the afternoon: again to Ghoya.

Friday, September 15, 1944—In the morning stand in line for Ghoya. Then go to the Gemeinde *[Jewish community]* and to Alcock and Ward Rd. Heim. Get soap. PCHQ. Find out there that Fritz Juliusburger is now provisional Sub-inspector. Lunch: Heim. To Chief Inspector Captain Weinberger. He is ready to accept me for the post of Inspector. Afternoon: stand *[in line]* at Ghoya's. Evening with supper to Uncle Martin's. Then alone to Uschi Sachs. Very nice.

Saturday, September 16, 1944—In the morning stand *[in line]* at Ghoya's. Finally get a pass till 10/10. Practice choir pieces that will take place at Alexanders' services.

A September 19th article in the weekly publication *Our Life* shed light on the observance of the High Holy Days in Shanghai.

High Holidays Observed with Solemnity by Jews in Shanghai

The High Holidays of Rosh Hashana and Yom Kippur were marked with especial solemnity this year in Shanghai. All Jewish shops and establishments closed their doors and many non-Jewish businesses give three days off to their Jewish employees. All the Synagogues in the city were overcrowded, but not as much as in previous years because the refugees attended prayers only within the Designated Area.

As to the Designated Area, the festive spirit was felt even more there than in other parts of the city, not only because all the cafes and shops remain closed, but because all the refugee street vendors and hawkers, who usually crowd the main streets of the Area, were conspicuously absent.

In all refugee Heime, special "holiday" cleaning was carried out, and the refugees for whom the Kitchen Fund cared received improved menus, or their equivalent in money, for the holidays.

The Synagogues in Hongkew were attended by a record number of people praying. While Russian and Polish Jews prayed mainly in the Ward Rd. Synagogue, at the Community Kitchen on Muirhead Rd., and at private homes, the German refugees attended "liberal" services at the Eastern Theatre (with organ playing and choir), and "conservative" services took place in the S.J.Y.A. School, camp halls, etc.

According to refugees, the most impressive services were those in the Community Kitchen, in which Cantor Antmann participated, and in the Eastern Theatre, where Cantor Warschauer participated.

Sunday, September 17, 1944—Erev Rosh Hashanah *[Rosh Hashanah eve]*. Loveliest European summer weather. Help at Alexanders' place to build the Aron HaKodesh *[the Ark where the Torah is kept]*. To services at the Eastern Theatre. Have a seat in Row 5 ($200). After that to Alexanders. Just in time for prayers. Invited to remain for dinner.

Monday, September 18, 1944—First day of Rosh Hashanah. Morning at the Eastern *[Theatre]* for services. Afternoon: pick up Fritz J. and Gerda A. Together pay a New Year's visit to the Sachs family. Then with Mrs. Sachs, Uschi, and Gerti Langer to evening

services held at the Alexanders. TRA *[Theo Rolf Alexander]* leads
the prayers. Alexanders ask me to stay for supper. Inv.: Allied
parachutists land in Holland.

Wednesday, September 20, 1944—ALARM NO. 23
Morning: work at home for *Jüdisches Nachrichtenblatt.* PCHQ.
Looser in bed with a cold. Evening: cultural group. Arthur Kornick Chairman. Schaefer *[speaks]* on the history of the newspaper
business.

Thursday, September 21, 1944—To the Country Hospital to
visit Dr. Gerendasi. PCHQ. 11:25: Precautionary. 11:50: all clear.
Dr. Kardegg had recommended me to the Captain as Inspector.
Looser and Bromberger were opposed *[it is not clear why]*. As a
result, I resigned last Saturday from my post of Assistant Chief
of Pao Chia. Today, I was present for the first time at a meeting
of the Inspectors' Council. Weinberger tells me that by Monday's
meeting he will probably have spoken with Kardegg. Since I already had spoken to Kardegg and he had not replied to me, I not
only agree but am very much in favor and in hopes of becoming
an Inspector.

Tuesday, September 26, 1944—Barber. Kol Nidre *[refers here
to the evening services for Yom Kippur, the Day of Atonement and the most
significant Jewish holiday of the year]*. Invited to Alexanders' to eat
before fasting. Pick up Ushi to go to services at Alexanders'. Sleep
overnight at A's.

Wednesday, September 27, 1944—Yom Kippur. Services at
Alexanders'. Chief Cantor Wartenberger and Theo Rolf lead the
services. Both *[of my]* parents are mentioned at Yizkor. I chant
Maftir Yonah in English and German. *[This was the first time Fritz
chanted this portion. Doing so became an annual honor that led to a lifelong
fascination with the character of Yonah (the prophet Jonah in the Hebrew
Bible) and an extensive collection of art objects portraying the prophet and the
"big fish."]* Stay at Alexanders for Break the Fast *[the daylong fast on
Yom Kippur generally ends with a celebratory meal called Break the Fast]*.
Then with Theo Rolf for a bottle of beer at Gruenfelds.

Friday, September 29, 1944—Still did not get to see Yosh.
Choseingo since yesterday was a holiday (Confucius's birthday).

Saturday, September 30, 1944—Radio Office. To a concert at
the Kadoorie School.

Fritz continued his series of inoculations, but did not define the nature of his physical problems. Although he was treated by excellent doctors in Hongkew, they were often hampered by the unavailability of medications. Two of the doctors whom Fritz mentioned had played an important role in medical circles in pre-Nazi Europe: Dr. Theodor Friedrichs (Berlin) and Alfred W. Kneucker (Vienna).

In 1940, Dr. Friedrichs was elected Chairman of the Hongkew Physicians Association and held this position until he resigned in 1944. He became interested in traditional Chinese medicine and studied the effect of Chinese herbs. He also made time to found and edit a journal, *Communications of the Association of the Emigrant Physicians in Shanghai*, which was published monthly in German and English, and also in Chinese. *[See Bibliography for Dr. Friedrich's 2007 memoir.]*

Dr. Kneucker was a renowned Austrian urologist. Besides practicing medicine, he wrote articles and a biographical novel based on his experience in Shanghai. Dr. Kneucker believed that Chinese doctors were limited by their centuries old traditions, and that they had difficulty accepting Western medical methods.

In spite of his poor health and inadequate living conditions, Fritz found comfort, even joy, celebrating the fall Jewish festivals with his close friends.

Sunday, October 1, 1944—Erev Sukkos *[the evening before the first day of the Feast of Booths, a harvest festival]*. Morning: at home. Bring back lunch from Heim. Go for services at the school in the evening, then to the dedication at the Corso Garden of the community sukkah. Get wine and challah *[special braided bread eaten on Friday night and festivals]*. *[The sukkah, erected during the eight days of the festival of Sukkot, is a representation of the temporary shelters, or booths, in which the children of Israel lived during their 40 years of wandering in the wilderness of Sinai. Such booths were also used as temporary shelters by farmers during the fall harvest in ancient Israel. The central theme of Sukkot is thanksgiving for the abundance of the harvest. On each of the eight days, observant Jews eat their meals in the sukkah and recite prayers.]*

Tuesday, October 3, 1944—Second day of Sukkos. Morning: with Theo Rolf and Gerti to services at the Kadoorie School. With Theo Rolf, receive an aliyah *[the honor of being called to the Torah during the worship service]*. Theo Rolf: Hagbah *[lifting the Torah scroll for the congregation to see]*, me: Gelilah *[dressing the Torah]*. Make a donation *[for the honor]*. At the end, Kiddush *[the blessing over the wine]* in the sukkah. Start preparations for Simchas Torah. *[This* *holiday celebrates the conclusion of the public reading of the Five Books of Moses and the beginning of the new reading cycle starting with Genesis 1:1.]*

Wednesday, October 4, 1944—ALARM NO. 24
In the evening go with Looser to Alexander's culture group. 20:45: precautionary. Around 21:45: all clear. Around 22:15: acute alarm. 22:30: all clear. The alarms prevent most from coming. The lecture is cancelled.

Saturday, October 7, 1944—To Wong. Get 50 mill *[million, signifying incredible inflation]* deposit. To Yosh. Still owe 20 mill. Take the merchandise by pedicab to the Wong factory. Lunch: Chinese, Szechuen Rd. opposite the Radio Office. In the evening with Theo Rolf, Gerda A., Mrs. A., and Gerti to a movie. Then to Alexanders' around midnight. Play Roulette.

Tuesday, October 10, 1944—Because I was unable to get a pass for French Town *[the French Concession]*, could not meet Mr. Woo. Foo (Standard) helped me by passing a sample from Crate 10. Later confirmed this by a phone call. Since the price is too high the merchandise is not accepted.

Wednesday, October 11, 1944—Special pass expired yesterday. Must wait at least another week since Ghoya is off. Evening big Simchas Torah party. $52 per person.

Saturday, October 14, 1944—Shabbat Beresheet *[the Sabbath when the Torah annual reading cycle begins again from Genesis]*. With Theo Rolf to services. Afterward: Kiddush. Afternoon to Oneg Shabbat *[literally, enjoyment of Shabbat; reception following worship services]* organized by Mendel Lewkowitz–H. W. Katz in the McGregor Rd. Synagogue *[located in the Kadoorie School]*. In the evening, bring a bottle of vodka to Uschi with Theo Rolf and Gerti. Brotherhood drink with the girls *[they start addressing each other with the familiar "Du" instead of the formal "Sie"]* (although for some months Uschi and I already used "Du" when speaking to each other). We do this in the traditional way with kisses. A delightful evening.

Sunday, October 15, 1994—Afternoon: with Theo Rolf to a wedding in the Ward Rd. Synagogue, according to traditional *[Orthodox]* rites. Marriage ceremony performed by Rabbi Ashkenazi *[Chief Rabbi of the Russian Jewish Community who had established excellent relations with the refugee community]*. Then to visit Rabbi Dr. Silberstein who is ill. With Looser to the opening of the Asia Seminar at the Kadoorie School. Finally, a lecture by Dr. Kneucker about physics and culture.

Thursday, October 19, 1944—In the morning to Ghoya. In spite of receiving Kitchen Fund support, I still get a pass because I am single. In the evening go alone to Uschi. "Evening of confidences." She talks to me of her plans. *[A peculiar series of numbers and letters follows, apparently written in a code devised by Fred to keep secrets from prying eyes.]*

Friday, October 20, 1944—Before lunch to Yoshikiu on North Szechuen Rd. Crates 8 + 11 have also arrived. Make calculations. To Missie. To services. Election of gabbaim *[wardens of the synagogue].*

During my walk home from a rehearsal I suddenly hear from a dark spot in Muirhead Rd. some loud meows, then a cat runs after me. When I bend down to look at him, he jumps on my shoulder. I take him home and look at him in the watchman's booth. He is pretty as a picture and clean and I take him—just on a trial basis—to my room. The long and short of it is we keep the cat. His name is Augustus and he is our great joy. *[Many refugees kept cats because of the prevalence of rats and other vermin.]*

Saturday, October 21, 1944—In the morning to Wong. He buys crates 8 and 10. Library. Play poker with TRA and Fritz J. Go to Gruenfeld at 11:30. Vodka and great waffles. After that read a 3-page Swiss magazine photo reportage titled "Bombed Berlin." Very much impressed. *[Unfortunately, Fritz does not relate how he got hold of this type of material, which was prohibited by the Japanese.]* Russ.: Belgrade.

9

Superfortresses over Shanghai

After every U.S. air raid the Japanese always claimed success, often using standard wording such as in the following excerpts from news releases: "Sirens sound here as U.S. planes scout around and scurry off, having sustained severe damage in frontal clashes with the Japanese Air Force." "Enemy machines beat a hasty retreat upon being detected by Japanese planes."

In reality, Japanese fighter planes could not reach the U.S. B-29s, which flew at 30,000 feet with deadly speed and caused great devastation within minutes. Although the Japanese had designed a special plane, the Raiden (Thunderbolt), to fight the B-29s, production was advancing very slowly as a result of deteriorating conditions in Japan.

On October 26, 1944, the same day that the Japanese were claiming successes, there was an item on the front page of an English language newspaper: "The Shikishima unit at the Kamikaze Special Attack Corps, at 10:45 hours on October 25, 1944, succeeded in a surprise attack against the enemy task force including 4 aircraft carriers."

The Kamikaze Special Attack Corps? This was the first time most Shanghai residents had ever heard of it. On page 3, an article titled "Kamikaze—Divine Wind" clarified the origin of the term. It is said that when Kublai Khan attempted to conquer Japan in 1281, the gods created powerful typhoons that destroyed the would-be Mongol invaders. Hence the term *"Kamikaze"* (literally, Divine Wind), which the Japanese used to describe their heroes on suicide missions who attempted to dive into Allied warships.

The paper ignored yet another Japanese disaster that occurred on October 26, 1944: U.S. victory in the naval battle of Leyte (Philippines), which forced the remnants of the Japanese Combined Fleet to withdraw in defeat. In effect, Japan had lost the war at sea in the Pacific.

People in Shanghai knew important events were being hidden from them by Japanese censors, but they still did not realize the extent of Japan's losses. They sensed that Japan's long series of victories were a matter of the past. The U.S. had fully rearmed and successfully reorganized its armed forces. Contrary to Japanese theories, the "pampered" American people were fighting back with courage and power. What would happen? Would the Japanese remain true to the Samurai Code, and fight to the death, drawing with them the population of the foreign lands they occupied?

Thursday, October 26, 1944—Reports in the daily press that yesterday planes bombed the suburbs of Shanghai but did no damage.

Wednesday, November 1, 1944—Get rest of the sum for crates 8 + 10. Cash bank check. Dr. Tonn's seminar: "Chinese Festivals." Evening: Alexander lecture group. Schaefer: "The Jewish Mentality." Chairman: Kornick.

Fritz never gave up his attempts to create new business opportunities, no matter how minimal, since he was always short of funds. At last, his persistent efforts to receive buttons from Japan paid off. The goods arrived in Shanghai, and he managed to sell some of them. After this small success, despite relentless perseverance, he had a difficult time concluding any other button deals, and when he did, it was a small quantity at a very low price. He then resorted to selling shirts but, alas, also without success.

Sunday, November 5, 1944—PCHQ. 6–8 seminar: Tonn— "Cultural History of China II." Rainy weather for one week.

Wednesday, November 8, 1944—To CSC, Yates Rd. *[one of the offices of Yoshikiu, with whom Fred did business]*. Interested in the merchandise. They keep the samples. Library. Lunch: Heim. With Theo Rolf, Gerti, Kornick to Asia Seminar. Lecture: Looser— "The Meaning of Jewish History." With supper to Uncle Martin.

Yates Road, nicknamed "Underwear Road," where Yoshikiu's firm was located, was famous for silk, embroidered lingerie, handkerchiefs, slips, nightgowns, and panties. There, one could also find Chinese dresses, mandarin jackets and coats, and fake antiques. These businesses continued hobbling along during the Japanese occupation.

Thursday, November 9, 1944—Air Defense Day. Many alarms. Get up at 5 o'clock in the morning. In the morning to CSC. Is not taking any merchandise. Heim. In the afternoon go with selected first aid team and two stretchers to the big exercise at Tongshan and Dent Rds. I lead our people. Evening: till 21:00 blackout. Dead tired to bed. President Roosevelt reelected.

To the refugees, Roosevelt was a god-like hero who would one day save them. The Japanese, of course, vilified him, calling him "a man of brutal force lusting for power." They even spread the Nazi lie that he was a Dutch Jew named "Van Roosevelt."

From this point on, the air raid alerts increased in frequency, sometimes occurring more than once a day. It is probable that Fritz was the only person to number the alarms as they occurred in Shanghai. However, he and Looser, as well as the other young people were not afraid, and—despite the danger and the strict prohibition against doing so—they went up to their roof to watch the American planes. After the raids, they continued with their daily lives as if nothing unusual had happened.

There were no actual shelters in Hongkew, and very few cellars. In the Heime, residents simply assembled on the first floor. Some Jews gathered in the basement of the well constructed Ward Road Jail for protection; others simply ignored the alerts. Some walked around with cooking pots on their heads for protection. Outside, they jumped into ditches in the street. Surprisingly, a number of former refugees who were interviewed for this book, including several who were teenagers in Shanghai, maintained that they did not remember the alerts at all.

Fred's helmet—to which he referred quite frequently—was like a hard hat, part of his gear as a member of the Pao Chia. In contradistinction to such functional headgear, women in Japan sewed useless headgear for themselves and their children that was supposed to protect them in the event of an air attack. They were ordered to carry these "helmets" suspended from their shoulders at all times. Should they forget to do so, they were strongly reprimanded by officials and teachers.

Saturday, November 11, 1944—ALARM NO. 26

In the morning we suddenly hear the sounds of loud explosions. Two minutes later sirens screech acute warning. I lie low, because I think the bombing is now over. But after a while it starts again. And then in shorter and shorter intervals. The AA *[antiaircraft)* fire is deafening. Shrapnel falls in our courtyard. It becomes rather dangerous to remain outside. The early morning cloudy sky clears slowly. I go to our roof garden (which is forbidden) with Looser, wearing a steel helmet according to ARP instructions. We want to observe the American planes. During the alarm (4½ hours), I go to the Seward Rd. Heim to eat lunch. Then to congratulate Uncle Martin, whose birthday it is. *[See Figure 13 for photo of Uncle Martin.]* At 13:15: precautionary. 14:25: all clear. In the evening we are informed that several American B-29s entered the outskirts of the city and caused damage. 2 dead and a number wounded by shrapnel. In our corner, a Chinese house was seriously damaged by shrapnel.

In the afternoon go with Looser to Alec. Gerti and Kornick also there. Actually, we had wanted to discuss Looser's lecture, but since we are still completely awed by this morning's events, we don't get around to doing this.

Sunday, November 12, 1944—ALARM NO. 27
Heim. In the afternoon with Theo Rolf and Gerti to the sports ground. Then alone to the Asia Seminar. Tonn lecture: "Chinese Cultural History III." After dinner to Marcuses. Morning: 9:55: precautionary. Everyone very nervous. 10:55: all clear.

Tuesday, November 14, 1944—Shanghai. My sample returned. Nothing is bought. Library.

Friday, November 17, 1944—ALARM NO. 29
Morning: 8:20: precautionary. Weather bad again. I again grab all my equipment. 8:35: acute. Roof garden. See only two Japanese fighter planes. Nothing else happens. 10:10: precautionary. 10:15: all clear.

Sunday, November 19, 1944—ALARM NO. 31
Morning: PCHQ. Looser resignation [as Chief] accepted. Captain Bluehdorn becomes new Chief. With Looser to Asian Seminar: Lecture by Tonn: "Chinese Cultural History IV." Hardly 10 minutes there, around 20:46: acute. I hurry home in pitch darkness. Around 21:50: precautionary. 22:15: all clear. The whole evening is ruined without anything happening.

Tuesday, November 21, 1944—ALARM NO. 33
Awakened in the morning at 7:30 by precautionary alarm. Put on complete air raid protection outfit. 7:40: acute. A little later a few explosions, longer pauses, then more explosions. AA not as active as the last time. As a result, fewer shrapnel splinters. Only one in our yard. I go to the Heim for lunch around 12:00 since nothing further is happening. Just as I finish eating, some horrible explosions. As I look up to the sky, I see 5 B-29s flying in formation. There are thundering sounds from all sides. I hurry home and go to the roof garden in my air defense uniform. A little later, 3 more planes arrive and drop bombs. Their strong effect and a few fires can be seen. 15:40: precautionary. 16:00: all clear from only a few sirens. In the evening: no electricty. Arrange that all strangers entering the SACRA Compound hand in their Residence Certificates. Police orders: 2 men and 1 officer must be on duty throughout the night. I myself am on duty from 23:00.

Wednesday, November 22, 1944—ALARM NO. 34
Around 1:10 lights return. However, since no street lights
functioning, continue my duty. At 3:00 Bluehdorn relieves me.
Afternoon: Pao Chia work. Tonn seminar: "Indian Literature."
To Theo Rolf. To Uschi. 21.05: precautionary. 21:07: acute. 22:40:
precautionary. 23:00: all clear.

Thursday, November 23, 1944—Morning: Shanghai. No
streetcars. Library. Customers. Pao Chia work. Evening: Pao Chia
meeting. Looser says good-bye. Bluehdorn takes over. I speak
about air raid protection. Applause.

Friday, November 24, 1944—Walk to customers in the city.
Chung Hwa button business keeps samples. They want a part of
the goods, but at very low price. Will give my reply tomorrow. To
services. With supper to Uncle Martin. His pass taken away and
he received a beating.

Saturday, November 25, 1944—On bike to Shanghai. In spite
of bad price, deliver *[the rest of the merchandise]* to Chung Hwa.
Evening: Theo Rolf, Fritz J., Gerti, with a bottle of vodka and ¼
lb. cookies to Uschi. Take radio along.

Tuesday, November 28, 1944—Yesterday, the tramcars start
running again for the first time. A notice about this in today's
paper. However, when I come to the tram station, *[I]* see that all
trams are going back to the depot. Rent bike. Library. Wong pays.
Gives me letter for extension of pass. Pay Yoshikiu the balance.
Lunch: Heim. All day horrible weather. Afternoon: PCHQ.

Wednesday, November 29, 1944—Raining. Afternoon:
to Ghoya. Get a pass till December 30 without any problem.
PC—work with Bluehdorn. Evening: with Looser to Theo Rolf's
cultural group. Discussion about Looser's lecture of November 8.

Thursday, November 30, 1944—Work with Bluehdorn in PC.
Evening: District meeting. Hendl explains again why I have still
not been appointed Inspector. Irritating. However, I am fully recognized as such. That's why I am invited to the meeting. During
the meeting, I am publicly praised. Afterward, it is decided that
I should train Bluehdorn and participate in the inspection group
of Weinberger, since it appears I don't want to remain in the Pao
under present circumstances.

By December 1944, Shanghai was a different city from the one Japanese forces had occupied after Pearl Harbor. The streets, never clean,

had become even filthier. Popular British double-decker buses had disappeared and single-decker bus service was irregular. Moreover, due to the lack of gasoline, a new contraption with a pipe spewing black smoke, which the French called *gazogene*, was fitted on the front of most buses. The limousines of high-ranking Japanese officers had been likewise converted. Electric trams also became unreliable and ran infrequently. Clumsy wheelbarrows clogged the streets transporting people, goods, and farm animals. Prices rose constantly. Many Chinese could no longer afford to buy rice. One newspaper headline was vividly descriptive: "Man Gives Child to Hawker for One Sack of Rice."

In a deteriorating city, Fritz and other Jewish refugees faced increasing problems. Nerves were frayed by constantly increasing numbers of air raid alarms. The biting cold weather in 1944 added to the difficulties. To stay warm, Fritz and the other refugees had to wear just about every piece of clothing they owned; some whose clothes and outer wear had worn out were never able to escape the cold.

Sunday, December 3, 1944—Nice weather, but terribly cold. Morning: to Eastern Theatre for "Das Dreimaederlhaus" *["House of Three Girls," a comedy accompanied by Franz Schubert melodies]*. Very nice. Home: to clean with boy *[male Chinese servant]*. Asia Seminar: lecture by Tonn: "Chinese Cultural History VI." Besides my suit, wearing the following: street jacket, flannel pajama top, coat with belt, scarf around my neck, a beret, black gloves with torn fingertips, and Augustus *[his cat]* on my lap. *[The Chinese Fritz knew described each winter by the number of coats needed—i.e., a "one-coat winter," "two-coat winter," etc.]*

Monday, December 4, 1944—Wanted to go to the city. After standing 1½ hours at the tram station still cannot get a ride and give up. PCHQ. Flower pot with charcoal keeps the room a bit warmer. Cook semolina *[cream of wheat]*.

Thursday, December 7, 1944—Shanghai. Yoshikiu, Peking Rd. Crate #12 now in NSR *[North Szechuen Rd.]* office. Work with Bluehdorn. Finalize my resignation. Evening home. Bitter cold.

On December 7, 1944, an earthquake of 7.9 magnitude, the *Tonankai*, caused tremendous damage in Nagoya, destroying most of Japan's aircraft industry, which already lagged far behind that of America. Also in December, U.S. B-29s based in the Marianas increased bombings in Japan proper, as well in the territories it occupied, including Shanghai.

Sunday, December 10, 1944—Erev Chanukah. *[Chanukah eve.*

This Jewish festival commemorates the victory of the Maccabees over the Syrians in 165 B.C.E. after several years of fighting. Judah Maccabee and his followers rededicated the Temple in Jerusalem, which had been desecrated by the Syrians. According to Jewish tradition, there was enough oil for only one day, but a miracle occurred and the Eternal Light burned for eight days. For this reason, Chanukah is celebrated for eight days.] With Theo Rolf to services. With supper to Alexanders. Then pick up Gerti. With the entire family. "Gottes Segen bei Cohn" *[a card game].* 1:30 to bed.

Friday, December 15, 1944—Shanghai. Get Wong's money immediately without any problem. Cash the check. Afternoon: services. 6th day of Chanukah. With supper to Uncle Martin.

Saturday, December 16, 1944—Icy cold. Yoshikiu, NSR. New price of bread: $84 per lb. Black market: $200. per pound. Evening to Fritz Juliusburger's birthday party. Very nice.

Monday, December 18, 1944—Klaus comes over. Teaches me dancing. *[See Figure 14 for a photo of cousin Klaus.]*

Tuesday, December 19, 1944—ALARM NO. 37 8:28: precautionary. 9:35: all clear. 10:30: acute. 12:00: precautionary. 12:39: signals for acute.15:00: precautionary. 15:45: all clear. In the afternoon several explosions can be heard and shrapnel can be seen. Not on duty.

Increasing night air raids and deep blackouts seriously affected visibility on Shanghai's streets. As a result, Japanese authorities published strict warnings for pedestrians to be cautious. Japanese military vehicles loaded with soldiers and arms often raced through Shanghai to unknown destinations. At night, because of the blackout, no headlights were permitted.

Pedestrians Are Urged To Keep off Roads At Night To Check Accident Toll

Walkers must keep to the pavement on the left side of the roads and where there is no pavement, as far as possible in the roads, in accordance with traffic rulings. Motorcar drivers under the present conditions at night are often unable to spot pedestrians walking on the streets and consequently it is essential that the public obey.

Wednesday, December 20, 1994—The daily newspapers report that yesterday morning one—and later in the afternoon—10 enemy *[American]* planes flew over Shanghai and bombed its south and east areas. 50 houses destroyed and 100 Chinese wounded.

Morning: to Yoshikiu and pick up merchandise. Take it to Chung Hwa on Hankow Rd. Get a check. Preparations for New Year's eve. Practice dancing.

Sunday, December 24, 1944—To Gerendasi. Business reckoning. Asia Seminar lecture: Tonn—"Chinese Cultural History IX." 21:00: precautionary. 21:05: acute. 22:30: precautionary. 22:45: all clear. 23:05: acute. 23:45: precautionary. 23:50: all clear.

Tuesday, December 26, 1944 to Saturday, December 30, 1944—ALARM NO. 41
During the entire week big preparations in Theo Rolf's apartment for the New Year's Eve party. 27.12.44 *[December 27, 1944]* at 20:45: precautionary. 21:00: acute. 21:50: precautionary. 22:00: all clear. 23:50: acute. 1:05: precautionary. All clear.

Sunday, December 31, 1944—Morning and afternoon: preparations for party. Pick up Uschi. Some 30 people there. Ego *[I] [am]* Maitre de Plaisir *[in charge of fun]*. With Fritz J. and Uschi present a skit: in a Japanese travel office (shipping of a dog to Australia). Then Ego: New Year's greetings. Then drinks **with** Uschi on my lap. Enjoy it until 4:30. Go to sleep there. Leave for home at 8:00 in the morning.

10

Depressing Days

In the first days of 1945, life in the Designated Area was becoming increasingly more trying. Former refugees recall escalating hunger, wornout clothing, growing poverty, more suicides, continuing angry clashes between family members, and an overall subdued mood.

Fritz exemplified these taxing times as he reported on the failures of his business ventures and the frightening possibility that the Kitchen Fund subsidies, on which he depended, could end. He described in detail every morsel of food provided by the Heim, where he lunched daily. It is obvious that his diet was deteriorating. He harangued himself for not accomplishing more than he was. Further, he slept longer and more often during the day, a certain indication of depression, from which he sometimes suffered later in life. Yet, amidst all these travails, he was temporarily buoyed by the joyful New Year's Eve celebration with his friends and his budding romance with Uschi.

Monday, January 1, 1945—Eat lunch in bed. Then get money from KF. To Theo Rolf. Clean up. 6 o'clock: go home. To bed.

Tuesday, January 2, 1945—Morning: Shanghai. Do not achieve any results. A holiday. Afternoon: sat in the courtyard in the sun. Work at home. Clean up. Finances bad but mood good, since the New Year's party was terrific. Impressions: Uschi was very affectionate. Hope we will continue to get closer and understand each other well. Also there: Inge, Theo Rolf, Gerti, Gerda, and Fritz J. We sat on couches, covered with coats. Uschi was really sweet to me. Bluehdorn brings me Deputy Chief nomination letter.

Wednesday, January 3, 1945—Morning: at home. Lunch: Heim. Vegetable soup. Go to Klaus (since the 24th I have been going there every day, [as] Klaus has jaundice). PCHQ. Get new armband. Gerendasi's fur coat stolen. PCHQ. Disciplinary proceedings. Pick up Uschi. Alexander's cultural group. Lecture: Kornick: "The Technique of Newspaper Production."

Saturday, January 6, 1945—ALARMS NO. 43/44

Air raid alarm wakes me up. 8:20: prec. *[precautionary]* 9:30: all
clear. Lunch: Heim—kasha *[porridge made of wheat, buckwheat, oats,
millet, rice, potatoes, etc.]* with clear soup and meat.12:45: precautionary. Sit in the sun—delightful. 15:10: all clear. Evening: with Uschi
at Theo Rolf's. Post New Year's eve celebration. Drink the rest of
the drinks. At 1:44 to bed.

Sunday, January 7, 1945—Grey day. Bitterly cold. A few
snowflakes. Morning: rest in bed without breakfast. Lunch—
Heim: white beans, sweet sour, 1 hot dog. Spend 2 hours at the
sports grounds. Completely frozen. Return home. Work. Asia
Seminar: Tonn's lecture—"Asia's Cultural History XI." End of
semester.

These past few pages and those that follow reflect Fritz's mood and the
freezing temperatures. The ink is very pale and very difficult to read.

Tuesday, January 9, 1945—Lunch: Heim—vegetable soup.
On foot to Shanghai. Library. Then on to 2 unsuccessful business
attempts. Horribly cold but dry. Completely frozen. Have a cup of
house coffee at Fürenberg's. In the evening go home in the dark
since it is Air Defense Day. Thank God not on duty ever since
Air Commanders of Pao for ARD have taken over air defense.
Nevertheless, we work together, but I am on duty only in case the
situation is serious.

My financial situation does not appear to be too rosy at the
moment. No more merchandise is arriving from Japan. I am
almost broke. Possibilities to make money are bad. Klaus has been
working for some time as a thread puller in a wool spinning business. I could possibly get work there too but the decision is hard
to make. The work hours are from 8 a.m. till 6 p.m. with a 1 hour
break. Then there is the horrible cold there that makes the decision even harder. Will I be able to stand this physically? On the
other hand I am tempted by the pay of $300 per day. So, I think I
will try to start working there since I feel down and lead a life like
a bum. I cannot get out of bed in the morning before 8:45. That
must be changed.

The truth is that I have never in my life done hard physical
work. In the present situation, it is becoming evident I must undertake something. I will do whatever is in my power to work my
way up. With God's help, a better time will come.

Wednesday, January 10, 1945—Hot water will be increased
from $10. to $20.

Thursday, January 11, 1945—Morning: Shanghai. Load
buttons for Diestel. Pick up a letter form from the Red Cross.
Lunch—Heim: carrots and beef. Crisis imminent at the Kitchen
Fund. Numerous American landings in Luzon.

Friday, January 12, 1945—Notice from the Kitchen Fund.
They want to cut off many recipients, and especially to cancel
the evening food subsidy. In the morning to the Alcock Heim
for coupons. I am lucky and get coupons for evening meals till
the 15th. Hopefully also after that. Pick up family records from
the Jüdische Gemeinde. Lunch: Heim. Red beans and noodles.
Shanghai. Pick up soap and sugar. Visit Theo Rolf. Services. With
supper to Uncle Martin. Reply from Klaus: no chance to get a job
at the spinnery until after Chinese New Year.

During these trying wartime years, many poor Chinese lived side
by side among the Jewish refugees. It is indeed remarkable that these
neighbors never showed resentment or antagonism toward the Jews.
In fact, relations between the two groups were always cordial. Refugees
who returned to the Designated Area after the war were—without exception—warmly greeted by former Chinese neighbors. Many even came to
see their old friends at the reunion of refugees held in Shanghai in 2006.
Not one refugee interviewed for this book expressed anything but friendship and gratitude toward the Chinese people.

Saturday, January 13, 1945—Morning: Shanghai. Diestel not
interested in the buttons. Lunch: Heim—kasha, clear soup, and
beef. Sleep at home. Buy Gert's food ticket and have the second
meal at home. In the evening to the Sachses.

Monday, January 15, 1945—Morning: sell a case for $700,
which brings me a little cash so I could pay the washman. Lunch:
Heim—vegetable soup. PCHQ. Theo Rolf. Played "Mensch
ärgere Dich nicht" *["Man, Don't Get Annoyed," a very popular German
game, similar to "Snakes and Ladders," played with dice and little colored
figures that are moved around a board]*. Russ.: Since yesterday huge offensive on the East front from East Prussia to Budapest.

Wednesday, January 17, 1945—ALARM NO. 46
Morning: at home. Lunch: Heim. Lentils, sweet and sour. Sit in
the sun. 15:10: acute. Can hear engines, antiaircraft guns, and
bombs exploding. *[Go to]* roof. Several big fires to be seen outside

the city, but quiet. 16:00: precautionary. 16:45: all clear. Sell trans-
former to Klingel for $1,500. Russ.: great breakthrough—Warsaw,
Radom.

Thursday, January 18, 1945—ALARM NO. 47
Morning to KF Payments in Alcock Heim. Many cuts. Finally
get my turn. Thank G. *[God]* got everything, nothing cut out or
diminished. PCHQ. Lunch: Heim. Carrots with sweet potatoes
and beef. 13:05: precautionary. 13:10 acute—uniform. Go on duty.
A big fire is visible, but don't hear anything. 15:10: precautionary.
15:50: all clear. Visited Theo Rolf. Russ.: 3 radio announcements
—1. Warsaw, 2. Duchbugam on Narev, 3. Radomsk.

Friday, January 19, 1945—Library. Lunch: Heim. Red beans
and noodles. Services with Theo Rolf. For the first time *[held]* in
Embankment Cafe, Chusan Rd. Russ.: radio announcements—Pi-
otrkov, Warsaw suburbs. By the time the Red Army entered
Warsaw in January 1945, the city had been completely razed by the
retreating Germans. Over a million of its prewar population were
dead.

Monday, January 22, 1945—ALARM NO. 50
Since yesterday slightly warmer. Sit in the sun. Lunch: Heim.
Millet with sauce and beef. Go with Mr. Uhlmann as translator to
Reifenvulkani-Sierongs Anstalt *[a tire repair service]*. 1 hour. $200.
PCHQ. 10:30–10:45: precautionary.

Tuesday, January 23, 1945—Rain, snow, and slush. Lunch:
Heim. Sleep at home. Go with Uhlmann *[again as translator]*. $200
for 1 hour.

In January 1945, the Japanese blockade of China was broken. The
Ledo Road from Burma to China, built to replace the old Burma Road,
was finally completed and was subsequently renamed the Stilwell Road by
Chiang Kai-shek. Although this news was generally unknown in Shanghai,
increased rumors were whispered in the Designated Area about Japanese
defeats.

Saturday, January 27, 1945—ALARM NO. 51
Shanghai. Wong. Get application for pass. *[Go to]* Harada. *[After
Ghoya was removed from his post, he was replaced by Harada, who was
reputedly more lenient.]* Pass renewed till 1.3 *[March 1]*. 14:12: precautionary. 14:45: acute. 15:00: precautionary. 15:10: all clear. Russ.:
1) Allenburg, Nordenburg, 2) Marienburg, Stuhm, Muehlhausen,
Tolkemit (East Prussia cut off), 3) Hindenburg.

In February 1945, the U.S. intensified raids over Shanghai. B-29s appeared and disappeared rapidly, leaving long white trails in the sky. The Japanese called these planes "B-ni-ju-ku," a literal translation of B-29. Umbrella-like shapes were created by Japanese antiaircraft shells exploding well below the B-29s. At first, many Shanghai residents mistook these for parachutes. As the situation worsened for the Japanese, new problems arose in Shanghai. Electricity was cut by 50% and there were sudden unannounced blackouts that paralyzed the entire city. Electric trams became even more unreliable, forcing everyone to walk long distances. For the first time, Fritz made reference to the rumors and gossip that were circulating and admitted to feeling very depressed.

Friday, February 2, 1945—Morning: with empty stomach to Ward Rd. Heim, to visit Mr. Hirsch, who is in charge of regulations. Gave him an application to be accepted in OD.

The OD—abbreviation for Ordnungsdienst—were the police who were hired by the Jüdische Gemeinde to work within the camps. Their duty was to keep order and guard food and medical supplies and to monitor people going in and out of the Designated Area. They wore blue uniforms and special armbands on their sleeves. Each camp had its own police chief, actually a general director, who sat in his own office at the Gemeinde. He was aided by an assistant, the second highest official of the camp police. Special passes were issued to camp policemen when they had to leave the Designated Area for work in the Broadway facility outside the Designated Area where some refugees were housed.

To supplement his meager income, Fritz wanted desperately to become a member of the OD. With acceptance, he would receive not only a small salary, but one and a half portions of food each day. Because his hunger was never satisfied, this was an important aspect of his desire to join. He would also receive a sort of uniform. In a recent interview, his friend Heini *[his nickname]* Meyer recalled that Fritz very much enjoyed wearing this status symbol. *[Figure 15 shows the OD uniform as worn by former refugee Erich Callmann.]*

Acceptance into the OD required both interviews and recommendations. Once again, Fritz's old friend and dentist, Seppi Gerendasi, through whose auspices he had become a volunteer member of the Shanghai Fire Brigade in the years prior to internment, helped him by writing a letter on his behalf. The drawback for Fritz in joining the OD was that he had to give up his pass to leave the Designated Area. Nonetheless, it took him only one day to make up his mind to do so. He therefore obtained the necessary release papers from his business associate Mr. Wong, whose previous letters had enabled him to obtain the passes to leave the Area.

Friday, February 9, 1945—Air Defense Day. Payments from Alcock Heim. Alexanders. Lunch: On foot to the city, since no trams running between 10:00 a.m. and 16:00 p.m. Get sugar from Domberg. Evening: at home. At 9:00 p.m. everything turns dark as electricity suddenly goes out.

Sunday, February 11, 1945—Evening: on foot to the Marcuses. Nobody opens the door. Go to bed feeling very depressed.

Monday, February 12, 1945—Lights are turned on again, supposedly only for 3 days (Chinese New Year). In the morning at 6:10, awakened by the clinking of windows. What's happening? At 6:50 a frightful explosion that forces the windows to fly open. Some further explosions, then quiet. What is their cause? No solution.

U.S. pilots appeared to know exactly which objectives they were targeting. Several Russian Jews who had access to shortwave radio broadcasts heard an announcement stating that, among other damages in downtown Shanghai, a building where Japanese military met Chinese puppet officials had been totally destroyed. *[Russian radio broadcasts were permitted since at that time Japan was not at war with the Soviet Union. However, the news reports they broadcast covered only the situation in Europe and not the details of the Pacific War.]*

Tuesday, February 13, 1945—Chinese New Year. Trams are running and lights on.

Monday, February 19, 1945—Go with Theo Rolf regarding sole agency for Wurst *[sausage]*. Library. Walk back because trams running only from 8–10 and 16–19. Sleep at home. Visit Horowitz (might get nougat representation). Meet Braun at the Wiener Konditorei. PCHQ.

On this day the U.S. invasion of Iwo Jima (Sulphur Island) began. The U.S. dispatched 495 warships, including 17 aircraft carriers and 1,170 planes—an unprecedented number. There was no hint of these important events in Fritz's diary, which indicates that he and his friends had no inkling about their occurrence.

Wednesday, February 21, 1945—Negotiate with Domberg regarding Wurst representation. Till the next electric meter reading on the 25th, no light.

Saturday, February 24, 1945—Lunch: Heim. The past few

days it is considerably less cold and the weather has become more
spring-like. However, today stormy and much rain. The huge price
increases at present are very worrysome. In particular, the bread
situation is really critical, since the flour mills don't have enough
electricity to grind grain. The rumors and gossip make people
quite crazy. However, it is simply useless to worry in advance. My
principle is to let things develop and drink tea *[a German saying]*.
Somehow things will work out and must work out.

Prices of all necessities were increasing at astronomic rates because
of steep currency depreciation, scarcity of all goods, and disruption of
transportation and communication. Many godowns stood empty. Food
products disappeared from grocery shelves and sometimes reappeared
on the black market, in spite of strict regulations against such trade and
severe punishment for those who disobeyed.

Beggars multiplied on the streets of Shanghai. Many lay ill, eyes bright
with fever, wounds oozing pus. Before Pearl Harbor, there had been a
beggars union headed by a much feared ruffian. He managed to collect
funds for the beggars by negotiating payments with rich Chinese in return for a commitment that no guests at a celebration would be roughly
approached by wailing beggars as they entered. Obviously, the Japanese
had put an end to these theatrics, and now the beggars simply died of
starvation and disease on the streets. Fritz passed these dead bodies in
the morning and fervently hoped that they would be removed before his
return home later in the day.

Sunday, February 25, 1945—To the opening of Spring
Semester 1945 of the Asia Seminar at the Kadoorie School. Dr.
Friedlander: "The Influence of Antiquity on Modern Times." *[Dr.
Fred Friedlander was a journalist who contributed articles to several refugee
newspapers, among which were the* Morgenblatt *and the* Chronicle.*]* No
lights in our building. Only a few blocks of houses have electricity.
At 22:00, the street lights go out.

Monday, February 26, 1945—Shanghai. Pick up application
for pass from Wong. To services: Erev Purim. *[The Jewish holiday
of Purim, which begins at sundown, is a joyful commemoration of Queen
Esther's heroism in saving the Jews from destruction at the hand of the
wicked Haman.]*

Tuesday, February 27, 1945—Morning: Pick up bread and
food tickets for March from the Alcock Heim. Sell a case *[probably
Wurst]. [Obtain]* Margarine from ERU. *[After the refugees were segre-*

gated in the Designated Area, Theo Rolf got a job working for the ERU, the European Refugee Union, an organization that purchased food wholesale and sold it to refugees at cost.] To the city on foot, regarding Wurst sales. In vain. Evening: District committee meeting.

Wednesday, February 28, 1945—Harada renews my pass until 28.3 *[March 28]*. Work at PCHQ. On foot to the city. Exactly like yesterday—no luck. Home. Asia Seminar. Lecture by Dr. Kneucker. Russian breakthrough near Konitz: Schlochau, Baldenberg, Düren.

Despite his efforts to sell various items, including nougat candy, wurst, and, later, dress designs by Gerti, Fritz was not a successful salesman, whch made his financial situation even more precarious.

Thursday, March 1, 1945—Alcock Heim. Shanghai. Then to the Further Education Higher Level Course at the Jüdische Gemeinde. Get a card to attend course. 8:00–9:00—Dr. Kuttner: "History of Music." 9:00–10:00, Dr. Grosslicht: "Introduction to the Study of Hormones." Very interesting.

Sunday, March 4, 1945—Go to the Jüdische Gemeinde about my shoes *[the Gemeinde conducted an investigation before issuing new shoes]*. To Horowitz *[regarding]* nougat business. PCHQ. Asia Seminar—Dr. Friedrichs: "Hypnosis and Suggestion." Evening at home. Russ.: Rummelsburg, Pollnow.

Monday, March 5, 1945—ALARM NO. 55
At night at 1:00: precautionary. 1:10: acute. 2:00: prec. 2:15: all clear. Continue sleeping without paying any notice. On foot to the city. My Resident Card confiscated by Sergeant 112 of the Foreign Police because I walked along Seward Rd., which is forbidden. Since I can't and won't pay any squeeze, I must go tomorrow morning to the Intelligence Officer of the Wayside Police, eventually perhaps to Harada. Must see it through. Library. With Chen from Braun's office regarding rolled ham to Gordon Rd. Russ.: Barwalde, Tempelberg, Falkenberg, Dramburg, Freienwalde.

Tuesday, March 6, 1945—In the morning full of trepidation to Wayside Police Station. Must return tomorrow. To the Welfare Office of the Jüdische Gemeinde. Get a pair of black leather shoes. Visit Theo Rolf. PCHQ. Russ.: Stargard, Neugard.

Wednesday, March 7, 1945—Morning: to the police. Must return tomorrow with resident certificate and a passport photo. Visit Horowitz *[re nougat business]*. Asia Seminar—Looser: "Psychoanalysis and Psychology." Russ.: 1) Graudenz, 2) Belgard, Grafenberg.

Thursday, March 8, 1945—ALARM NO. 56

Morning: Police Station. Long questionnaire. General personal information taken down. Must come again in the afternoon. Library. Home. Again to the police station. Special pass will be taken away from me for 3 days. PCHQ. Soap distribution in Ward Rd. Heim. Supper: at home. 17:10: prec. 17:40: all clear. Go to District Meeting in HQ. Then to "History of Music" and "Study of Hormones" in the Jüdische Gemeinde.

Friday, March 9, 1945—Lunch: Heim. Pick up ERU margarine. Visit Theo Rolf. To services. Evening: blackout because Air Defense Day. Late in the afternoon an announcement by the KF according to which people aged 18-55 will get, in the best case, bread, lunch, and a $1,000 allowance every 10 days. Apparently, the situation is again critical for me, although it is said the KF has a lot of money. Go to bed depressed.

Unbeknownst to Fritz and the other refugees, a daring bombing of Tokyo by B-29s had been ordered by Major General Curtis LeMay on March 9th. Although the pilots were trained to fly at 20,000 feet, LeMay ordered 325 B-29s with incendiary bombs to fly to Tokyo at only 5,000 feet so as to avoid the jet stream, which had previously caused these bombers to miss many targets. During the night of March 9–10, the massive firebombing virtually destroyed 16 square miles, killing 100,000 civilians. LeMay intended to follow up this raid with similar attacks on all major industrial installations, but he ran out of incendiary bombs. The March 9 bombing, with its indiscriminate slaughter of civilians, crossed a divide. It was this new course of action that, many experts believe, helped pave the way for dropping of atomic bombs in August on Hiroshima and Nagasaki.

Since almost all the Japanese men were mobilized, fighting the fires depended on neighborhood associations (there was a Pao Chia system in Japan, too). Methods were primitive, and included bucket relays, hand-operated pumps and fire extinguishers, and the use of damp mops to douse the sparks from the incendiary bombs.

The Japanese cabinet had previously considered building air raid shelters, but by then it was too late. There were simply no materials available for their construction. An alternative solution—protective tunnels—was also studied, but this required a prolonged effort, and time had obviously run out.

Most likely Fritz didn't know about the fire bombings because Japanese censors kept the information out of the newspapers.

Sunday, March 11, 1945—Morning to Pao Chia meeting in Alcock Heim. Get nougat collection from Horowitz. Hear lecture in seminar on Endocrinology. Russ.: Lemenburg.

Monday, March 12, 1945—Early to the police to pick up my pass. Wait a long time for the arrival of the Japanese who had the pass in his desk. He doesn't come. *[It was a Japanese tactic to make people wait for long hours.]*

Tuesday, March 13, 1945—Early to the police: get my pass back. Went all along Bubbling Well Rd. with the nougat business. No results. Russ.: Linz on Rhine.

Wednesday, March 14, 1945—*[Get]* payment Alcock Heim. Only $1,000. But better than nothing. On foot to the city. Library. Then attempt a new business: Gerti designs fashions and I want to try and sell the drawings to Chinese dressmakers. Have success and sell 16 sketches in Hongkew. *[Gerti had studied dress design while residing in England, where she was sent on the Kindertransport from Austria to avoid annihilation by the Nazis. As an older teenager, she traveled alone by ship to Shanghai and reunited with her parents there. After her arrival, she worked for a couturier, but it became impossible to hold that job after compulsory transfer to the Designated Area. See Figure 16 for one of Gerti's designs.]*

Friday, March 16, 1945—Shanghai. No success for Gerti. With nougat *[again]* as far as Uptown cinema. Still no luck. Exhausted from going back and forth on foot.

Saturday, March 17, 1945—Warm up lunch for supper. With Fritz J. to Sachses. Long discussion about Uschi's general estrangement. Closer friendship apparently not going to happen. We separate on good terms. Inv.: the Americans cross the Mosel at Koblenz.

Wednesday, March 21, 1945—Pouring rain. Unsuccessful with Gerti's pictures on Bubbling Well Rd. Russ.: 1) Braunsberg, 2) Altdamm *[an important airfield]*.

Thursday, March 22, 1945—Morning: pick up letter from Gerendasi for OD. To Hirsch. Wants to employ me, but I must give up my pass. Must make up my mind by Saturday. Get bread and food cards till April at the Alcock Heim. Lunch: Heim. Pea soup and ground meat. Evening: music lecture at the Jüdische Gemeinde. Inv.: Worms, Kaiserslautern.

Sunday, March 25, 1945—Morning: to Hirsch. Accepted into Ordnungsdienst. Many application forms. Will receive: armband, cap, lumber jacket, trousers. Will have a medical checkup, get food tickets with OD stamp (1½ portions). 1st Duty: 13:30–21:30 in the Chaoufoong Heim. ½ hour: coal site, ½ hour: border of sports grounds, ½ hour: gate, ½ hour: standing on watch. Since the weather is very nice, this duty really pleasant. Wedding for someone in the Heim: 2 cups of coffee, 5 slices of cake. Very tired, very satisfied to bed. Russ.: Leobschütz, Neisse.

Monday, March 26, 1945—Morning: payment Alcock Heim. 2nd Duty: 13:30–21:30. ½ hour coal site, ½ hour standing on watch. Easier than yesterday. Again coffee and cake from the wedding. Russ.: 1) Breakthrough: Hungary. 2) Heiligenbeil. Crossed the Rhein at Wesel and Oppenheim. Pacific: Allied landing at Ryukyu Islands. Nice weather. Cloudy but mild.

On March 26, the invasion of the Ryukyus began with the landing of the 77th Division on the Kerama Islands, 15 miles west of Okinawa, the biggest and most important of the Ryukyu Islands. The Ryukyus were critical to the Allies as a base for the planned invasion of Kyushu, the most southerly and westerly of the four main islands of Japan.

Six days later, on April 1, the largest amphibious fleet of the Pacific War approached Okinawa. When Fritz referred to the invasion of the Ryukyus, he was not aware of the total picture. The Japanese did not at first resist the assault, but holed up in caves and concealed garrisons in the mountains. During a bruising, 82-day battle, Allied forces destroyed the Japanese resistance cave by cave. The victory came at a terrible cost: 12,000 American casualties, among whom were many killed by bombs dropped by 325 Japanese planes manned by Kamikaze pilots.

Tuesday, March 27, 1945—ALARM NO. 58
3rd Duty: 21:30–5:30. ½ hour: coal site, ½ hour: patrol, 1 hour in readiness. Mild, moonlit night. Inv.: Breakthrough till Aschaffenburg, Itanau or Hanau. Darmstadt, Dinslaken.

Saturday, March 31, 1945—ALARM NO. 61
Morning at 10:00: muster for OD in Ward Rd. Heim. General instructions. Visit to Alexanders. Take a shower in Seward Rd. Heim. Pick up food. 13:75: prec. 14:05: acute. 14:30: prec.: 15:35: all clear. 6th Duty: 21:30–5:30. As usual. Russ.: 1) Komarow, 2)

Danzig, 3) Places in Austro-Hungarian border. Inv.: Giessen,
Wetzlar, Bad Nauheim. Buelon, Wildungen.

U.S. bombs whizzed downward and landed with loud explosions ever
closer to the Designated Area. As Fritz's health deteriorated, he spent more
time in his room. He was tired, slept late, sometimes until noon, rested
during the day, and lay on a "small cot" when on watch. Sometimes his
friends delivered meals to him from the Heim, presumably because he
was not well enough to go there himself. Very short of money, he again
sold some of his food. Nevertheless, he struggled to lead a semblance of
normal life, attending an operetta and a lecture, continuing to enjoy the
cinema, and going to Passover services.

Sunday, April 1, 1945—ALARM NO. 62
Warm weather. Very tired during night duty. Sleep in the morning.
Have someone pick up the food for me from the Heim. Get my
first payment from Chaoufoong Rd. 14:10: precautionary. 14:30:
acute. Bombing and sounds of AA follow. On duty at Chaoufoong Rd. Heim. 15.15: all clear. Some clouds of smoke on the
horizon. With ODF *[Ordnungsdienst Führer, or OD Leader]* Korn
to "Der Zigeunerbaron" *[The Gypsy Baron, an operetta by Johann
Strauss]* at the Eastern Theatre. Evening at home. Russ.: Ratibor,
Nitra, Slovakia. Crossed the Waag *[river in Hungary]*.

Monday, April 2, 1945—ALARMS NO. 63/64
7th Duty: 5:30–13:30. At 9:00 o'clock sent to report to ODL *[Ord-
nungsdienst Leiter, or OD Chief]*. At 10:00 back to Chaofoong Rd.
Heim. 10:20: acute. Explosions. Plane (P-51) in clouds of smoke.
11:00: prec. 11:30: all clear. 11:45: prec., acute, precautionary.
12:30: all clear. Rest at home. Visit Alexanders. Russ.: 1) Sopron,
2) Glogau, 3) Near Bratislava.

The P-51, which Fritz mentions for the first time, was a very efficient
fighter plane the U.S. produced in 1941 at the request of the British Air
Purchasing Committee. P-51s were used by the Allies to escort heavy
bombers in Europe, but also saw some action in the Pacific Theater.

Tuesday, April 3, 1945—Morning at home. Bring lunch from
Heim. 8th Duty: 13:30–21:30. Weather cloudy and stormy. Get
second helping from Seward Road Heim *[he received this extra portion because he got a job taking lunch tickets at the Heim—see next entry]*.
Inv.: Kassel, Warburg, Bruchsal.

Wednesday, April 4, 1945—10–13 o'clock: first Knipsdienst
[Clipping Duty]: tear out lunch tickets for distribution in Seward

Road Heim. 7th day of Pesach. Soup with rice. Meat. Stewed dates. Huge portions. Sell some of it to Looser and Keuvik for $300.00 each. Afternoon: big cleaning. Sleep awhile. 9th Duty: 21:30–5:30. Very dark. Cold. Some rain. Russ.: 1) Wiener Neustadt 2) Inv.: Entschede, Ibbenbueren, Melsungen. Bad Orb, pushed into Meiningen.

Thursday, April 5, 1945—Sleep a little. Then to services and Yizkor (8th day of Pesach) in the Kadoorie School. Lunch in Chaoufoong Heim—ask comrades to bring it to me. PCHQ and some shopping. Short rest in bed. Get up for light supper. Russ. Bratislava. Inv.: Osnabrück, Gotha, Lingen, Arnstadt.

Saturday, April 7, 1945—PCHQ. Get lunch from Heim. 11th Duty: 13:30–21:30. However, before that go to First Aid course in Ward Rd. Heim. Interesting lecture by Dr. Loewinsohn about "Fainting and Gas Poisoning." Then to duty in Chaoufoong Rd. Heim.

Japanese censors in Shanghai blacked out news of a great U.S. victory on April 7, 1945: the sinking of their giant battleship *Yamato* by bombs and torpedoes. The *Yamato* had been built secretly by the Japanese in 1941 and completed in 1942. Fritz, like others in Shanghai, had obviously not heard the startling news of its final sortie.

Wednesday, April 11, 1945—Daily bread ration from 12 oz. down to 8 oz.

Friday, April 13, 1945—ALARMS NO. 65/66/67
With supper to Uncle Martin. Sleep. I awaken suddenly from a terrifying sound of explosions. Shortly after: acute air raid alarm. From the roof, can see a big fire in the direction of Broadway-Kungpin Rd. Go to Chaoufoong watch. 0:10: acute. Home to bed. 2:00: prec. 2:10: acute. Back to Chaoufoong watch. There, rested a little on a cot. 3:00: all clear. Toward morning: again big explosions. Sound of motors. 4:40: acute. 6:30: all clear.

Unbeknownst to the residents of Shanghai, the Bergen-Belsen Concentration Camp was liberated by British troops on April 15. Its Commander, Josef Kramer, the "Beast of Belsen" had received 60,000 prisoners (mostly Jews) evacuated from other camps as the Allied invasion advanced. By the time Bergen-Belsen was liberated, only 50,000 internees remained, most of whom were barely alive, and about 20,000 of whom were critically ill. More than 13,000 inmates died after the liberation. Kramer was tried and executed in November 1945. After all the inmates were removed, the camp was burned down by the Allies to prevent an outbreak of typhus.

Just a few days before, the Buchenwald Concentration Camp had been liberated by the 6th Armored Division of the U.S. Third Army. Some 65,000 people had died there in horrible ways, including being hung from meat hooks or burned alive.

In Shanghai, this news was censored, and Fritz made no mention of it in his diary. It wasn't until after the war ended that some Jewish refugees discovered to their horror that their family members and friends had perished in various Nazi concentration camps.

Saturday, April 14, 1945—ALARM NO. 68
President Roosevelt died suddenly of a stroke.

President Roosevelt died on April 12 *[April 13 in the Far East]*. Shanghai media revealed Roosevelt's death on April 14. The news came as a painful shock to Shanghai Jews, many of whom continued to believe that Roosevelt was their only hope in defeating the Nazis and the Japanese. Although Fritz did not mention it, and the Japanese were unaware of it, memorial services for FDR took place in the Designated Area.

Sunday, April 15, 1945—13:30–21:30. 17th Duty. Russ.: 14.4 *[April 14]*: Vienna. Moedling. Reached Elbe near Magdeburg. Bad Rodach near Coburg. Weissenfels in Thüringen. Baden-Baden. Weimar.

Tuesday, April 17, 1945—Sleep till noon. 13:30–17:00: special duty at the Alcock Heim—payouts. Home. Russ: Germans inform that a big Russian offensive is beginning between Kuestrin and Neisse. Inv.: Bamberg, Erlangen, Bayreuth, Hagen. Leipzig. Halle. Food prices going sharply up. Sugar from $1,100 to $1,600. Rice from $600 to $1,400. Evening to Eastern *[Theatre]*. Very entertaining.

Thursday, April 19, 1945—Morning: shower in the Seward Heim. Lunch: at home. 20th Duty. 13:50–21:30. Get pay from Office at 1 Ward Rd. Pick up seconds *[of food]*. New guard duty in new grocery storage in the sports ground area.

Friday, April 20, 1945—6th Knipsdienst: 10:30–12:30. 14:30 watch muster for OD inspection. Change. To barber. PCHQ. Memorial service for Yahrzeit *[Yiddish term meaning anniversary of a death; observed on Hebrew date]*. Then to 66th birthday party for Sammy Marcus. Although I have night duty, get time off thanks to kindness of ODF Hirsch.

Saturday, April 21, 1945—21st Duty. 21:30–5:30. Two guard
duties, 1 patrol. Very cool night. Sleep till noon. 14:15: First
Aid Course in Ward Rd. Heim. Inv.: Lünesburg. Russ.: Bautzen.
Spremberg.

Sunday, April 22, 1945—ALARM NO. 69
1:15: prec. 1:25: acute. So far hear nothing and sleep through.
Wake up only by prec. at 2:50. While dressing, all clear at 3:15.
Back to bed. 22nd Duty: 5:30–13:30, 4 guard duties (storage and
laundry in the sports ground). Coal site. Gate. Russ.: Reach Berlin
proper.

Tuesday, April 24, 1945—8th Knipsdienst. 10:30–12:00 in
Seward Heim. Get 50% salary increase to $340 daily, retroac-
tive to April 1. Evening: at home. Russ.: 1) Frankfurt on the
Oder, Wandlitz, Oranienburg, Birkenwerde, Karlshorst, Pankow,
Koepenik; 2) Kotbuss, Lübben, Zossen, Liebenwalde, Rangsdorf,
Feltow; 3) Troppau. Inv.: Dillingen. 24th Duty: 21:30–5:30.

Wednesday, April 25, 1945—Rest. 9th Knipsdienst. 15:30–
17:00 in Seward Rd. Heim. Russ.: Nauen, Fürstenberg, Guben.
Inv.: Ulm. It.: Ferrara. Speier. Opening day of the Conference in
San Francisco.

At the San Francisco Conference, convened on this date, nearly 300
delegates representing 50 nations met to reach an agreement on an international organization designed to keep the peace in the postwar world.
The Charter of the United Nations was adopted by the conferees on
June 25, 1945.

Saturday, April 28, 1945—ALARM NO. 71
10th Knipsdienst. 10:30–12:45: Seward Heim. Big cleaning. Realize I did not attend the First Aid course. Hope that I will get away
with a warning. *[Despite this oversight, Fred did receive his certificate of
completion for the course in June 1945.]* 37th Duty. 21:30–5:30. While
I'm on duty, Theo Rolf, Gerda, and Fritz J. come to visit me. Suddenly at 22:55 low sound of engines. An airplane appears. Flak
directed from all sides toward the plane. Then also bombing. The
friends go quietly to the Heim. I open emergency exits, etc. After
10 minutes the street lights go out. No sirens. Again bombers fly
over. At 23:45 street lights go on. Shortly after that, plane visible
again. Then big noise. Street lights go out again. Around 2:00,
3 big planes are visible in the sky. At 3:00 the street lights go on
once more. No sirens. Russ.: 1) Uniting of Russian troops with

British and American troops in the area of Torgau; 2) Rathenow, Spandau, Potsdam; 3) Prenzlau, Angermünde; 4) Wittenberg. Inv.: Eger, Konstanz, Lanzberg (near Augsburg), Regensburg. It.: Mailan *[Milan]*, Verona.

The encirclement of Berlin was completed on April 25 (U.S. date, April 26 Shanghai date). Nearly 500,000 Germans were isolated within the city. Allied and Russian troops met in Torgau on the Elbe. In Shanghai, the Soviet radio station broadcast on April 28: "Men from either side met and embraced in this moment of great triumph, ideological differences did not obstruct the effusion of warmth. Together as comrades-in-arms they celebrated the eradication of great evil . . . .

Sunday, April 29, 1945—Sleep for 3 hours. Take over Knips-dienst for a colleague: 10:30–12:00 in Seward Heim. Eat at home, rest. Afternoon to "Der Orlow" [That Man Orlow, *an operetta by Ernst Marishka and Bruno Granichstaedten]* at the Eastern *[Theatre]*. Evening: at home. Russ.: Strasbourg, Templin.

Monday, April 30, 1945—28th Duty: 5:30–13:30. PCHQ, Sup-per at home. Inv.: Allies enter Munich. According to news reports, during ALARM No. 71 *[see April 28 above]* two B-24s bombed Shanghai and one of them was shot down.

11

Victory in Europe

May 1945 was marked by two significant events: the unconditional surrender of Germany and Hitler's suicide. Fritz referred to these occurrences
only in passing, and neither had much effect on the harsh and difficult
circumstances still faced by the refugees.

Fritz continued with his OD duty, engaged in social activities, dealt
with the lack of electricity at home and on the streets, and fought the usual
illnesses and infections. He remained oblivious of the fact that in the war
on Japan the tide was turning, and that on May 20, the Japanese began
to withdraw their troops from China in preparation for a likely attack on
their mainland by the Allies.

The refugees were also completely unaware of the difficulties the
Japanese were facing at home where the great majority of Japanese
citizens followed strictly their army's National Self-Restraint Campaign,
which encouraged them to share the privations of the soldiers at the
front. They ate a rigidly minimal diet, refrained from smoking, and gave
up all entertainment.

> **Wednesday, May 2, 1945**—ALARM NO. 72
> **Adolf Hitler died on 30.4.45** *[April 30, 1945]*. News of Hitler's
> suicide did not reach Shanghai until May 2.

> **Thursday, May 3, 1945**—13th Knipsdienst for a colleague:
> 15:30–17:00. Russians report alleged suicide of Hitler and Goeb-
> bels. Grand Admiral *[Karl]* Dünitz *[is]* the new Führer. Capitula-
> tion of German and Italian troops in Italy and Austria. Russ.: 1)
> Berlin, 2) Liquidation of German troops in Berlin, 3) Rostock.
> Warnemünde. Inv.: Wismar, Lübeck.

> **Saturday, May 5, 1945**—32nd Duty: 0:30–13:00. In the of-
> fice of the Jüdische Gemeinde watching over the stored summer
> clothing belonging to the Welfare Office. Then to First Aid course
> in Ward Rd. Heim. Inv.: capitulation of German troops in Hol-
> land, Northwest Germany and Denmark. Hamburg and Prague
> declared open cities. Hamburg occupied by Allies.

Tuesday, May 8, 1945—Unconditional surrender of Germany to America, England, Russia. *[He neglected to list France.]* The war is over.

The unconditional surrender of Germany actually took place on May 7, 1945, at General Eisenhower's headquarters at Reims, France. Because of the international dateline, this was May 8 in Shanghai, and that is the date Fritz reported it. He and his friends had a low-key celebration, but not until May 12.

Thursday, May 10, 1945—Read report of Reuter correspondent from Berlin, Harold King: "City of the Dead." Deeply moved. Spring leaves me somewhat restless. Something must happen. 36th Duty: 21:30–5:30.

Friday, May 11, 1945—Morning: sleep. Afternoon: 18th Knipsdienst. 15:30–17:00 in Seward Heim. Evening at home. Because of badly done blackout, Japanese Sergeant cuts off electricity. Both *[SACRA]* houses in darkness.

Saturday, May 12, 1945—37th Duty, 5:30–13:30, then to First Aid course in Ward Rd. Heim. Evening at Theo Rolf's. Uschi, Gerti, and Fritz J. also there. Small victory celebration with Kao Liang *[a clear, fiery spirit distilled from sorghum]* and cookies till 1 o'clock.

Sunday, May 13 till Tuesday, May 15, 1945—Wake up on Sunday at 5 o'clock with strong vomiting and diarrhea. At 6:00 and also at 8:00: 100.4 degrees temperature. To the clinic. Reported to OD I am sick. At home taken care of by Dr. Götz. Enterosan Acetan *[medication]*. Fever up to 102.7 degrees. Monday and Tuesday: no fever but in bed. Visited by Theo Rolf, Klaus, Fritz J.

Wednesday, May 16, 1945 *[21st birthday]*—No fever. Doctor allows me to get up. But lightheaded and *[feel]* general weakness. Morning: congratulated by Looser with Augustus. Had ordered a round of mocha for breakfast during my tour at the ODs. Result: at 7:30 ODF Hirsch appears personally, to congratulate me and to hand me a package of cigarettes. Very nice. Get up in the evening and dress. Standing in the yard when Gerda, Gerti, Theo Rolf, and Fritz J. appear. Theo Rolf hands me in the name of all of them, as well as that of Looser and Braun, a big 5 lb. thermos bottle. Such a spendthrift bunch! The kids bring along their dinner and stay for a delightful evening till 10:30 at my place. Klaus also drops in during the evening to congratulate me. A lovely birthday in the circle of the people I love.

Although he was not completely well, Fritz was able to celebrate his 21st birthday on May 16 with his dearest friends. He deeply appreciated their thoughtful gift, since there was no running hot water in his building, or in most other Hongkew buildings. The large, new thermos bottle enabled him to keep on hand a much needed supply without going so often to the man selling hot water in the lane.

Thursday, May 17, 1945—Morning: to the clinic. Get results of my urine and stool tests. Everything OK. 1) Get heart medicine (strychnine drops) and 2) a general strengthening medicine (Nervolzis). Make a short appearance at the watch where the watch leader congratulates me. Afternoon: buy socks and do other chores. Supper at home. Very boring since no light. Dr. Kneucker ran away from his wife.

Saturday, May 19, 1945—2nd Day Shavuot. Early to services and Yiskor [*Memorial Service*]. Afternoon: with supper to Alexanders. Evening to Marcuses.

Sunday, May 20, 1945—Morning: shower in Seward Rd. Heim. Lunch at home: mung beans, boiled potatoes, 2 eggs. Speak to Dr. Götz. From tomorrow on will go on duty again. Evening: celebrate my birthday at Alexanders after the fact. Present: Theo Rolf, Gerda, Theo Rolf's parents, Looser, Gerti, Fritz J., and I. Ordered 3 pieces of cake per person with a cup of coffee with milk and sugar. Great evening.

Thursday, May 24, 1945—40th duty: 5:30–13:30. New post: stand near the broken wall of the Sports Grounds, so that I have hardly any free time during my watch. At 4:30 a.m. hear loud noise and sound of plane engines. Streicher arrested. Churchill resigned.

Julius Streicher [*publisher of the infamous* Der Stürmer, *see p. 7*] was tried at Nuremberg and found guilty of crimes against humanity. He was executed on October 16, 1946, shouting the words "Heil Hitler" as he was forcibly led to his death.

Sunday, May 27, 1945—Sleep till noon. To the barber. Dress to go to the birthday of Alexander Sr. Take supper and eat there. Evening: with Gerti, Gerda, Theo Rolf, and Fritz J. to Barcelona [*a restaurant/night club*].

Wednesday, May 30, 1945—In the morning to clinic, Chaoufoong Rd. Heim, for follow-up checkup by Dr. Götz. Get

prescription for 5 injections. 21st Knipsdienst. Evening 45th duty
21:30–5:30. During the night notice a big fire at about 22:00 and
think I hear planes.

Hunger was on the increase in Shanghai, especially among the Chinese
poor. Unable to direct their anger towards the hated Japanese occupiers,
they turned against other foreigners. Thus, a Chinese SACRA employee
warned in a threatening manner of forthcoming violence by a group of
50 Chinese.

As for Fritz, he was often forced to miss work due to lack of healthy
nutrition, and he worried constantly about losing his job.

> **Monday, June 4, 1945**—Yesterday an employee (Chinese)
> from our Heim water shop threatened an emigrant in SACRA
> that early today 50 Chinese from the Kitchen Fund water shop
> (which was opened several weeks ago) would storm into the
> Chaoufoong Rd. Heim. That is why they wake me up at 6:15 and
> I gather others to reinforce our watch. On watch till 8:30. Then
> to Alcock Heim for summer headgear. Personal chores. At 11:00
> get an order to reinforce the watch. All the gates must be closed
> and the number of men doubled. In the evening with Theo Rolf
> to Gruenfeld and for a walk. Theo Rolf's worries: 1) Engagement
> of Gerda to yeshiva bocher *[yeshiva student]*, 2) Telling Dr. Langer
> about his serious intentions toward Gerti *[whom he wants to marry]*.

A group of 300 Mirrer students of Talmud, *yeshiva bocherim [among them
Mechuel Abramchik, Gerda's boyfriend]*, landed with their rabbis in Shanghai
in August 1941. Their group was officially named the Mirrer Yeshiva Far
Eastern Rabbinical College, Shanghai.

Mir was a small town in Poland renowned for its Jewish learning. Rabbi
A. Kalmonowitz, head of the Mirrer Yeshiva, worked ceaselessly—and
successfully—in the U.S. to organize the escape of the yeshiva students
from Nazi persecution. With the help of the U.S. State Department, he
convinced the British consul in Lithuania to certify that all Mirrer Yeshiva
members were Polish citizens. This first step was pivotal in their ability
to leave the country.

In 1940, two Dutch students from the Telshe Yeshiva petitioned Jan
Zwartendijk, the acting Dutch consul in Kaunas, Lithuania, to provide
them with visas to Curacao. Zwartendijk, who was sympathetic to their
plight, informed them that no visa was necessary for Curacao, and entered
a statement to that effect in their passports. The two then went to Chiune
Sugihara, the Japanese Consul in Kaunas, who issued them transit visas

for Japan. With these documents, they were able to procure Soviet exit visas. Zwartendijk then agreed to stamp the passports of other refugees with the words "No Visa to Curacao necessary." Word spread quickly and Zwartendijk was deluged with applicants.

Sugihara, against the wishes of his government, cooperated and issued transit visas to as many as 2,400 Jews before he was forced to stop. Both Sugihara and Zwartendijk have been honored by Yad Vashem as Righteous Gentiles.

The refugees, among them the students and teachers of the Mirrer Yeshiva, traveled first to Vilna, then to Moscow, where they boarded the Trans-Siberian Railroad to Vladivostek. From there, they went by ship to Kobe, Japan. They remained there for several months, well treated by the Japanese and helped by the small Jewish community, until the authorities sent them to Shanghai. There, they received the full support of Chief Rabbi Meir Ashkenazi, as well as that of the Sephardi and Ashkenazi communities.

Because they had more food and extras due to the additional monetary aid received from the Orthodox community in the U.S., there was some envy of the members of the Yeshiva on the part of the Central European refugees. These feelings were exacerbated by the cultural differences between the two groups.

Wednesday, June 6, 1945—ALARM NO.73
Morning: got 4th Panfos injection in the clinic. Then to Seward Heim to take a shower. 11:40: prec. 12:30: all clear. 49th duty: 17:00–0:30 *[a.m.]* in the Jüdische Gemeinde. Recently colossal price increases. 12 oz. of bread from $450 to $1,270. Evening *[meal]* ticket from $500 to $900. No increase at all in salary. The state of my health worries me. In spite of injections, have strong pains in the heart, and am coughing somewhat since tonight. Hope it will pass because if I am sick too often, or my heart weakens too much, I may lose my job.

Thursday, June 7, 1945—Three times one airplane *[flew over]*. Bombing and flak shelling during the night.

Monday, June 11, 1945—ALARM NO. 74
Morning: 8:30–10:00 special duty during payouts *[to refugees]* at Alcock Heim. Double allowance ($1,800) for supper. Bread now: 12 oz. $1,450. 53rd Duty: 0:30–6:30 *[a.m.]* in the Jüdische Gemeinde. 1:45: new precautionary signal. Before that heard 2 bombings.

Tuesday, June 19, 1945—Injection. Then 25th Knipsdienst in Seward Heim. Afternoon at home. Big cleaning. Evening:

with Looser to Alexander's cultural club. Schaefer: "About the English." Chair: Kornick. 59th Duty: 0:30–8:00 in the Jüdische Gemeinde.

Wednesday, June 20, 1945—From 13:30–16:00 on special duty: payments in Alcock Heim. To PCHQ. Hand in my resignation.

Thursday, June 21, 1945—60th Duty: 5:30–13:30 in the afternoon. Pick up money from Alcock Heim. Since cash is short, the KF pays us ⅓ in cash and ⅔ in coupons.

Tuesday, June 26, 1945—8:00–11:00: special duty in Alcock Heim during payments. Afternoon: 65th Duty. 17:00–0:30 in the Jüdische Gemeinde. Okinawa fell.

The news of the fall of Okinawa reached Shanghai late. In fact, by June 21, organized resistance in Okinawa had disintegrated. General Ushijima and his staff committed harakiri *[ritual suicide by disembowelment]*. American casualties were estimated at 49,000; Japanese military and civilians, 100,000. Civilians had been prevented from surrendering by the Japanese army, and committed suicide with hand grenades or bayonets.

After the defeat in Okinawa, the Japanese government changed the ideographs used when referring to the Pacific War from "*kessen*" (decisive war) to "*ohinamagusai*" (war to the death). The *Mainichi*, one of the largest papers in Japan, described the battle of Okinawa as "an attempt at the mass murder of women and children who had no connection with the fighting."

Friday, June 29, 1945—67th Duty: 5:00–13:00 Afternoon: to ERU. Supper at home. Then with Theo Rolf to Gerti. Weather hot. For the first time this year sleep on the roof.

With the sweltering heat came another irritation: mosquitoes. The commonly used mosquito netting made it uncomfortably warm in bed, and did not shut out the constant buzzing of the insects. Fritz derived a rather satisfactory solution to the problem when he discovered that by turning on a light, the mosquitoes instantly flew to the wall. This enabled him to swat them and then return to a more peaceful sleep.

Another remedy against this annoyance was to burn dark green coils that were infused with a chemical. These gave out a slight medicinal smell, which repelled the bugs. Besides mosquitoes, the army of pests included flying cockroaches, fat spiders, large centipedes, aggravating lice, and bedbugs.

12

Direct Hit in the Designated Area

Aside from the oppressive heat that continued to envelop Shanghai, life proceeded uneventfully during the first half of July 1945. In his precise, German way, Fritz continued to mark down the number of each duty and where it was served. The only air raid alarm he noted during these two weeks was on July 15. Then, on the 17th, an unforgettable event occurred in Hongkew, one that remains permanently imprinted on the memory of every refugee: the bombing by American planes of the Designated Area. Thirty-one refugees were killed, and another 250 wounded. In addition, many Chinese died (the figure ranges from 250 to 4,000), and several hundred more were wounded. Rumors flew that the Americans had attempted to destroy secret military and naval communications installations or a radio station or a synthetic fuel plant hidden in Hongkew. Some scholars, however, insist that in the overcast weather, bombs were mistakenly dropped too early.

The house of siblings Ruth and Erich Callmann was completely destroyed when the roof fell in. Ruth and her mother were miraculously saved because they happened to be standing at the point of least stress from the collapsed roof. Fortunately, neither Erich nor his father were home at the time of the bombing. From the 19th to the end of the month, almost daily air raid warning alarms were heard.

Saturday, July 7, 1945—29th Knipsdienst: Chaoufoong Heim. 73rd Duty (like yesterday). Salary increased by 170% *[to]* $2790.

Sunday, July 8, 1945—30th Knipsdienst Seward Heim. Afternoon: at home. 18:30–22:30: with Theo Rolf, Gerda, and Gerti at the SJYA *[Shanghai Jewish Youth Association, the Kadoorie School]* for an outstanding program, stage anniversary of Heinz Ganther. Very nice. *[Ganther, a stand-up comedian in Germany and then in Shanghai, was also publisher of the newspaper* Laterne, *and a well-known M.C. He was close to Theo Rolf's family, probably the reason why Fritz was included in this celebration. In 1942, Ganther had published a book called* Drei Jahre:

Immigration in Shanghai, *a thorough overview of the refugee experience in Shanghai during 1939, 1940, and 1941.]* 74th Duty: 0:30–6:45 in the Jüdische Gemeinde.

Saturday, July 14, 1945—78th duty: 5:30–18:30. Last Tuesday, Gerda got engaged to Mr. Mechuel Abramchik and I am introduced to him. A. also lives with us in SACRA.

Sunday, July 15, 1945—ALARM NO. 76

79th Duty: 13:30–21:30. At night go home and take my sleeping stuff to the roof. Soft sound of engines. Then can see a column of fire in the distance. Later hear explosions and sound of engines and at once the flak goes into action. At first, not very loud, medium ammunition, but then heavy caliber. On the roof, everyone jumps up and runs down the stairs in panic. Rush past the crowd and get to my room. Put on my OD uniform, belt, and steel helmet and then to the Chaoufoong Rd. Heim. At 22:35: acute alarm. On watch standing in front of house #77, then after ½ hour sent back home. Again go to sleep on the roof. 23:55: prec. 0:20: all clear. The sound of sirens does not cause general surprise, because in general the alarm is sounded when big formations of planes approach.

Tuesday, July 17, 1945—ALARM NO. 77

Awakened by preparatory alarm sirens and at 12:50 *[another]* prec. Then at 1:00: acute. Dress and go to Chaofoong Rd. Heim. While I am dressing the sound of engines can already be heard getting louder and louder. However, the sky is overcast and nothing can be seen.

Halfway to my destination, which is nearby, all hell breaks loose. I press close to the wall of a building and look around. A series of explosions is followed by black smoke across Point Rd. through the District, up to the Whangpoo. Glancing to the left of Muirhead Rd., the world seems to have come to an end at Point Rd. Only a wall of black smoke can be seen. Then all is quiet, and I hurry to the Heim entrance. I call out to my comrades who are on watch there: "Come out and look around!" My voice is cracking because I am afraid for the safety of my house. Without delay, I hurry back to my room. Find Looser getting dressed. I grab all my identification papers and all of my cash and say to Looser: "This is all I can do. We must leave the rest to God."

I get out on the street and meet ODF Rosenzweig, who is going in the direction of Point Rd. I join him to see what is going on, because the smoke has now become less dense. The old composer, Leopold Maas, is coming toward us. He is completely black and asks me how to get to the clinic. Rosenzweig leads him. I go further on. A number of Chinese have fled to the open space between our house and the corner of Point Rd. A man from Chaoufoong Heim reports that there have been a number of wounded. Some First Aid people arrive with stretchers.

I go out of the Heim, across Point Rd., along Muirhead Rd. There are two large bomb craters on the street where the asphalt pavement stops. A dead Chinese is lying there. Again the sound of roaring motors. I seek cover in the entrance of a house. Luckily, nothing happens. The noise stops again. I see clouds of smoke that appear to come from the direction of Dent-Yuhang Rd. and go back to the corner of Dent Rd. Then an official runs past me and shouts: "For Heavens sake, send help to the SACRA *[on]* Yuhang Rd. There was a direct hit there!" *[This turned out not to be the building in which Fritz lived.]* This news upsets me very much and I rush to Chaoufoong Rd. Heim. Three colleagues have already arrived there with a stretcher.

I tell them about the misfortune and we all run without stopping to SACRA. As we get closer to the corner of Yuhang Rd., more splinters and broken pieces cover the street. When we turn, we see that the SACRA entrance has been badly damaged. We quickly cross a bomb crater to the courtyard. Hardly had people caught sight of us, when we hear from all sides cries of: "First Aid! Come here! Help my husband!" etc. Without pausing, we turn to a wounded man and the three men surrounding him. The wounded man is lying on his stomach. His shirt is torn and smeared with blood. He is wearing shorts and has eliminated in his pants. He stinks terribly. While my colleagues put him carefully on the stretcher, I get the man's name and address from people standing around. Max Goldbaum, room 225B. We march on quietly carrying the wounded man. We have a long way to go and the man is heavy. On the way, some civilians help us out. There is the sound of loud explosions. It is only mortar fire. Finally, we reach Chaoufoong Heim. There are some wounded Chinese on the grounds of the Heim trying to find the clinic. I tell them to come with us. We reach the clinic.

There is much pressure from people with medium and light wounds, mostly Chinese. We carry in our stretcher and I remain

there, while my colleagues go outside. I bring over Dr. Grünberg.
He removes the bloodied shirt from the wounded man's back.
In the lung area, I see two deep holes. Dr. Grünberg insists that
the patient must be undressed. In his present condition, this is
an unpleasant thing. I am filled with disgust, but what can I do
in this situation? The face of the wounded man looks like he is
dead. When the patient was on the stretcher, he had begged for
water. Now his mouth is open and his eyes look glassy. I ask the
doctor. "Should we carry him outside?" "Just a moment." The
doctor listens to the patient with his stethoscope. "The heart is
still working. Sister [Nurse], give him a caffeine-strychnine injection immediately."

Since the clinic is taking care of the patient, I leave the room
with the bloody stretcher to go on watch. On the way, I meet several other stretchers. One of the patients tells me: "Mr. Marcus,
please go to the watch, because I am ill." To my surprise, I see
that my colleague Reinhaus is on the stretcher. At the watch, I fill
in his report and add mine. All around are big clouds of smoke
and I run to my room to put on my rubber boots. I discover that
a big piece of plaster from the wall has fallen on my couch.

Out again to Yuhang Rd. SACRA. From there, I am led with
some other people by Mr. Koenig, who lives in the SACRA. We
check various destroyed rooms in the house to see if there are
dead or wounded. I had already heard from colleagues at the
watch that one of our men, Raphael, is dead. I find him on the
first floor of the house where his room was. The roof had caved
in and fallen on him. He now lies buried under the ruins. We get
hold of Dr. Salomon and he confirms his death. Our small group
then goes on further from room to room. Almost everywhere,
the Chinese cooking ovens are still burning. They are endangering
the entire complex and we would like to put them out. At first we
have no water. We get help from a pot of still warm coffee and
potatoes boiling in water. The search through the rooms continues. Fortunately we find no more dead or wounded. We reach Dr.
Kardegg's room. It is empty. I see that a window pane is shattered. A neighbor tells me that Dr. Kardegg was wounded and
was bandaged. I assume that his injury was light.

I go to the courtyard where I hear an order to check if people
are buried in the rubble. Go together with two men, hooks and
shovels, to a site situated in Yuhang Rd. Here, a direct hit seems to

have occurred. Instead of 4 houses there is only a space filled with rubble. Several immigrants are standing at 2 spots and are pointing to places in the rubble from which sounds of voices can be heard. Now we begin a difficult exhausting job that lasts 2 hours. We are divided into two groups and rescue 5 Chinese. We also find an apparently dead baby. I am completely covered with pieces of white plaster.

I go back to SACRA after having completed the rescue and am told that #416 Tongshan Lane (the Gemeinde) is burning and has to be evacuated. I think there is a fire and I immediately hurry there. I see a Japanese fire engine stopped at a fire hydrant. From all sides immigrants are rolling out hoses while I run from place to place to couple them together. Before that is completed the water starts running, and there is no nozzle. I dash from spot to spot to try and get a nozzle. I go to a Japanese fire engine and beg the Japanese officer to give me a nozzle. Apparently, he doesn't understand me, but he allows me to step onto the place where nozzles are kept. A Japanese fireman understands what I want. Commandant Mann begins to search, but does not find any. They turn off the water, precious minutes are lost, and the entire corner of Seward Rd. Heim goes up in flames. 2 immigrants come running from the opposite side and bring a nozzle.

In the meantime a second Japanese fire engine arrives. The water is turned on again. We are looking for water hydrants. The immigrants are unable to deal with the hoses and don't know how to attach the nozzle. I am able to connect it in a few seconds. Finally the Japanese take over the hoses. (The next day I am being praised for my "brave" efforts.) I enter the lane of the Gemeinde. The house is badly damaged from the air raid. In the back the fire patrol keeps pouring water on the houses that the Japanese fire department is already working on in the front. I suggested that they turn their efforts to the third row of houses to make sure the fire doesn't reach them. After a few minutes they follow my advice.

As I leave the lane, I meet my colleague Fred Schlesinger with another colleague and their civilian assistants carrying stretchers. They need another man, so I drag myself forward to help them. *[See Figure 17 for a photo of stretcher bearers, one of whom might well be Fritz.]* They had laid two dead Chinese children on the pavement on a piece of cardboard and now place them on stretchers. We carry the bodies to the hospital of the Ward Rd. Jail. An emergency place has been set up there in the courtyard. We add our horrifying load to the site where dead and badly mutilated bodies have been placed.

Arms, legs, etc., are lying around. The main part of the court is packed with all kinds of wounded people: Chinese, Russians, immigrants, lying on the ground waiting for help. I notice in particular a Chinese wearing only his underpants and otherwise naked. He is obviously in great pain. His legs are up in the air and he is staring at his right arm. I realize just then that his arm is missing. At his shoulder, where his arm should have been is a spotless white bandage, which had been tied in a very professional manner. Who, I ask myself, could have done such work here in this courtyard? I look around and see several Chinese and Jewish nurses, Dr. Kneucker, Dr. Götz, as well as some others of our doctors standing nearby. The doctors are really outdoing themselves.

After a short discussion, we take our stretcher and go to the Ward Rd. Heim. In the Heim there is a constant coming and going. The wounded are taken to the hospital, the dead are carried out of the hospital. I find out that in contrast to the information I had received earlier, Dr. Kardegg was brought to the hospital with serious wounds, to which he finally succumbed. The big onslaught of wounded into the hospital appears, however, to be over. As a result, all the OD people must go to their own watches. So I make my way to the Chaoufoong Heim where I report and am given permission to go and eat. It is 8:00 [p.m.]. Immediately after, go back to the watch. The atmosphere there is frightful. A horrible sweet smell of corpses. In the hall, used to place the dead, three bodies are lying one next to the other on the bare floor. They are covered with bloody rags or sheets. A man points out a corpse to me and I go and lift the sheet. See open, glassy eyes and a severely wounded face. I remain at the watch until 10:00 o'clock. Then I go to SACRA Yuhang No.10. Then home. At 11:45 to bed.

Commenting on the Jewish reaction to the disaster, Dr. David Kranzler, author of *Japanese, Nazis & Jews: The Jewish Refugee Community of Shanghai 1938–1945*, told the authors: "In this moment of great tragedy, the refugee community pitched in to help, regardless of whether the victim was of Jewish, Chinese, or any other ethnic origin. Devoted doctors, nurses, health workers, those who helped carry the wounded, virtually everybody, worked selflessly in a cooperative effort never before witnessed in Shanghai. The Chinese were particularly grateful and offered to pay the doctors, who refused to accept any remuneration. This event brought out the best in the refugee community, and the impact on the Chinese community was incalculable. Thus, the refugees' greatest tragedy turned into their finest hour."

Heinz Bergmann, a German refugee living in the Designated Area was amazed at the close cooperation between the Chinese and Jews, the only positive aspect of such a calamity. "You know how poor the Chinese in Hongkew were," said Heinz, "but still they brought food and even money to the clinics to show their gratitude for the equally dedicated treatment given to one and all."

Wednesday, July 18, 1945—ALARM NO. 78

Although I have free hours, I cannot sleep. I am much too upset about what happened. After restless tossing and turning, have to carry out my 81st Duty: 5:30–13:30. Must go with my report book to the ODL. At the corner of Wuhang and Muirhead Rd.—which we jokingly call Potsdamer Platz *[a major square in Berlin]*—the Russian Auxiliary Detachment specially trained in air defense has set up a special Defense Corps, and laid out rows of dead Chinese. Body parts are lying on the site and the smell is so bad that I have to cover my mouth with a handkerchief. Several groups of SPBC *[Shanghai Public Benevolent Cemetery Society]* are already there and are moving the bodies to the site where they are stored, at the corner of Point and Muirhead Rds. They are carrying a head, an arm, a leg, body parts to the site where they are thrown in one big pile. I am overcome with nausea.

As we approach Chaoufoong Rd., everyone rushes into the houses. Doors and windows are closed. I feel like I am a messenger of the apocalypse. Behind me, men are carrying bodies taken out of the site where they were stored. "Marcus, go and relieve the men," says Korn, "Sometimes, I also need half an hour's rest!" I reply. I go to the storeroom where the vegetable kitchen is working and sit down comfortably. Hardly have I sat down when at 12:00 there is a preparatory alarm, then at 12:10 there is an acute alarm. Great excitement in the vegetable kitchen.

I get an OD steel helmet at my post and start my duty. We hear an increasing noise of motors. It is the same sound we heard yesterday. I look up at the ceiling of the vegetable kitchen. On the rafters I can see red roof tiles. The whole thing is a ridiculous protection. So I decide to stay outside opposite the ORT on a patch of grass where I squat. The sky is blue with big white clouds. One can see clearly between them a formation of planes flying very high. The sound of motors gets louder and ebbs. Fear, yes, now there is real fear. Not the fear of death. I am on my own, independent, but fear of being crippled, fear of becoming a tortured mass of flesh and blood, such as the dozens I have seen yesterday. A great need to escape overwhelms me and I must fight my instincts. I go back to the vegetable kitchen. Here I feel safer. After a few minutes I realize that the loose roof tiles signify an even greater danger but instinct still conquers reason.

During a pause in the roar of motors, the people on duty in the vegetable kitchen have run off home. Only two young serving guys remain behind. Added to the sound of planes, antiaircraft flak can be heard, and also distant bombings. We build ourselves an emergency shelter out of a table and several iron kitchen pots, under which we crawl. A veritable Witches Sabbath breaks out as sounds of flak, bombs, and mortars burst out. After the noise dies down, I am relieved and soon after, at 13:15, there is a precautionary. Then at 13:45 an all clear.

At least half an hour later, we finally get our lunch. Eat it at home. Then around 16:00 to the Ward Rd. Heim from where the first funerals of the victims, including that of OD Commander Dr. Kardegg, are to start. Isaak appoints me to take part in the honor watch transporting the bodies. Finally, a truck arrives to pick us up. Ten of us from the honor watch climb in. First we go to the hall where the bodies are stored in Chaoufoong Heim. A second truck is already there to pick up three Polish victims for the funeral. However, we must all wait because we have not yet received the necessary authorization. In the Heim front office, Osano [*possibly Okura's replacement*] from the Bureau of Stateless Refugees Affairs is sitting with another Japanese. They are filling out the forms. The Poles load the bodies and drive away. We have to wait because an acute alarm is announced, but this turns out to be wrong information. Finally, we also get our permits and drive off fully packed with 12 coffins, which exude a terrible smell. Ten of us OD people, our faces covered with handkerchiefs, gravediggers, body carriers, as well as men from the Chevra Kadisha drive off at 18:30 past the Ward Rd. Heim, past the Yangtze, up to Point Rd. Cemetery. (I am, of course, standing on the running board.)

At the entrance of the cemetery, a huge group of mourners is waiting for us. They had been brought by two other trucks. The leaders of all the top Jewish organizations are present, as well as officers of the Foreign Pao Chia Corps. Several coffins are carried to their graves. Everyone gathers around Dr. Kardegg's grave. Mr. Wachsner gives a general funeral speech. Then Rabbi Dr. Kantorowski and Engineer Rechenberg speak about Dr. Kardegg. The many cantors present then take care of the actual burial of the 12 victims. Then we drive back in the trucks and reach Ward Rd. Heim around 20:45. We, the OD people, are sent to the hospital kitchen (after first washing with Lysol in the pharmacy) where we get fried potatoes and black coffee. Then go home, where I drop dead tired into bed.

Thursday, July 19, 1945—31st Knipsdienst in the Chaoufoong Rd. Heim. At 17:00 had duty in the Jüdische Gemeinde. However, get permission to come later so I can participate in a second funeral, which includes my colleague Raphael. Go to Ward Rd. Heim. Am again selected to take part in the honor watch. Go by truck to Chaoufoong Heim. Take coffins to the Point Rd. cemetery. It starts to rain and in the cemetery the rain is streaming down. Terribly depressed mood. Get home drenched to the bone at 19:00. Have supper. Change my uniform. Then to the Jüdische Gemeinde. The Gemeinde building at 416 Tongshan Lane, which was damaged in the air raid, had to be evacuated. 82nd Duty: 20:00–0:30.

Saturday, July 21, 1945—ALARM NO. 79
14:00: preparatory. To the watch. Nothing happens. In the afternoon with Fritz J. and Looser to Gerda–Abramchik engagement at the Alexanders.

Sunday, July 22, 1945—ALARM NO. 80
83rd Duty: 5:30–13:30. Go with my report book to early duty. On the way see a man who is obviously insane. He is speaking loudly and gesticulating wildly. It appears that a bomb had been dropped on his house while he stood there, and his life was spared by some miracle.

On my way to Alcock Heim, at 10:30 I hear: precautionary. At 11:00: acute. I go to the common room of Alcock Heim. Payments that were being made are stopped immediately. A large number of people are present. ERU employees, including Theo Rolf, come in. I was stupid enough to leave my steel helmet in

Chaoufoong Rd. After some time louder and louder noise of engines. The noise grows very loud and there are explosions of bombs. Everyone throws themselves on the floor. Women and children are screaming. Then the bombing seems to occur somewhat further away. The Alcock Heim phones all the other Heime. Nothing has happened anywhere, but it is very upsetting. 12:05: prec. 12:10: all clear.

The attack on the 17th *[was]* by some 100 American planes. *[This appears to be an exaggeration. Most sources indicate that the raid involved only 25 planes, twin engine A-26 bombers that took off from Okinawa.]* Current attacks are by the same number of planes, mainly B-24s and P-54-51s. Today's attack is in the Yangtzepoo district *[the industrial section of Shanghai that included the Shanghai Power Company, the Shanghai Waterworks Company, and the Shanghai Gas Company]*. The Point Rd. cemetery is damaged (30 graves). *[The raids on July 22 were carried out by many more bombers than on the 17th, perhaps as many as 250 from the U.S. Fifth Air Force, which targeted military sites outside the city.]*

Monday, July 23, 1945—ALARM NO. 81
8:00: special duty in Alcock Heim. Just as I finish and am on my way home, hear at 11:15: prec. I run home like a crazy person with my steel helmet on my head. God be praised, nothing happened. At 12:15: all clear. 84th Duty: 13:30–21:30.

Tuesday, July 24, 1945—ALARM NO. 83
8:00 in the Welfare Office of the Jüdische Gemeinde. At 10:10: prec. At 11:00: acute. After half an hour the planes come. I am together with Zeidler from the Jüdische Gemeinde in the emergency shelter which he had made. We hear the planes come in several waves. Flak is very active. We can also hear nose-diving planes and MGs *[Maschinengewehr, machine guns]*. This nerve-racking situation lasts two full hours, but it feels like centuries. Then 13:00: prec. And 13:15: all clear.

Wednesday, July 25, 1945—ALARM NO. 83
Afternoon: shopping (ERU). Clement Atlee British Prime Minister.

Thursday, July 26, 1945—ALARM NO. 84
86th Duty: 5:30–13:30. 10:45: prec. Nothing further. Afternoon: to washman. Then with Looser to the Kadoorie School, where the people who were bombed out of their homes are lodged.

The bombing on the 17th left many refugees homeless. As it was summer vacation, they were housed in the Kadoorie School. Meals were supplied by the East Seward Road kitchen. Ruth Callmann, whose family lived at the school for some time due to the damage done to her family's home, relates that the young people managed to enjoy themselves even in these makeshift quarters. Something interesting was always going on, she stated. Now and then, Mrs. Hartwich, the principal of the school, played the piano. There was even dancing in the courtyard.

Friday, July 27, 1945—33rd Knipsdienst in the Chaoufoong Rd. Heim. 87th duty: 13:30–21:30. We are supposed to take a third lodger in our room. In the given circumstances, we cannot, of course, refuse. We are to take in the old composer, Maas, who is senile and ill. This, however, we refuse to do. A big wallah-wallah *[Shanghai Chinese expression to signify a "row"]* takes place. We have to take in Maas. Back to duty.

Saturday, July 28, 1945—ALARM NO. 85 88th Duty: 8:00–17:00. Jüdische Gemeinde. At 9:00 for general muster in Ward Rd. Heim. OD thanks everyone for the help beyond duty during the watch on the 17th. He cites most of us by name, including me, and hands envelopes (with $10,000). *[This figure demonstrates the enormous inflation of Chinese currency at the time.]* Back to my duty. Prec., acute, prec., all clear. Thank God, nothing happens. Maas moves in. 89th duty: 0:30–8:00. Jüdische Gemeinde. Potsdam Conference: Am., Eng., Russ., and Chinese. Send the Japanese an 8-point ultimatum to end the war. In our house we have light again.

Fritz mentioned the Potsdam Conference for the first time on July 28. Possibly, news of the conference reached Shanghai only on that date. In point of fact, the conference began in Potsdam, a suburb of Berlin, on July 17, and concluded on August 2.

Fritz also erroneously cited China as one of the participants, which was not the case. In attendance were the "Big Three": Harry Truman, Josef Stalin, and Winston Churchill (who was replaced by Clement Atlee after his election as Prime Minister of Great Britain). Most important to Fritz and his fellow refugees, the Potsdam Declaration outlined the terms of surrender by Japan and issued an ultimatum that Japan agree immediately to unconditional surrender or face "prompt and utter destruction." The latter statement is a clear indication that Truman must have shared with the other heads of state the creation of the atomic bomb.

Sunday, July 29, 1945—Amazingly, Maas moves out again. In the afternoon short visit with Fritz to Theo Rolf. Evening at home **with light!** Japanese take no position on ultimatum.

13

Japan Surrenders!

The Pacific War is at last surging towards its end, but Fritz had heard so many false rumors that he was skeptical of all whispered reports. His doubts finally evaporated when the official declaration of Japan's defeat was broadcast on the radio and published in the Shanghai press. Sadly, Fritz's joy was dampened by thoughts of his beloved father and life without him when normal times would eventually return.

> **Friday, August 3, 1945**—Pick up money from Alcock. Put Augustus, who obviously was ill, to death (apparently a tooth fistula and half of his face full of pus). Bury him. 93rd duty. 17:00–0:30. I have been working for months to become a permanent employee of the Jüdische Gemeinde.

> **Sunday, August 5, 1945**—95th Duty: 6:00–14:00. Go to Parnes (Vienna Soap Works, Point Rd., who have started food storage for the Kitchen Fund). 96th Duty: 0:30–8:00 in the Jüdische Gemeinde with Sondlaud. S's bride has baked a large chocolate pudding for me, with vanilla sauce, which costs me $6,400 but is really worth it.

> **Tuesday, August 7, 1945**—97th duty: 6:00–14:00 at Parnes. Small notice in *The Shanghai Times* that Hiroshima in Japan was bombed with a new type bomb. A second report stated that President Truman and Prime Minister Attlee announced at the same time the news that for the first time an "atomic" bomb had been dropped.

> **Wednesday, August 8, 1945**—36th Knipsdienst in Chaoufoong Heim. Then 9th Duty: 13:30–21:30. The atomic bomb was dropped attached to a parachute. Tremendous effect. Get confirmation of my release from Pao Chia.

Fritz learned about the atomic bomb hitting Hiroshima from sources like the Tokyo *Mainichi* that were reprinted in Shanghai:

ATTACHED TO PARACHUTES

A small number of B-29s penetrated into Hiroshima on August 6 shortly after 8 a.m. and dropped a number of explosive bombs, as a result of which a considerable number of houses in the city were destroyed and fire broke out at various places. It seems the enemy dropped new-type bombs attached to parachutes which exploded in the air. Although details are under investigation, their explosive power cannot be made light of.

Thursday, August 9, 1945—ALARM NO. 86

In the morning go to the KF Dentist, Ward Rd. clinic: 1 root extraction, 1 root treatment, and filling. 37th Knipsdienst in Seward Heim. 99th Duty: 0:30–8:00. Jüdische Gemeinde. At 4:00 a.m. a plane can be heard. Very near. Then 3 explosions. Flak or bombs? Then quiet. At 1:00, Russia declares war on Japan.

Friday, August 10, 1945—An exciting day. First, sleep after returning from night duty. When I wake up, feel terrible. Have a temperature of 100.2 degrees. Stay in bed. In the evening 101.6 degrees. Still, want to try to go on early duty tomorrow. Awakened by Warschauer around 23:30. There is a fire somewhere. I jump out of bed and run to the window. Black clouds of smoke rise over the courtyard. Warschauer comes in again. I tell him that the fire must be under our corridor window, on the low roof of a public convenience there.

"By the way, the war is over," Warschauer informs me. Since I am very skeptical, he tells me that it's definitely true. *[Fritz seems to be unaware of the Nagasaki atomic bombing. Presumably, that news had not yet reached the Designated Area.]* The people, who are standing around, find it more important to celebrate the end of the war than to put out the fire, which is already burning brightly. I run upstairs again with Warschauer and together with my neighbors begin to carry basins and buckets full of water to the window, where two other people pour the water out of the window on the fire. Somewhat later, I jump out of the window down onto the still burning straw and put out the fire completely. The neighbors pull me back through the window.

As might be expected, the refugees were ecstatic at the news that the war with Japan was at last over. Their excessive behavior demonstrated their relief and intense joy.

Warschauer decides to leave and find out the latest news. After

a few minutes he comes back. He did not even get as far as the
Chaoufoong Heim. Inside *[my building]* all hell has broken loose.
The people are acting wildly and screaming. The OD makes
every effort to keep them in check. I change immediately into my
uniform to go to the Heim. On the way, I hear that the entire OD
has been mobilized. Everyone has to check in at the watch. All the
occupants of the Heim seem to be up. The OD people are patrol-
ling up and down to quiet groups when they become too loud. I
and another couple of colleagues decide to go on a tour outside
the Heim. We stride through the streets. Here and there, where
immigrants live, excited people are congregating in front of their
doors. As we go by, we are offered vodka, cookies, etc.

There was great jubiliation in the Heime as the news of the surrender
circulated. Judy Urman, who lived at the time in the Chaoufoong Heim,
had gone to see the movie "Camille" that evening with her boyfriend
Ernst (later her husband). Ernie was feeling very down because he had
seen Japanese bunkers being built at many intersections, one of which
had machine gun emplacements that faced the Chaoufoong Heim. Ernie
had confessed his fears that they would not survive the war and would
all be killed.

Judy was already in bed when Mrs. Moses, the cook for the children in
the Heim, ran through the camp shouting, "The war is over!" Judy jumped
down from her bed so fast that she hurt her ankle. As she loudly took up
Mrs. Moses's cry, her roommates told her she was crazy and to go back
to sleep. Instead, she joined the many others who had gone downstairs.
There was great excitement, but also a nagging fear that this was just another rumor. When Judy discovered it was the truth, she and Ernie both
skipped going to work that day. "Who could work after hearing this kind
of news?" she said with a smile.

    Saturday, August 11, 1945—It is almost 2 o'clock *[a.m.]*. There
is such an uproar in the corridors and stairways that it is impossible to fall asleep. I bound out of bed. *[Fritz and Günther and other
refugees tear down their blackout curtains.]* Then I dress and go out
once again. In Tongshan Road the traffic is still lively. Nobody appears to be sleeping. Looser and I separate from the others, since
we want to look for Theo Rolf. When we reach his house, we see
that he has just returned after visiting Gerti and is in the process
of getting undressed. He dresses again, and the three of us go on
a futile search through the neighborhood for something to drink

until we finally meet Herbert Braun, who directs us to Schoenberg on Wayside. We settle happily there at 3:30. Two glasses of beer, potato salad, and eggs. Braun pays. We break up in time for me to go home and change, since I have early duty. 100th Duty: 5:30–13:30.

The evening papers say that Japan has accepted the Eight Points of the Potsdam ultimatum, but demands that the Emperor remain and keep some imperial privileges.

Sunday, August 12, 1945—In the morning, go to the dentist in Ward Rd. Heim. Root extraction. 101st duty: 14:00–22:00 at Parnes. The Allies are negotiating about the Japanese note. The judgment seems to be advantageous. War in Manchuria and heavy bombing continue. Various calls for the population to keep calm and orderly.

Monday, August 13, 1945—After my root extraction, my left cheek rather swollen. 102nd Duty: 17:00–0:30, Jüdische Gemeinde. No new developments. Some people are doubtful, others depressed, because the rumors that circulated on Friday are misleading.

Indeed, puzzling rumors were spreading in Shanghai. Some whispered that the war had not really ended, that Shanghai should prepare for an eventual U.S. atomic bomb attack, and advised that everyone wear white clothing. (It was thought then that people in black were more vulnerable during an atomic bomb explosion.) In the Designated Area, the Japanese attempted to reestablish control. Pao Chia duty was enforced again since, on Friday, some immigrants had ripped off the signs at the borders of the District. (Years later, in 2006, Gary Matzdorff displayed one of these signs to 110 former refugees at a reunion in Shanghai. The sign has since been displayed in three German cities in an exhibit, "Heimat und Exil—Jüdische Emigration aus Deutschland nach 1933" (Home and Exile—Jewish Emigration from Germany since 1933).

Tuesday, August 14, 1945—In the morning go to the clinic to see Dr. Salomon. Prescribes stool examination. In the evening with Fritz J. to the cinema *[Eastern]*: "Petermann Ist Dagegen" *["Petermann Is against It"]*. Now it is very amusing to see German propaganda films on Strength through Joy, etc. Of course, some people have to whistle. We only laugh. The Nazis have lost and we have survived! *[We hear another]* rumor that the war is now definitely ended. Japanese military patrol the streets.

Wednesday, August 15, 1945—103th Duty: 6:00–14:00 at
Parnes. Toward lunch Hirohito, Japanese emperor, speaks on
Radio Tokyo. He declares that the war is over. Japan has accepted
all conditions. Confirmation of this by President Truman. 15:20:
Cabinet meeting. Suzuki *[the prime minister of Japan]* resigns. In the
evening buy Chinese liquor. Klaus at my place. Drink to peace.

Shanghai radio stations rebroadcast the Japanese Emperor's Rescript,
which he had delivered in Tokyo. After listening to the "Kimigayo" *[the
Japanese National anthem]*, the Emperor's "good and loyal subjects" heard
for the first time the Voice of the Crane (Imperial symbol). The message
was clear—an admission of Japan's defeat from the highest level: "We
have resolved to pave the way for a grand peace for all the generations to
come by enduring the unendurable and suffering what is insufferable."

Friday, August 17, 1945—105th Duty: 22:00–5:00 at Parnes,
where 4 men must remain temporarily at their posts. The Nanking
government has dissolved itself. The Japanese Emperor broadcasts a cease fire order to all the troops. Admiral Chester Nimitz
commands the Allied Naval Forces to stop firing. Blackout here in
Shanghai is lifted.

Saturday, August 18, 1945—No special news. Delegates from
various countries on their way to Manila, where the cease fire will
be signed.

Sunday, August 19, 1945—106th Duty: 5:30–13:30. When I
am on watch, hear a report that the August 20 night duty in the
Welfare Office of the Jüdische Gemeinde is cancelled. Will people
lose jobs? The highest official of the Joint, Mr. Siegel, supposedly was released yesterday from camp. Perhaps the changes are
already a result of this. *[Manuel Siegel, an official of the Joint Distribution
Commitee, arrived in November 1941, shortly before Pearl Harbor, to work
with Laura Margolis in the Shanghai office. Unfortunately, he did not have
time to accomplish much of importance before the Japanese interned him as a
U.S. enemy national, to be released only after the Japanese surrender. Laura
Margolis, too, was incarcerated for the same reason in 1943. However, she
was released for health reasons several weeks later.]* 18:10: Loud noise
of aircraft engines. By the time I get to the window, everything is
already over. Several minutes later, the same thing. When I lean
out of the window, I see an American plane fly very low, above
the house. Go to the roof. While the American plane, with clearly
visible markings, flies over us several times, and also drops leaflets

over the city, everyone celebrates and waves handkerchiefs. Great enthusiasm!

On Tuesday, *The Shanghai Times* published a report about this incident. The plane was a Curtis C-46, a big American transport plane, that brought a "humanitarian mission" consisting of 26 American officers whose task it is to take care of the clothing, food, and accommodation of the internees. The leader of the Mission is Colonel Shoemaker, who is residing at Kadoorie's Marble Hall on Bubbling Well Rd. Content of the flyers (2 kinds): calling the internees to remain quietly in the camps until the arrival of the Allied troops. Forgot to note down that the newly formed Japanese government will be led by Prince Higashi-Kuni. A civilian cabinet also includes Prince Konoye and Admiral Yonai.

Monday, August 20, 1945—39th Knips duty in Chaoufoong Heim. Then 107th Duty: 13:30–21:30. No changes, as suspected yesterday, at the Alcock watch. Japanese arrived in Manila yesterday. Negotiations began at once. *[The Japanese ceased fighting in China on this date.]* Radio station XMHA *[see pp. 17–18]* starts broadcasting *[again]* today at 20:05.

Tuesday, August 21, 1945—Pick up a one-day pass from the Bureau of Stateless Refugees Affairs. Reason: Want to try to apply for a job at my former company *[the Shanghai Fire Brigade, or SFB.]* Chinese Senior Officer Chang Loong-Zu, with whom I actually wanted to speak, died in December. The Brigade is in a stage of transition. The Chinese are trying to manage on their own. The Japanese are still there as advisers. With Braun to the interest carrying account on Woochang Rd. To Yangtzepoo. Pingliang Rd. Camp *[a Japanese internment camp for enemy nationals]*. Visit Captain Reid. Joyous reunion. Get back home dead tired at 6 o'clock. After signing agreements, the Japanese mission returns from Manila to Japan with instructions for the Allied occupation of Japan. 108th Duty.: 22:00–6:00 at Parnes. Completely worn out.

Wednesday, August 22, 1945—Return the pass at the Bureau of Stateless Refugees Affairs. To Seward Heim to take a shower. Pick up my repaired rubber Shanghai Fire Brigade boots from the Welfare office, which were damaged during the rescue work of 17/7 *[July 17]*. Repair work wonderful. Would have cost me $80,000. Rested for 2 hours after eating, then work at home. The days are full of small joys, thanks to a return to normal times, *[which]* give spice to life.

As long as I have been able to think independently, I have become accustomed to restrictions, bans, and laws. I accepted all this as self-evident, so that now it strikes me as a hardly comprehensible wonder that these bans have been lifted. In general, we cannot as yet digest our great luck—even though our future is not yet clear.

The emigrant interpreter in the Bureau of Stateless Refugees Affairs tells all who come up timidly to the table of the Japanese: "Speak! Speak up! Don't be self-conscious! These times have passed!"

The various Heime have received large banners from the KF: blue and white with the Star of David. Also the Chaoufoong Heim. A large flag now flutters on a mast that was mounted on one of the posts of the gate. The entrance of the Heim makes the impression of a colonial station in the jungle, such as one sees in films. Yesterday, in the Heim, there was great rejoicing, since the supply of electricity was doubled and it was permitted to keep lights on all night. For the first time American marches are again broadcast on the radio.

It is announced on the radio that the Japanese general who had introduced "suicide tactics" has committed suicide.

Currency and precious metal have fallen sharply, but are somewhat recovered today. The KF is, of course, hit hard. The highest exchange rate for the Swiss Franc was $50,000 and fell to $10,000. Various merchandise was dumped dirt cheap on the market. Yesterday, on the street, I bought a pack of 20 "Kores" cigarettes for $2,000, which was being sold in stores for $10,000.

Figure 1 (above): Fritz and his father
at Gertrud's gravesite, 1938

Figure 2: Semmy Marcus, World War I
soldier

Figure 3: Semmy and
Fritz on the beach at
Heringsdorf, 1929

Figure 4: Gertrud Kowalewski
before her marriage to Semmy
Marcus

Figure 5: Fritz with *Schultüte* on the first day of school, 1930

Figure 6: Fritz with Pardi at the Berlin Zoo, August 1938

Figure 7 (above): The Bund, circa 1940

Figure 8: The Ward
Road Heim circa
1939

DIARY #1

THIS BOOK was given to me by my great aunt Anna and my great uncle Hermann for
my benediction.

Begun on: May 8, 1937 (destroyed) (begun again) on May 5, 1944.

Ended on: August 9, 1944

Changes in my signature as time went by:

23.VI.I944 (signature)
26.VI.1945 (signature) ------------

"'Forsan et haec olim meminisse invabit." (Aeneas)
Perhaps this too will be a happy memory.

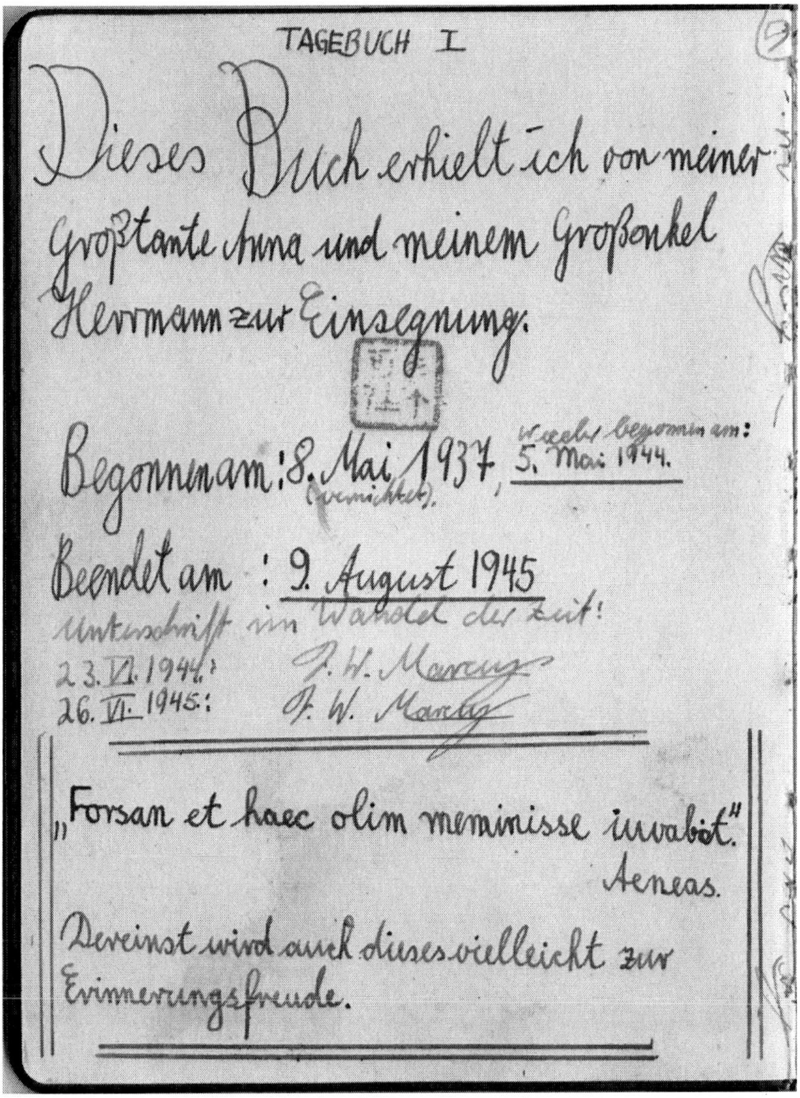

TAGEBUCH I

Dieses Buch erhielt ich von meiner Großtante Anna und meinem Großonkel Herrmann zur Einsegnung.

Begonnen am : 8. Mai 1937, *neech begonnen am:* 5. Mai 1944.
(vernichtet).

Beendet am : 9. August 1945

Unterschrift im Wandel der Zeit!
23. VI. 1944: J. W. Mercus
26. VI. 1945: J. W. Mercus

„Forsan et haec olim meminisse iuvabit."
Aeneas.

Dereinst wird auch dieses vielleicht zur Erinnerungsfreude.

Figure 9 (above): First page of Fritz's first extant diary

Figure 10 (opposite page): Translation of first page of Diary #1

Figure 11: Refugees lined up for passes at the Bureau of Stateless Refugees Affairs; Ghoya is in center in dark sport coat

Figure 12 (above): Fritz as a member of the Shanghai Fire Brigade Reserves, 1942

Figure 15: Erich Callmann in Ordnungsdienst uniform

Figure 13: Uncle Martin, known as "Tino"

Figure 14: Cousin Klaus Marcus, Martin's son

Figure 17: Stretcher bearers after July 17, 1945 air attack

Figure 18: The
Pagoda at Lunghwa

Figure 19: Wedding photo of
Ted and Gerti Alexander,
June 9, 1947

Figure 16: One of Gerti
Alexander's dress designs

Figure 20: The Alexander Family (l-r, Mechuel, Gerda, Kaethe with Chuna, Hugo, Gerti, Ted)

Figure 21: Fred and Henry Meyer (a.k.a. Heinz or Heini)

Figure 22: Frank and Helene DeGroodt at Broadway Mansions

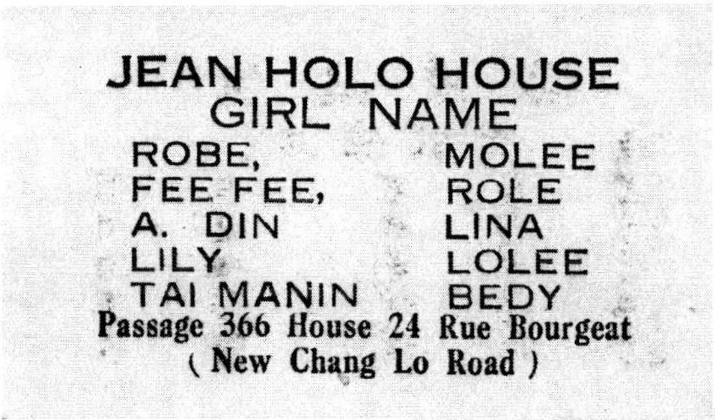

Figure 23: Business card from Shanghai brothel

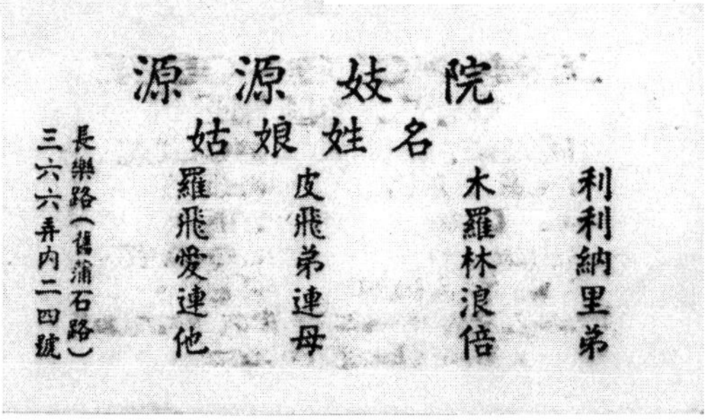

JEAN HOLO HOUSE
GIRL NAME
ROBE,   MOLEE
FEE FEE,   ROLE
A. DIN   LINA
LILY   LOLEE
TAI MANIN   BEDY
Passage 366 House 24 Rue Bourgeat
(New Chang Lo Road)

院
名
木羅林浪倍
利利納里弟

妓
姓
皮飛弟連母

源
娘
姑
羅飛爱連他

源
姑
長樂路（舊蒲石路）
三六六弄内二四號

Figure 24: Reverse of business card

CARD OF IDENTIFICATION
No. 4309 D

Photo with Signature of Bearer
ISSUED BY
INTERNATIONAL COMMITTEE
FOR GRANTING RELIEF TO
EUROPEAN REFUGEES
SHANGHAI   P.T.O.

Figures 26: Theo Rolf Alexander's identification card from the International Committee for Granting Relief to European Refugees

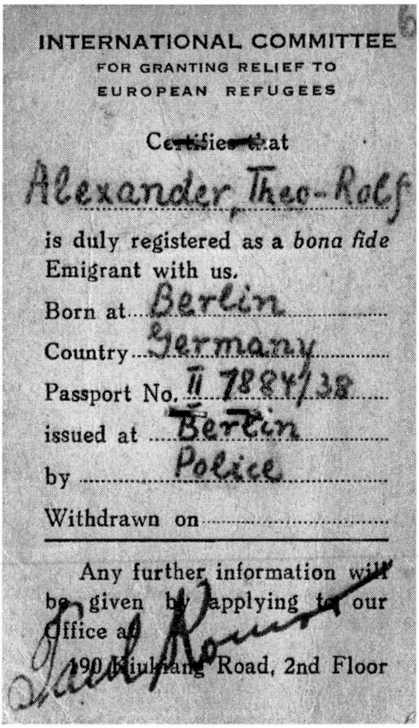

INTERNATIONAL COMMITTEE
FOR GRANTING RELIEF TO
EUROPEAN REFUGEES

Certifies that

Alexander, Theo-Rolf

is duly registered as a *bona fide* Emigrant with us.

Born at... Berlin

Country... Germany

Passport No. II 7884/38

issued at ... Berlin

by ... Police

Withdrawn on

Any further information will be given by applying to our Office at 190 Kiukiang Road, 2nd Floor

Figure 27: Reverse side of Theo Rolf's identification card

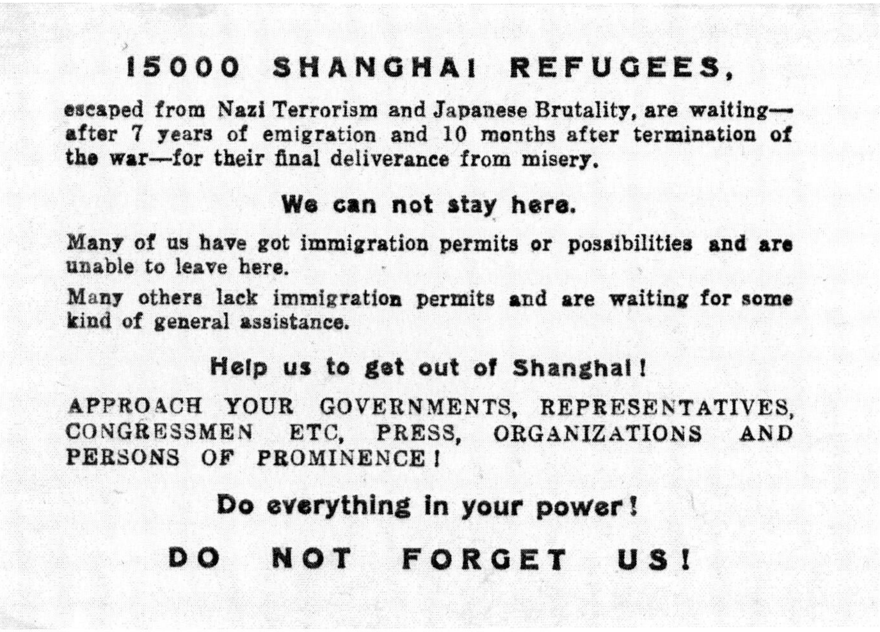

15000 SHANGHAI REFUGEES,

escaped from Nazi Terrorism and Japanese Brutality, are waiting—after 7 years of emigration and 10 months after termination of the war—for their final deliverance from misery.

We can not stay here.

Many of us have got immigration permits or possibilities and are unable to leave here.

Many others lack immigration permits and are waiting for some kind of general assistance.

Help us to get out of Shanghai!

APPROACH YOUR GOVERNMENTS, REPRESENTATIVES, CONGRESSMEN ETC, PRESS, ORGANIZATIONS AND PERSONS OF PROMINENCE!

Do everything in your power!

DO NOT FORGET US!

Figure 28: Card sent by refugees with plea for help to family and friends in Europe

Figure 29: Sticker for envelope containing plea for help

Figure 25: Fred's dearest friend, Ted Alexander

Figure 30: Grave
of Samuel Semmy
Marcus, Columbia
Road Cemetery,
Shanghai

Figure 31: Fred with Kay at Kiaochao, April 6, 1947

Figure 32: Photo of Fred taken at Josepho Studio, May 27, 1947

Figure 33: Fred, a proud teacher and his students, March 22, 1948

Figure 34: Seppi Gerendasi and Fred on hike in Mokanshan, August 1947

Figure 35: Fred relaxing in pagoda at Mokanshan, August 1947

Figure 36: Fred having fun at the Race Course, 1948

Figure 37: Thea playing wee golf at the Race Course, 1948

Figure 38: Fred at the Ming Tombs in Nanking, February 12, 1948

Figure 39: Fred on bike
ride, January 1947

Figure 40: Fred's 24th birthday, May 16, 1948 (standing l-r, Karl Gelbard, Haas,
Karl Epstein, Relly Gutmann, Heinz Guttmann, Jimmy's wife, Jimmy, Karl
Maehrishel; seated, l-r, Lilly Epstein, Thea Gellert, Fred, Stephen Wu, Trude
Gelbard; in front, Sylvia Maehrischel)

Figure 41: Chinese laborers carrying sedan chairs up Mt. Lushan

PART II:

AFTERMATH OF WAR

14

Postwar Euphoria

On August 24, 1945, the U.S.S.R. and China signed a Treaty of Alliance. All Japanese fighting in China had ended four days before. The despised Japanese soldiers vanished from the streets. The refugees exuded unabated joy that was reinforced by the constant din of exploding fireworks. As Nationalist troops made a triumphant entry into the city and the Japanese formally surrendered, a renewed sense of hope enveloped the Designated Area.

Wednesday, August 22, 1945—For the first time the Russian radio station XRVN broadcast at noon today, again in German. Before that, an old march, and also the same announcer. Just like in old times, only my Pappi is missing.

When I went yesterday down Nanking Rd., there at the corner of Shanse Rd., *[was]* a better dressed old Chinese man who said aloud in English, I don't know to whom, perhaps he meant to me: "This is a happy day! The Japanese enemy is beaten. Peace is restored. The foreigner is my friend." The Americans will land in Japan this coming Sunday. **District definitely open** *[meaning that people can freely come and go]*.

Saturday, August 25, 1945—Hunting for metziahs *[Yiddish for "bargains"]* in Hongkew. Jam, underwear, Japanese uniforms sold very cheaply. 111st Duty: 22:00–6:00 at Parnes.

Sunday, August 26, 1945—41st Knips duty—Tongshan Rd. Evening cinema: "Black Sea Navy" *[at the Eastern]*. Russian war film about the fight for Sebastopol.

Monday, August 27, 1945—112th Duty: 6:00–13:30. First at Parnes, then at the watch. In the afternoon with Fritz J. to the Reunion Club on Avenue Foch to see a documentary film:

"Moscow-Berlin." A very pleasant evening. Thousands of people throng the streets. Everything is brightly and colorfully lit once again. On Nanking Rd., in the area of the Wing On, we hear firecrackers thundering in our eardrums. We have already crossed Chekiang Rd. and are away from the big hustle and bustle, when everything that happened before is put into the shadows. While we look around with astonishment, we are dragged back by a flood of people to the corner of Chekiang Rd., and to our amazement we see a line of trucks with Chungking *[Nationalist]* troops. Only a narrow lane is left open within the enthusiastically wild crowd. Firecrackers are popping, and the racket increases constantly, because people are rushing in from all the side streets. I drag Fritz out of the milling crowd. Our situation is not too safe. There are no foreign troops around, and one never knows what stupid ideas the excited people may suddenly get. We hear the earsplitting noise of firecrackers all the way to Hongkew. We go home with the knowledge that we have experienced something extraordinary: the arrival of the first Chinese troops in Shanghai. 383 Allied warships in Tokyo are waiting to land. They have been delayed by typhoons. Russian-Chinese friendship agreements on Manchuria are signed. Dairen is declared an open port. Port Arthur is now a Russian Navy base.

Tuesday, August 28, 1945—113rd (light) Duty: 13:30–21:30. Visit of American Welfare Mission announced for tomorrow. They will visit all the Heime, the bombed area, our SACRA, as well as the Kadoorie School.

Wednesday, August 29, 1945—42nd Knips Duty—Seward Heim. Especially good food. Visit of the Americans postponed for 24 hours. Everywhere, everything is nicely decorated, especially in Chaoufoong Heim *[and]* in my house. I also buy paper flags for myself from the U.S.A., Britain, China, and Russia and place them over my couch, where they make a nice wall decoration, together with a crack that had been caused by the 17/7 *[July 17]* bombing. 114th Duty: 22:00–6:00 at Parnes.

Thursday, August 30, 1945—Dress to go for lunch and to wait for the Americans. I go to the Kadoorie School, along with many others living in our house. There, in one of the classrooms, a table has been set for coffee. The members of the Welfare Mission, led by Major Schoyer, and the leaders of the emigrants' organizations are sitting there. Later the Americans come out to the lawn to witness the ceremonial hoisting of the American flag. Schoolchildren sing the American and British national anthems, "God Bless America" followed by "Hatikvah." It is very festive and everyone is beaming with happiness. The Americans then leave amid much jubilation. Admiral Nimitz arrives in Tokyo Bay. The first big landings begin in Japan.

Admiral Chester W. Nimitz (1885–1966), Chief of Naval Operations, arrived in Tokyo on Admiral Halsey's flagship, the USS *Missouri*. The formal surrender of Japan would take place on this ship on September 2. Nimitz was much admired and very popular with the entire U.S. Armed Forces.

The atmosphere of euphoria continued among the refugees, as joyful victory celebrations took place in homes, in the lanes, and in the SACRA. The exultant mood was not marred by the exceptionally heavy rains. When huge formations of American planes flew over the city and the 7th Fleet docked in Shanghai, the excitement was palpable. The bright lights of the city went on again after years of blackouts. Festive flags were raised, and the refugees experienced their first taste of freedom in a very long time.

Saturday, September 1, 1945—In the evening a victory party given by our SACRA, in the open air, with dancing and cabaret. Herbert Zernik *[a much loved comedian who entertained the refugees on the Jewish holiday of Purim as well as on other occasions]* brings along a poem about the monkey "Go" *[obviously meant to be Ghoya]*. A very pleasant evening!

Among other things, we buy 2½ bottles of sake and, as the evening goes on, we become tipsier than on last New Year's eve. I drink a brotherhood drink with Günther Looser. Theo and I cannot walk straight. While Looser dances with Ulla and Gerti dances with someone else, Theo and I sit at the table (chairs, tables, and something to drink had to be brought along) and sing to a tango melody: "We are both sitting here and are nicely tipsy. We are both sitting here and looking at everyone," etc., etc. Around 2:30 a.m. we stagger into my room. Both girls sleep on one couch, I sleep on the second one. Günther opens the folding bed and Theo Rolfchen *[Little Theo Rolf, a pet name]* camps out on the floor.

Sunday, September 2, 1945—We are awakened early by large numbers of Mustang fighter planes that fly close above our houses. Each one of us buys a delicacy and then we have a breakfast such as not one of the four of us had ever eaten in Shanghai. The atmosphere is one of a honeymoon, of a celebration, which is simply fantastic. Gerti says: "You are really wonderful people, because you are in such a good mood so early in the morning."

Large numbers of *[American]* planes are constantly flying over us. We count 70 of them at one time. In the evening go to the opening of the Winter Semester of the Asia Seminar at the Kadoorie School. Tonn lecture: "Culture and Construction." Armistice officially signed this morning on board the U.S. super warship, the USS *Missouri.*

The *Missouri* and other Allied ships were anchored in Tokyo Bay. Hanging on the door of Captain Stuart Murray's cabin on the surrender deck was the flag Commodore Perry had flown as he sailed into the bay in 1853 to open Japanese ports to American ships. Some assert, however, that the American flag the *Missouri* flew was the one that had flown over the Capitol when Pearl Harbor was attacked by the Japanese, although Captain Murray disputes this. The deck of the ship was crowded with media correspondents, dignitaries, and military officials from many countries.

The Japanese representative was Mamuru Shigemitsu (see p. 20). Both he and General Yoshiji Umezu signed the surrender documents (one in Japanese and one in English) on behalf of Japan. Then General Jonathan M. Wainwright and Lt. Gen. Sir Arthur Percival added their signatures, as did Admiral Nimitz and other representatives of the Allied Forces.

Tuesday, September 4, 1945—117th Duty in the clinic. In the afternoon on foot to Shanghai. Library. Evening at Juliusburgers. V-celebration at Lane 305.

Thursday, September 6, 1945—119th Duty in the clinic. In the evening to Theo Rolf for the choir rehearsal for the Holy Days. Fritz J. also there. Notice from Siegel *[Manny Siegel of the Joint]* that there won't be any money transfers from Switzerland because of technical difficulties. At the same time, a very exaggerated article in *The Shanghai Times*: "18,000 European Refugees Facing Starvation."

Friday, September 7, 1945—120th Duty in the clinic. On the eve of Rosh Hashanah go to the Alexanders for services. Stay there for supper. Then with Theo Rolf to Gerti's.

15

A Real Job

From the time of his arrival in Shanghai until this point, Fritz had scraped together a meager living through attempts to maintain his father's importing business and by doing odd jobs and trying his hand—none too successfully—at sales. After the war, many more opportunities became available. Many refugees obtained jobs with the U.S. military; others were able to find satisfying work in businesses, both Chinese and British. Fritz was now seriously on the lookout for a "real job." At a dinner party in September, the first opportunity presented itself.

Tuesday, September 11, 1945—123rd Duty in the clinic. Evening at the Taubenschlags–Juliusburgers *[these two families were related]*. Mrs. Taubenschlag offers me a job in the company where she also works (Josepho Studio). I would be a shroff there. *[Josepho was considered the best photographer in the French Concession. Shroffs, mostly Chinese, collected payment for "chits"—informal I.O.U. notes—that customers signed. People usually paid all their "chits," since their credit was ruined if they did not. Many Shanghailanders—foreigners—went around without money and signed "chits," which were accepted by stores, bars, etc.]* However, I would also have to clean the office in the morning. My salary would be $500,000 monthly. I reply that I am keenly interested.

Wednesday, September 12, 1945—124th Duty in the clinic. Call from Mrs. Taubenschlag. I have to come for an interview early tomorrow morning. In the afternoon go to the KF administration. Gottschalk assures me that should I resign from the OD, I would not lose my turn getting supper. Then to ODFI *[Ordnungs Führer Inspector]* Isaak. Get leave for tomorrow morning *[for the interview]*. In the evening to the cinema *["Janosik" at the Eastern]*.

Thursday, September 13, 1945—To Josepho, 61 Nanking Rd. *[at Avenue Joffre, which was named after the famous French World War I general]*. Introduced to the manager, Ikey Goldfield, and am hired.

Library. 14:00 watch muster. Announce my resignation *[from the OD]* as of the 16th of this month. Stay there up to 20:00 for my 125th Duty. For the last 2 days Theo Rolf is again working at *[E. D.]* Sassoon Company as a storekeeper in Grosvenor House. *[Theo Rolf had worked for E. D. Sassoon prior to the time when he and his family were required by the Japanese to move into the Designated Area. After the Japanese surrender, he returned to his old job. He, as well as the other employees who had quit their jobs rather than work for the Japanese when they took over the company, received full salary for the months spent in the Designated Area.]*

Although he was soon to begin his job at Josepho, Fritz continued to seek other more interesting and remunerative employment. His big break came when Theo Rolf recommended him to the manager of the Cathay Hotels.

The elegant Cathay Hotel occupied part of the Sassoon House, which was built in 1929 by Sir Victor Sassoon, a wealthy Baghdadi Jew. The vast Sassoon offices were also located in the same building, the tallest building on the Bund. (Until the Cathay was built, the Bank of China was Shanghai's tallest building. Not to be outdone in height by the new arrival, the bank put up a tall flag pole on the roof of its building.) Greatly admired for its distinctive pyramid-shaped roof sheathed in copper, it was referred to as the "No. 1 Mansion in the Far East." The hotel featured marble floors, high ceilings, ornate woodwork, and art deco fixtures. Shanghai residents flocked to this mecca for the rich and famous and danced in the main ballroom, with its special spring floor. Renamed the Peace Hotel, it is still a much visited Shanghai landmark, and remains in operation.

While Sir Victor kept a penthouse at the Cathay Hotel where he resided occasionally, he also built an elegant villa, a half-timbered British country lodge at Hungjao, just outside of Shanghai. An enormous fireplace dominated the drawing room, and there was a gallery for musicians. His many holdings included the power company and the bus company, and he was legendary throughout the Orient because of his opulent parties, the beautiful women he escorted, and his race horses (actually Mongolian ponies).

Friday, September 14, 1945—Upon the recommendation of Theo Rolf to Lipsmann, the General Manager of the Cathay Hotels Co. Ltd., go for an interview at the Cathay Hotel. Must return on the 21st. Dentist. In the afternoon get money from the Alcock watch for repair of my shoe soles—through the aid of the watch duty management office. 126th and last Duty: 22:00–6:00 o'clock at Parnes.

Sunday, September 16, 1945—In the morning to the watch duty management to return clothing *[his uniform]*. Pick up my shoe soles from the ODW *[Ordnungsdienst Wache, or the OD guard house]*. In the afternoon visit Theo Rolf in Grosvenor House. The area is closed off since the 94th Army is billeted in the Cathay Mansions. Nevertheless could get in. Home. Then for services at the Alexanders. Kol Nidre.

Monday, September 17, 1945—Yom Kippur. To services at Alexanders'. Chant Maftir Yonah. Theo Rolf was Hazzan Musaf *[Cantor for the Musaf service, the additional morning service]*. In the evening stay there for a Break the Fast and dinner.

Tuesday, September 18, 1945—Started job at Josepho's. In the morning go along with P *[probably one of his employers]* to photograph an American Colonel in the Cathay Hotel. Free in the afternoon, since no bike available for me yet.

Wednesday, September 19, 1945—The American 7th Fleet arrives early this morning. 66 American and British ships are anchored between the Yangtze estuary and the French Bund.

Thursday, September 20, 1945—Morning: office. Afternoon: Ave. Joffre. Get a bike. Ride to collect cash *[he has at last begun his duties as a shroff]*. Evening: Theo Rolf and Gerti pop in to visit me.

Friday, September 21, 1945—Go with written recommendation from Ted to Lipsmann *[at Cathay Hotels]*. Must return on 2/10 *[October 2]*. Pick up shoes from the Jüdische Gemeinde. The *[photography]* company's bike is at my disposal day and night. I can use it for all my private chores. Lieutenant-General Albert C. Wedemeyer landed in Shanghai the day before yesterday. *[Wedemeyer was appointed the Commanding General of the U.S. forces in the China Theatre and Chief of Staff to Chiang Kai-Shek in October 1944, replacing Gen. Joseph Stilwell, who was recalled by President Roosevelt at the insistence of Chiang.]*

Saturday, September 22, 1945—Office. Lunch with Günther in Woochang Rd. Deliveries in the French *[French Concession]*. Many streets are flooded. Have no boots and my legs get wet. Never mind. The weather is warm. To the Golden Gate *[theatre]*. See my first American film *[since Pearl Harbor]*, "Anything for a Thrill." Very nice. Go home on bike via Bubbling Well and Nanking Rd.

Everything is illuminated bright as day. A fairy-tale dream.

Sunday, September 23, 1945—Morning to the tailor and visits to Alexanders and Juliusburgers. Evening at the Marcuses. Discussion about the deluge of gold resulting from the presence in Shanghai of the enormous Allied fleet. This especially affects goings-on with women *[bar girls, taxi dancers, prostitutes]*. Of course, make all my visits on bike, which is really a great pleasure.

Monday, September 24, 1945—Morning: office. Afternoon: deliveries, among which was one to Mrs. Kadoorie in Marble Hall *[wife of Lawrence Kadoorie]*.

The Kadoories lived in Marble Hall, an enormous stately residence built in 1924, with spacious grounds and a grand ballroom lit by 3,600 electric lights that turned various colors. Large quantities of Italian marble were imported, mainly for the many fireplaces, hence the name "Marble Hall." Groups of Jewish children were occasionally invited there and royally entertained. After Pearl Harbor, the home was occupied by Japanese "bluejackets" (marines). Today the building is the Children's Palace, a famous school for the arts.

The Kadoories were very charitable Sephardi tycoons whose motto was: "Wealth is but a sacred trust to be administered for the welfare of society." Lawrence's younger brother, Horace, handled most of the educational projects of the family. Among Horace's important responsibilities was the Shanghai Jewish Youth Association School (SJYA) in Hongkew (see p. 67).

After business closes, go to visit Theo Rolf in Grosvenor House. We go for an evening of fun to the Great World Amusement Center, Dah So Ga, on Avenue Edward VII, corner Yu Ya Ching Rd. Very interesting. *[The Great World Entertainment Center was notorious for its illicit pleasures, including a gambling casino and a brothel. It symbolized Shanghai's prewar reputation as a sinful city where gangsters ruled, opium was readily available, and anything was acceptable. The original Great World burned down, but it was later rebuilt. Today, it features more wholesome entertainment: karaoke, Beijing opera, and acrobats.]*

Tuesday September 25, 1945—Office. In the afternoon: deliveries, among which was one to Capt. Reid in Eastern Area Camp, Pingliang Rd. *[The internees had to remain in the internment camps until arrangements were made for housing and/or repatriation.]* Evening with Fritz J. to the Eastern *[The Sweetheart of Sigma Chi]*.

Friday, September 28 until and including Tuesday

October 2, 1945—Have flu and lie in bed. Klaus and Theo Rolf visit me. Since the 1st of this month, we get only cash from KF. At present receive $30,000 a day *[local currency]*. The family Knoche cooks for me.

Thursday, October 4, 1945—In the morning to Lipsmann. He appears to have a job for me. Must return early tomorrow. Office. Deliveries. Evening to the cinema *["Michael Strogoff" at the Eastern]*.

Friday, October 5, 1945—In the morning to Lipsmann. Wait a very long time. He does not invite me in. Just says en passant: "I am sending you with a couple of letters to the manager of the Cathay Mansions." The secretary then explains to me that I am to work on a trial basis for one week at the reception office of the Cathay Mansions. After one week they will decide if they will keep me. To the Cathay Mansions. Introduced to Manager Stahly. Will start early tomorrow morning. Reported at Josepho's that I am leaving the job. Dentist: Dr. Fraenkel.

Saturday, October 6, 1945—Start my job at the Reception Office of the Cathay Mansions. Heinz Meyer *[also works]* there. On duty till 15:00 hours. Ate lunch there.

Fred's diet improved substantially with his new job, as the Sassoon hotels were famous for their elegant dining facilities. Helene DeGroot, in a column written for *The Enquirer and News* in Battle Creek, Michigan, described the surroundings and the "marvelous French and Viennese cuisine" offered at "the three finest hotels in the city."

> Their elaborate dining rooms glitter with sparking crystal, silver, and important persons. The maitre d'hote and the dignified waiters almost overwhelm you with their old world gallantry, courtesy, and flawless service. Musicians serenade you with soothing dinner music. Food is served in a number of elaborate courses and when the diner picks up his check, he finds its total a fairly reasonable amount, and certainly worth the superb service.

How exhilarating it was for Fred to dine in such surroundings after his years of subsistence living! It was about this time that Fritz began to be called Fred or Freddy. Only his family members still called him Fritz, although they sometimes lapsed into a Germanized diminutive of the name, Fredchen, or the nickname Fredel. *[References to Fritz from this point on refer to Fritz Juliusburger.]* Theo Rolf changed his name to Ted, but to his parents he would always be Theo Rolf.

Sunday, October 7, 1945—Morning: washman. Then would like to go to the hotel, but the French trams are on strike. Traffic problems. Since I am afraid I may arrive too late, I call the Cathay Mansions from the Cathay Hotel. I am told that I should not come there, but go to the Metropole Hotel for duty. *[Built by the two real estate visionaries, Sir Victor Sassoon and Commander F. R. Davey, who was Director of the Sassoon Banking Corporation, the 16-story, 200-room Metropole was another of the E. D. Sassoon hotels. Now a budget hotel, it is part of the Shanghai New Asia Group of hotels.]* At the Metropole am introduced to Manager Rovere. *[Harry]* Burstein is at the Reception Office. I know him from OD. He was also employed in the hotel before the war. On duty till 20:00. A great deal to do since the hotel is full. Mainly U.S. Armed Forces. Have tea and dinner there. This post offers big opportunities, since besides Burstein and me, there is only a night clerk (Herzberg). Privately, though, I am afraid that I will also have to do night duty.

Wednesday, October 10, 1945—Chinese holiday *[Double Ten, see p. 198 for description]* and V-Day. Much noise on the streets. Am at the hotel first thing in the morning. Duty till 20:00. Meals in hotel. Breakfast: coffee, 2 eggs, jam, bread. Lunch: hors d'oeuvre, soup, meat, 2 side dishes, salad, dessert, coffee. Tea: tea, bread, jam, a piece of cake. Evening: soup, fish, meat, 2 side dishes, dessert, coffee, bread.

Thursday, October 11, 1945—Duty as usual from 12:00–20:00. Evening: visit Ted. The headquarters of the China Theater will be transferred from Chungking to Shanghai. In our hotel we get only *[American]* colonels, lieutenant colonels, and majors.

Sunday, October 14, 1945—In the morning visit Gerendasi's new office at 344 Hamilton House *[prestigious office and apartment building, built by Sassoons]*.

Wednesday, October 17, 1945—Library. Then duty as usual. Although my trial week ended on Saturday, have not heard anything further from the management, which is, of course, a good sign. *[The management was obviously pleased with Fred's job performance. When Ted checked up to find out how Fred was doing, Lipsmann said enthusiastically, "Send me more Marcuses!"]*

Thursday, October 18, 1945—Duty as usual. Mess room opened. Introduced to American mess personnel. Lt. Soudakoff (Russian born) and especially Sergeant Seidel (his father was German born). Get closer with Seidel who is 22 years old and comes from a ranch in Arizona.

Friday, October 19, 1945—Have breakfast with Seidel. Then library. Duty as always. Through my friendship with Seidel, I get—besides the hotel food—specialties meant for Americans. American butter for every meal, stewed fruit, pineapple, tomato juice. This is indescribable! My present situation appears to be so good, that I cannot completely grasp and believe it, and have an inner fear of something bad happening. Still, with God's help, things will remain as they are. I have, indeed, had so many sad experiences!

In his diary, Fred seldom dwelt on personal emotions—perhaps a plucky attempt to "keep his chin up." However, his unexpected avowal of "so many sad experiences" revealed his inner turmoil. Since his father's untimely death, Fred had fought a battle to survive poverty, illness, enemy occupation, bombings, and the fear of an uncertain future. At this point, it was no simple matter for him—as for others in Shanghai—to grasp the return of normalcy, to put the past into perspective. He was entering upon a period of enormous transition.

16

GI Joe

On August 30, 1945, General MacArthur, his ever present corncob pipe clenched in his teeth, had landed in Tokyo to take charge of the occupation of Japan. One of the greatest achievements in his long, illustrious career was as civil administrator of Japan. Among his first and wisest (albeit controversial) decisions was his insistence that the Emperor be left on the throne and not be treated as a war criminal. Thereafter, the Emperor cooperated closely with MacArthur and helped assure that his people did likewise. On January 1, 1946, Emperor Hirohito publically renounced "the false conceptions that the Emperor is divine."

In Shanghai, replacing the sullen Japanese soldiers in their ill-fitting uniforms, were smiling, impeccably dressed GIs who loomed above the rest of the population. These handsome U.S. marines, soldiers, and sailors were often seen riding in pedicabs too small for their size, with their feet sticking out from the sides. Some GIs distributed C-rations to curious Shanghai citizens, who eagerly ate this new "delicacy." Others handed women pure wool blankets, which skillful Chinese tailors transformed into elegant coats. Moss-green U.S. Marine blankets soon became the ladies' favorites. The ebullient and generous nature of the Americans immediately captivated the refugees.

One of the thousands of military descending on the city was Ed Diner, Navy Radio Operator First Class, a Jewish boy from Denver, who lived on his ship in Shanghai harbor during the winter of 1945–46. He and his buddies thoroughly enjoyed the Shanghai scene. In an interview, he recalled vivid memories of a noisy, vibrant, and crowded metropolis; innumerable fabulous nighclubs, some featuring girls who stripped naked and performed obscene acts onstage; constant, loud, and rapid-fire Chinese speech, and a multitude of rickshaws.

Shortly after the arrival of Ed's ship, four English ladies boarded and invited the sailors to a dance at the YWCA. There he met a refugee girl from Munich, and soon afterward joined her family in Hongkew for a Shabbat dinner. Despite their impoverished circumstances, they prepared a meal "fit for a king," which meant a lot to the young sailor who had been living on shipboard meals for three years. Ed still remembers his surprise at the lack of sanitation and the surrounding dirt. "Everyone was sick," he said, "some with rashes and oozing sores." The people were very resilient, but were still courageously facing many daily challenges.

All the refugees Ed met during many visits to Hongkew were interested in only one subject: America. They loved hearing details about everyday life there and expressed their deep longing to become Americans. Somehow, Ed remembered, they all seemed confident that they would eventually make it to the U.S.

Back on his ship, Ed pilfered a quantity of sulfa from the pharmacy and handed it over to the Jewish doctors in Hongkew. They were thrilled to receive this rarely available and much needed medicine, which was used as a disinfectant and an antiseptic. The Americans were also responsible for bringing DDT to Shanghai and conducting trainings in its use. Dr. Friedrichs (see p. 71) oversaw the use of this miracle fumigator to end the infestations of vermin in the camps.

Fritz, like other young refugees, was elated at the Allied victory and entranced by the happy-go-lucky, gum chewing Americans whose care-free *joie de vivre* he emulated. During frequent evenings spent with his new friends at Hamilton House, he learned American folksongs, which he found to be as sentimental as the German ones he knew. He began to smoke American cigarettes, mainly Camels and Lucky Strikes, chew gum, drank stateside beer, and devoured big meals of delicious, long unavailable treats. All of this he called "A1," another Americanism he picked up (the Shanghai expression was "Number 1").

> **Sunday, October 21, 1945**—Duty as usual. In the evening go with Burstein to the billet of our Mess Sergeant *[probably Seidel]* in Hamilton House. Sing along with the guitar. The Americans are really great guys! *[Under British influence, the expression "great" had not been used in Shanghai. Now, through contact with members of the U.S. Armed Forces, Fred—as well as many other Shanghailanders—was becoming quite Americanized.]*

> **Monday, October 22, 1945**—Have breakfast in the hotel in the morning. Then visit the office of the Gerendasis. *[Relax in]* Public Garden.

The Public Garden on the Bund (International Settlement) was comprised of an acre of reclaimed foreshore. It was the creation of Shanghai's British authorities, who engaged the services of a well-known Scottish landscape designer. The Scot reproduced a British garden with hollyhocks, roses, blooming bushes, lawns, and pebble-covered walks. Before the war, on weekends and holidays, the British Army Band would entertain visitors with polkas, jigs, and waltzes. On special occasions, the Scottish Highlanders marched through the park wearing colorful tartans and playing their bagpipes. Occasionally, the Shanghai Symphony Orchestra—in which no Chinese musicians participated—gave concerts in an elegant wrought-iron pavilion.

Entrance to the Public Garden was forbidden to Chinese residents, except for park employees and amahs caring for foreign children. The main reason for the exclusion of Chinese, so the British claimed, was an influx of Chinese beggars. When the Japanese occupied Shanghai, they opened the Public Garden to all Chinese, emphasizing British anti-Asian discrimination in their propaganda. Indeed, most Shanghainese fiercely resented a large sign erected by the British at the park's gate, which listed park regulations, including NO ENTRY TO CHINESE. Another sign refused entry to dogs. In anti-foreign propaganda, first used by Chinese students, the two signs were conflated to read "No Chinese and No Dogs Allowed." There was, however, no such sign in the Public Garden.

Located on the banks of the Whangpoo River, where cool breezes brought respite during Shanghai's unbearable summers, the Public Garden was a favorite place for relaxation. As this beautiful and restful spot was just a short walk from the Cathay Hotel where Fred worked, he enjoyed spending some of his free time there.

> **Wednesday, October 24, 1945**—Duty: as usual. In the evening go to the Capitol, which has now become a GI theater: "Where Do We Go from Here?" Relatives of the U.S. Armed Forces can enter free, as well as one guest. Before the main film, weekly news (Eisenhower in New York!); 1 propaganda film; 1 musical film with Bing Crosby. Everything very new and interesting.

> **Thursday, October 25, 1945**—Duty: as usual. Evening: with the guys in Hamilton House without Burstein. Introduced to beer with whiskey *[boilermakers]*.

Fred was overjoyed with his newfound freedom. The restraints imposed by the Japanese had ended; he was free to come and go as he pleased. The fear associated with daily air raids faded away, and his constant struggle to survive was over. The work in the Sassoon hotels was satisfying, he enjoyed excellent meals, and drank a quart of milk each day directly from the bottle.

Aside from French lessons, a new undertaking, Fred's main diversion was—as always—going to the cinema. He went with friends, with army personnel who were staying at the hotel, and often by himself.

Until the Nazis ruled that Jews were "not wanted" in movie theatres, Fred had been an avid movie-goer. This interest continued in Shanghai until the refugees were ordered into the Designated Area and the Japanese banned American movies. Before that occurred, the little red book, into which Fred had carefully entered the operas he attended as a child in Berlin, morphed into a record of all the movies he saw. (This is the source for the titles of the movies inserted in italics in various diary entries on the exact date when Fred saw each.)

At the Capitol, on May 26, 1940, he saw his first American film, *Babes in Arms*. Other well-known films he enjoyed include *Gone with the Wind, King Kong, Good-bye Mr. Chips, The Wizard of Oz, Northwest Passage,* and *Mutiny on the Bounty*. His tastes were eclectic, and his list included many B pictures as well as classics. A number of movie theaters were mentioned by Fred in the little red book, among them the Grand, Nanking, Cathay, Capitol, Broadway, Eastern, Ritz, Wayside, Roxy, Rialto, Golden Gate, Uptown, Doumer, Majestic, Astor, Lyric, Lyceum, Strand, and Metropole.

During the first days of November 1945, Fred performed his duty at the hotel, frequented the library, and saw a film every night but one. He listed *Cartoons & Comedies, Meet Me in St. Louis,* and *Radio Stars on Parade,* all at the Capitol Theatre. (The last film was preceded by a documentary about the Japanese surrender on the USS *Missouri*.) During the remainder of November, he saw another five films. His attendance did taper off in December, down to only three. This passion for movies, which was shared by most Shanghailanders, lasted all his life.

Fred's affection for and friendship with Ted was unwavering after the Allied victory, and Ted remained his chief confidant. They saw each other frequently and always celebrated together their birthdays and other significant occasions, such as New Year's Eve and Ted's engagement to Gerti.

Tuesday, November 6, 1945—Morning: at Grosvenor House. Congratulate Ted, on the occasion of his birthday. (The celebration will take place this coming Saturday.) Duty: as usual. My entire salary for October, including today's additional payment, CNC$30,000 in total. To that we must add another $1,865 side income. (Fred and the other hotel receptionists were able to supplement their income by exchanging currency at a small profit, buying cigarettes for guests, arranging tours, etc.) I am happy and satisfied. Things should just keep going on like this!

Wednesday, November 7, 1945—Duty: as usual. In the evening alone in Hongkew to the cinema *[Clouds over Europe at the Wayside]*. In the morning: French lesson with Knoche. Since yesterday, they have opened a PX (Post Exchange) in the hotel. U.S. army personnel can buy cigarettes there at the cheapest prices. I can get stuff through acquaintances. *[In 1945, there were more than 20 PXs in Shanghai and vicinity. Several were located in the hotels where military personnel were billeted. In addition to U.S. merchandise, some PXs also featured a snack bar, barber shop, photo shop, watch repair shop, dry cleaners, and tailor.]*

Saturday, November 10, 1945—Morning on foot with Günther to the city. In the evening with a PX employee Suzie Hahn by jeep to Ted's. We celebrate his birthday. Very nice.

Wednesday, November 14, 1945—Take a day off. Together with Private Dallas Erickson from Billeting go for a three-hour steamboat ride on the Whangpoo. This is a free of charge pleasure cruise, since it is sponsored by the American army. Sail up the river. Very interesting. See land and seaplanes landing. In the evening visit the three guys in Hamilton House.

Saturday, November 17, 1945—In the morning, buy a pair of black shoes. *[This was no doubt a significant event for Fred, after years of having worn shoes repaired or obtaining used ones from the Kitchen Fund.]* Duty: as usual. Evening: at home.

Thursday, November 22, 1945—Duty: as usual. Thanksgiving Day *[possibly the first time Fred celebrated this American holiday]*. Evening with Burstein at the guys' place in Hamilton House.

Saturday, November 24, 1945—Ted and Gerti get engaged. Official announcement coming soon.

Tuesday November 27, 1945—Ted has been promoted to Purchasing Manager at E. D. Sassoon Company.

17

Uncertainty Continues

Reports of the terrible fate that befell the Jews of Europe did not appear in the local newspapers until the fall of 1945 when *The Shanghai Jewish Chronicle* printed a series of articles called "Treblinka," which documented the gassing and incineration of Jews in German concentration camps. Shortly afterward, refugees were stunned by actual newsreels that documented the liberation of concentration camps. As the names of survivors were posted in Hongkew, the magnitude of the Holocaust became a horrifying reality. Synagogues held prayer meetings to memorialize those who had perished. Soon it was whispered from mouth to mouth that a number of Jewish refugees in Shanghai had committed suicide upon learning of the extermination of their families in the European death camps.

Now, even though they had experienced great deprivation and suffering in the Designated Area, the refugees became aware of their incredible good fortune in having escaped and survived. While Fred did not have any Jewish relatives who remained in Germany, many of his friends and acquaintances discovered to their horror that their families had been annihilated. The revelation of torture and mass murder of Jews by the Nazis shocked all Shanghailanders and increased their sympathy for the European refugees whose relatives and friends had suffered such a bitter fate.

> **Sunday, November 11, 1945**—Duty: as usual. In the evening go to see "British War News" at the Broadway cinema. Shots of V-1 and, especially, KZ *[Konzentrationslager, or concentration camp]* Belsen! This has to be seen. The dogs!

After the initial period of postwar exhilaration, Fred's spirits and health began to plunge. He fought a persistent cough and frequently felt unwell. There can be no doubt that his truly difficult physical and emotional experiences had left some permanent marks. In his typical way, however, he did not allow his illnesses to hold him back. Very soon, he was up and around, joining his friends for evenings of enjoyment in a city that was once again lively and exciting. Now a twenty-one-year-old young man with

a good job, he began to seek out female companionship. His preference
at the time seemed to be for Chinese girls.

There was underlying tension in all of Shanghai because of the
expanding civil war between the Chinese Nationalists and the Chinese
Communists. President Truman, well aware of the escalating danger, attempted to solve the problem by summoning General George Marshall
out of retirement and sending him to China on December 20, 1945, as
his special representative. Marshall's mandate was to urge Nationalist
leader Chiang Kai-shek to make some kind of accommodation with Mao
Tse-Tung, obviously a very complicated endeavor, and one that eventually failed.

In Hongkew, weakened psychologically and physically after long years
of segregation, European refugees were faced once again with mounting uncertainty regarding their future. Yet, at this point in time, Fred and
many young people his age were still caught up in the excitement of the
Allied victory over the Nazis and the Japanese, and, making every effort
to suppress their worries, they attempted to lead a normal life.

Saturday, December 1, 1945—Duty: as usual. In the after-
noon go with Looser to buy an engagement present for Ted and
Gerti. (Buy 2 Chinese bowls in a box.) In the evening: alone to the
Roxy *[Thirty Seconds over Tokyo]*.

Sunday 9th and Monday 10th December, 1945—Duty: as
usual. These words appear short and dry in every daily report. The
main reason for this is that in the evening I have neither the time
nor the desire to write at length. However, I still manage to write
in my diary at work, during quiet moments, also letters such as are
attached hereto *[unfortunately, no letters were found with the diaries]*. At
least, these record in a small way the uniqueness of hotel life. Evening: at home. Coughing a lot. Visit *[Heinz]* Meyer and the doctor.

Tuesday, December 11, 1945—In the morning to the Chaoufoong Heim clinic to Dr. Götz. Apparently, I don't have TB, but
chronic bronchitis. *[Perhaps Fred's poor health was exacerbated by the
extremely cold winter in Shanghai that year. The coal mines had stopped pro-
ducing, and there was often no heating available.]* At 1:00 o'clock back to
Hongkew to the Ward Rd. Synagogue for Gerda Alexander's wedding to Michuel Abramchik. Pay in the Ward Rd. Heim for shots
prescribed by the doctor. Duty: as usual till 8 o'clock. Dr. Saper (a
Pole from London), who is Director for Displaced Persons at the
UNRRA *[United Nations Relief and Rehabilitation Administration]* and
moved to our place recently, wants to borrow a radio. Since I am

seldom at home, I lend him mine for $7.00 a month (out of which I give Burstein $1.00).

Saturday, December 15, 1945—Duty: as usual. Evening with Gerti, Ted, and Fritz. Again to the Park Hotel. Eat a big dinner. *[The Park Hotel was a 22-story hotel at the junction of Nanking Road and Bubbling Well Road. It was famous for its outstanding Filipino band. The exclusive restaurant in the hotel had a beautiful view of the Race Course across the street. Today it is operated by The International Hotels, Limited.]* Go home by pedicab. *[Rickshaws were cheaper, less "classy."]* Fritz J's birthday today. However, we will celebrate tomorrow, since I have a date tonight with the night bookkeeper's daughter. Ted made a big fuss, claiming that I should not go out with the daughter of my subordinate. Luckily for me, the girl stood me up. Great plans and discussions about what kind of girls Fritz and I should take out on New Year's Eve. Taxi dancers? *[Girls in nightclubs who were paid for dancing with customers were called taxi dancers. Often, after a few dances, the girls would join the customer for a drink at his table. They would order "whiskey," and were routinely served tea. The customer, of course, was charged the price of an expensive imported drink. Some taxi dancers were actually prostitutes; others offered favors only to select clients. The 2005 Merchant-Ivory film* The White Countess *is about a fictitious Russian taxi dancer.]*

Sunday, December 16, 1945—In the morning first injection at the Chaoufoong clinic. 2 ampoules of vitamin B and 1 ampoule of calcium. French lesson. Duty: as usual. Go together with Ted, Gerti, Steffi Taubenschlag, and Fritz (at Fritz's expense) to have dinner at Wing Hwa. Then, on our joint account, for coffee to Ciro's. *[The expensive, art deco Ciro's, built by Sir Victor Sassoon, was the first nightclub in Shanghai to have air conditioning—a citywide sensation.]* I invite Steffi for next weekend. Must finally learn how to dance!

Monday, December 17, 1945—Second injection. Duty: as usual. Evening to Ballet Master Pasqual! 10 private dance lessons: $8:00. Pay in advance. I must be able to dance, more or less, on New Year's Eve. *[Pasqual came from Vienna. His school was one of two competing dancing schools in Hongkew.]*

Sunday, December 23, 1945—Sixth injection. 4th dance lesson. Duty as usual. Health: very bad. Coughing for weeks. Cough has now become quite horrible. Who knows? *[Even after the diagnosis by Dr. Götz, Fred was still concerned about the possibility of tuberculosis, which afflicted many refugees.]*

Monday, December 24, 1945—5th dance lesson. Duty as usual. Get a *[Christmas]* gift from the No. 1 Hall Boy of ½ dozen handkerchiefs, and ½ lb. of cheese from the kitchen. Since I am feeling very ill, I just sit in the office. In the evening go at once to bed.

Tuesday the 25th till Sunday the 30th December, 1945—In bed with pleurisy.

Monday, December 31 to Tuesday, January 1, 1946—In the morning and afternoon, chores in Hongkew for the New Year's Eve preparations. In the evening, invite Günther Looser to the Delikat. Then to a party at Ted's. Bring a cabaret number *[possibly a taxi dancer from the cabaret]*. Dance and flirt till 6:00 in the morning. Then to bed and sleep 3 hours. To the Hotel. Duty: as usual. To bed early in the evening. Traffic changes to the right. *[The British had established left-hand traffic. When the Americans came, they changed it to the right.]*

By the beginning of 1946, Fred's life had settled into a pleasant routine, marred only by continuing health problems. Enjoying his newfound freedom, Fred began a pattern of frequent drinking. Looking back, none of his old friends thought this practice of his was excessive or called it problematic. Nevertheless, this imbibing continued throughout the rest of his Shanghai years, possibly caused by a need to escape from the reality of his peculiar situation. Although his life had taken a huge turn for the better, he was still trapped in alien surroundings and continually worried about what the future had in store for him.

Monday, January 7, 1946—Afraid that since the trams are running later at night, I will have to be on duty till around 10:00. *[In Shanghai, the local designation for cars that ran on rails was trams. Trolleys, on the other hand, were connected to overhead electric wiring and ran directly on the street. Russian immigrants called a trolley kukushka (cuckoo), and in the plural, kukushi.]*

Tuesday, January 8, 1946—French. Duty: as usual. In the evening with Billeting Private Erickson to the Majestic: "The Nuremberg Trial" (Goering, Hess, Streicher, etc.).

Tuesday, January 22, 1946—Short visit to Gerendasis. Duty: as usual. Evening to group circle dance lesson at Pasqual's. During the lunch hour: big demonstration of unemployed Chinese who, since the war ended, can no longer work at machines that are now out of use. An American sailor and many pedestrians try to get through the demonstration that is blocking traffic, and are mis-handled by the Chinese. MPs *[U.S. Military Police]* and SPs *[U.S. Navy Shore Patrol]* close ranks with the police and the Chinese military to bring order. After the demonstrators are held back from the SMC *[Shanghai Municipal Council]*, they go to the garden of the Holy Trinity Cathedral, and remain there until late in the evening. *[The Anglican cathedral was built on a grand scale in 1869 as the Holy Trinity Church. After Pearl Harbor, the Japanese used it as a collection point for the enemy nationals they interned in camps. It was closed in 1949 after the Communist takeover of Shanghai, and is presently undergoing restoration for the "postdenominational" Protestant churches in China.]*

Monday, January 28, 1946—Transferred to the Cathay Hotel. (Among others staying there are Generals Wedemeyer and Strate-meyer.)

The most important of the military top brass stayed at the Cathay Hotel, including Gen. Albert C. Wedemeyer, Commanding General of the U.S. Forces, China Theater, and Gen. George E. Stratemeyer, Commanding General of the China-Burma-India Theater. In his capacity as a receptionist, Fred became acquainted with all the top brass. At one point, he also met Maj. Gen. Claire Chennault of the Flying Tigers and Morris "Two-Gun" Cohen.

Claire Chennault had been hired by Chiang Kai-shek as an advisor to the Chinese Air Force in 1937. He trained Chinese pilots, and helped convince the U.S. to supply the Nationalists with 100 Curtiss fighters. With 100 volunteer pilots recruited from the U.S. armed services, he formed the American Volunteer Group (AVG), which was dubbed the Flying Tigers by *Time* magazine. The group flew many dangerous missions carrying supplies over the Hump from India to China after the Burma Road was cut off by the Japanese. (Some sources claim that the Flying Tigers were a covert entity of the Office of Strategic Serices, the wartime precursor of the Central Intelligence Agency.) After the war, Chennault founded the Civil Air Transport (CAT) in China, which was backed by the Nationalist Government and UNRRA. Using Flying Tigers insignia, CAT carried relief supplies to China's interior.

Morris Cohen was a well-known Jewish character who had been a bodyguard for Dr. Sun Yat-sen and later was appointed general in the Chinese army. It is said that when Dr. Sun Yat-Sen died, Cohen wept for the second time in his adult life (the first time was on the death of his own father).

Friday, February 1, 1946—Afternoon: visit to Gerendasis. With the doctor to the Seymour Rd. Synagogue. *[Ohel Rachel, a Sephardi synagogue near the Jewish school, see p. 43. Although permission can be obtained to visit this building today, all efforts to turn it once again into a synagogue have so far failed. In 2006, a comprehensive exhibit on the European refugee period was displayed there. In Spring 2008, the first Jewish wedding in 60 years was held there for the daughter of Maurice Ohana, Head of the Shanghai Jewish community, thanks to the efforts of Professor Pan Guang, Dean of the Centre of Jewish Studies Shanghai.]* To worship services by U.S. Chaplain Fine.

A few months later, a notice about the worship services conducted by the army chaplains Fine and Gordon appeared in the English supplement of *Our Life*:

Military Services at the Ohel Rachel Synagogue Becoming Popular

The Military Services held on Shabbat eve at the Ohel Rachel Synagogue under the spiritual leadership of Chaplains Alvin I. Fine and Morris Gordon are becoming popular not only with the members of the American Armed Forces, but also with members of our Communities. Last Friday, for instance, the spacious worship hall of the Synagogue was filled to capacity. Both Chaplain Fine and Chaplain Gordon are brilliant speakers and their sermons create a great impression.

Rabbi Alvin Fine was greatly admired by Jews from all three communities: refugees, Sephardis, and Russians. Jewish Shanghailanders welcomed all the American GI's of Jewish origin, and were especially thrilled to meet an American Jewish chaplain. A native of Portland, Oregon, Rabbi Fine later became the Senior Rabbi at Temple Emanu-El in San Francisco from 1948 to 1964. A staunch liberal, he was a pivotal figure in the civil rights coalition and a leader in interfaith cooperation. He died in 1999.

Saturday, February 2, 1946—Chinese New Year. In the morning: duty. After lunch move into my own room: No. 126. Am very happy.

Friday, February 15, 1946—Exchange duty with Meyer. Morning: with Knoche at the War Crimes Trial in Ward Road Jail. Around 16 Japanese who killed American flyers in Hankow. *[As described below, there were actually 18 Japanese on trial.]* Afternoon: duty.

While much has been written about the Nuremberg Trials and on the Tokyo War Crimes Trials, material on the 11 cases that were tried in

Shanghai appears to be scarce. Horst Eisfelder, a refugee, was allowed to take photographs at one such trial, which lasted from August 1946 until January 1947. In that trial, the U.S. charged 23 former German officials in Shanghai for engaging in intelligence and propaganda activities against the Allied forces after Germany's surrender.

The "Hankow Airmen" trial began in January 1946, but was postponed to February 7. Eighteen members of the Japanese gendarmerie were accused of humiliating, beating, torturing, and finally "cremating" three American fliers. Defense attorney Major Maurice Levin argued for acquittal on the grounds of superior orders. Another member of the defense team, Lt. Col. E. M. Hudgins, insisted that five high-ranking officers, who were missing from the trial, were really responsible. This trial ended on February 27. All but one of the defendants were found guilty. Five were sentenced to death and the other 12 to imprisonment for sentences ranging from 18 months to life. Fred attended this war crime trial on three occasions—February 15, 19, and 23. Very likely, he was one of the few refugees to do so.

In a subsequent trial that began on February 27, four Japanese officers were tried for their war crimes against eight of the famous "Doolittle Raiders" who made crash landings off the coast of China after a daring air raid on the Japanese mainland. (The 1944 film *Thirty Seconds over Tokyo* tells the story of this bombing raid.) Two of the original ten fliers died when their B-25 ditched. The other eight were captured and tortured. In addition, they contracted dysentery and beriberi due to the horrendous conditions of their detention. On August 28 of that year, three of the fliers were put on trial, but were not told the charges against them. This was a common practice during World War II. Japanese policy was to assume that foreign military prisoners were well aware of what crimes they had committed and simply had to admit their guilt. These three men were executed on October 15. Four of the other five remained confined on a starvation diet, surviving with only a Bible to ease their despair. They were finally freed in August 1945. The fifth man died. At their trial, all four Japanese were found guilty. Three were sentenced to hard labor for five years and the fourth to a nine-year sentence.

Saturday, February 16, 1946—Morning: duty. Evening with Fritz to Royal Hotel, Range Rd. dancing hall. Get to know young woman Wong Mei-Lee. Make a date to go tomorrow to the cinema. Have a lot in mind. Fritz also has a date for the same time.

Sunday, February 17, 1946—Morning: duty. Then to the rendezvous. Both Fritz and I stood up by the girls. Share double pain. We sell our extra cinema tickets and go alone to the Grand *[Dumbo]*. Have dinner and wander around till 12:30 a.m.

Back at the Mansions, go on a rescue operation with Heinz Meyer. Eleven sailors *[without doubt Americans]* have been attacked in a dark alley by some Chinese and we rush to help, together with an MP. After half an hour of hitting around in a pitch dark lane, banging of house doors and loud swearing, we go back to my room, where we consume peanuts contributed by Meyer and get tipsy on several bottles of stateside Budweiser.

Tuesday, February 19, 1946—Morning: go with the Chief of Defense Lt. Col. Hudgins to the War Crimes Trial in Ward Rd. Jail (in Hudgins's jeep). *[Lt. Col. E.M. Hudgins was billeted in one of the Sassoon hotels, which is where Fred met him.]* Lunch with Hudgins. Afternoon: duty.

Wednesday, February 20, 1946—Morning: short visit to Burstein. Afternoon: duty. Günther comes to take a bath. *[Since most of the accommodations in the Hongkew area did not have hot water, Fred generously invited his friends to come to his room in the hotel to enjoy a hot bath.]*

Thursday, February 21, 1946—Early duty. Afternoon: a strike breaks out in the entire hotel at 17:30. Same thing in the Cathay and Metropole. Great excitement. Military Police occupy the buildings. At 19:30 negotiations succeed in persuading the Chinese to start work again. During the strike I was, of course, in the office. (*[I]* also saw the flyer that the Chinese were sending to all guests' rooms). In the evening go alone to the Astor *[Cobra Woman]*.

Saturday, February 23, 1946—Pappi's Birthday. With Marcus and Col. Hudgins (in his station wagon) to War Crimes Trial in Ward Rd. Jail. Meet Ted there.

18

A Pleasant Routine

Life in postwar Shanghai continued to change at a feverish pace. All over the city, blackmarketeers hawked items available at U.S. military PXs: cigarettes, toiletries, canned goods, clothing, household articles. Even essential pharmaceuticals were sold on the streets. In nightclubs and at home, people danced to the strains of "Don't Fence Me In," "I'll be Seeing You," "Sioux City Sue," "Rum and Coca Cola." New American expressions and words entered Shanghai's vocabulary: wolf whistle, stateside, Roger, okey dokey, and a phrase from a Glenn Miller song that infuriated the girls: "must be jelly cause jam don't shake like that!"

Fred resolved to adapt to life's bewildering changes, and to try to be a little looser about irregularities at work. He began to develop very pleasant and close friendships with officers who were billeted at the Sassoon hotels and with Americans who seemed willing to help him, should he eventually emigrate to the United States. However, by the time Fred reached America several years later, most of these relationships had dissolved. The reason, most likely, was that his new friends, who had gone through the trauma of war and separation from their families, encountered many problems themselves when they returned home. Fred's experience in this respect was similar to that of many Shanghailanders.

> **Friday, March 1, 1946**—Morning: duty. Negri tells me that I must transfer my room to the Cathay Hotel, because my room at the Mansions is needed. After end of the duty go to the Cathay. Very nice room. However, must share it with Herzberg (night clerk at the Metropole). No private bath, but hot and cold water in the room. To Hongkew: French lesson. Evening to Cathay cinema [*Madonna of the Seven Moons*]. Then with Fritz visit Meyer in his room. Beer. Then read aloud a sketch I wrote, "The Friendly Receptionist." More beer. Then on to "Boilermaker." Finally, a straight whiskey. In between finish stock of stateside beer and order more from the bar.

Thursday, March 7, 1946—Morning: French lesson. Afternoon: duty. Fritz and I have received permission to fix up for ourselves a windowless room that was used till now for storage. We make it very nice with the help of the housekeeper. Since Fritz always works at night (in the morning he goes to the university and in the afternoon he sleeps in the room), I can use the room for myself at night. Now, I actually have 3 rooms: SACRA, Cathay [Hotel], and Cathay Mansions. During the afternoon duty bring the rest of the things to my room.

Thursday, March 14, 1946—Start bookkeeping course with Kornik. Unfortunately, due to my duty times cannot attend the course regularly.

Saturday, March 16, 1946—Morning: duty. Meet Chinese girl, Julia Fong. She comes often to the lobby to use the telephone. I invite her to go to the cinema tonight. I also get to know Mr. Max Lamm, an American importer-exporter (and a member of B'nai B'rith), and a nice, generous man. He invites Heinz and me for dinner in his room. I get a gift of shaving soap, razor blades, and a completely new American lighter.

Sunday, March 17, 1946—In the evening I have the date with Fritz and the two sisters. The four of us drive to Wing Hwa restaurant. We get a private room and have a good Chinese dinner with Chinese wine and everything that goes with it. My date is attractive and very well dressed in Chinese style. Her name is Weih-Ing and the sister who is with Fritz is called Feh-Ing. After dinner, we decide to go to the Paramount *[a swanky nightclub, the largest in Shanghai, located in the French Concession]*. Neither of the girls speaks English, so the conversation takes place in Chinese. *[By this time, Fred spoke Chinese quite well.]* In the busy traffic of Nanking Rd. at night, the lights of department store illuminations are reflected. A fresh wind is blowing. Weih-Ing and I, Feh-Ing and Fritz get into 2 pedicabs. The cover of our pedicab is turned up. *[Pedicabs had removable waterproof covers at the front for protection against rain, wind, inclement weather.]*

It's a long way from Wing Hwa on Nanking Rd. to the Paramount Ballroom at St. George's. At first, I chat with Weih-Ing about this and that. Then the conversation stops. Suddenly, my arm is around her shoulder and she presses herself very close to me. We ride on a while, cheek pressed to cheek, mouth to mouth. Then all my shyness vanishes and I put my hand under her fur coat. She allows it to happen, and sighs and trembles a bit. Weih-Ing has an exceptionally good figure. When we reach the Para-mount, I am in high spirits. We get a table for four on the balcony and suddenly I can also dance, even if only slow fox trot. Weih-Ing dances charmingly, so charmingly that I close my eyes and bump into a sailor, so charmingly that fired by impulse I bite her ear playfully while we dance, and she whispers to me: "Please not here. People can see us here." We chat, we flirt, we dance: we are happy. I take Weih-Ing home by pedicab, then go on to the Cathay Hotel, where I arrive at midnight.

Tuesday, March 19, 1946—Pick up an enquiry from HICEM from Julius Tuchler of New York, a friend of Friedel Brennecke *[Fred's mother's closest friend in Berlin].* Tuchler is looking for Dad and me and wants to help us in our need. *[HICEM stands for a combination of HIAS, Hebrew Immigrant Aid Society, located in New York, and JCA, Jewish Colonization Association, headquartered in Europe. The American office is called HIAS, while in Europe and other countries, it was known as HICEM. The organization was founded in 1927 to advise European refugees regarding emigration. When World War II broke out, they had offices all over Europe, South and Central America, and the Far East.]*

Wednesday, March 20, 1946—See Gerti and Ted's new apartment at #639, Hamilton House. *[Because of his job as an executive of E. D. Sassoon, Ted was able to rent this studio apartment at a discounted rate. He and Gerti furnished it with custom-made furniture and moved in on June 9 after their wedding.]* This writing (since the 11th of this month) is being done with an American "Eversharp" fountain pen that I got from Sergeant Corbin, together with a bottle of American fountain pen ink, in exchange for U.S. $2.50 plus my old Mont Blanc.

Wednesday, March 27, 1946—Morning: duty. Afternoon: write letter to Tuchler in New York. Evening: With Lamm, Heinz, and Fritz, learn how to play gin rummy.

Sunday, March 31, 1946—Morning: duty. Afternoon: to the cinema *[The Pied Piper at the Cathay and Pagliacci at the Lyceum].*

The Lyceum Theatre on Avenue Joffre is still a landmark. Before the Japanese occupation, it had been the home of the Shanghai Amateur Dramatic Club (ADC). Besides plays performed in English, White Russian companies used the Lyceum to stage operettas and ballets, the Symphony Orchestra gave concerts there, and famous visiting artists attracted full houses. Later, American, British, and German movies were screened at the Lyceum, which was renamed Shanghai Art Theatre.

Saturday, April 13, 1946—Early duty. As a result of differences between the Russian chief cook and the native kitchen personnel, a Chinese riot. They have to be subdued by the American military police carrying revolvers. Afternoon: French. In the evening invited by Günter, who had a birthday the day before yesterday, to the Wing Hwa.

Monday, April 15, 1946—Evening: for first Seder to the Alexanders. *[The Seder is a Passover meal during which the story of the Exodus is told. Special foods are served, prayers said, and lively songs sung.]* A very lovely Seder with excellent food and drinks. A jolly festive mood.

Saturday, April 20, 1946—Go with Lamm to the Victoria Cafe. Long conversation. I now see that I have been taking my duty too strictly. Certainly, I should have overlooked hundreds of small irregularities. I had put a stop to matters that were actually not part of my responsibility. All this in the interests of the company. Now, I must admit that this is not the right way. It is especially important to be generous in small matters that cost one nothing or very little. That can happen without harming one's principles. That's why I now intend to be considerate and obliging to everyone, be it guest or employee.

Sunday, April 21, 1946—Easter. Duty: 7:00–12:00; 16:00–19:00. After lunch, meet Maj. Warren. Go on an excursion to Jessfield Park and St. John's University.

Jessfield Park was no doubt Shanghai's most popular park. Before the war, during summer months, the Municipal Orchestra gave weekend concerts in its enormous shell-shaped pavilion. Children loved its zoo, especially a charming Javanese bear named Sister. The Park was named after Jesse, a little Chinese girl whom a wealthy American adopted after he heard her screams as she was being beaten. When Jesse grew up, he sent her to college in the U.S. She returned to Shanghai after graduation and eventually married her benefactor, whom she had grown to love. When the Japanese occupied Shanghai, they used Jessfield Park for military purposes.

Students from St. John's University (founded by an American Jew who had converted to Christianity), which was adjacent to the park, had to show their student I.D. cards to Japanese guards before walking through the park to their classes. In fact, the Japanese military had a strong presence in the entire area, which included an important railway station—a possible target for U.S. bombing. During the occupation, all the American professors disappeared from St. John's campus: they had either left for the States in good time, or had been incarcerated in Japanese internment camps. After that, the teachers were mostly Chinese. Several "non-enemy nationals" also taught there, among them a very popular young, stateless Russian Jew, who was a history teacher.

Wednesday, April 24, 1946—At night: storm. During the day continuing heavy rains. Early duty. Afternoon: together with George Kirkland of Albany, Georgia *[a field director with the American Red Cross, which looked out for the welfare of American troops in China]*. He is going tomorrow to Tokyo. As a farewell present from him, I get 1 Palm Beach suit and 1 shirt. In return, I give him a Chinese hors d'oeuvres dish. Visit the Metropole. Dinner at the Cathay. Alone to the Capitol, which is once again open to the general public *[Objective Burma]*. Will continue my relationship with Kirkland through correspondence. Perhaps, when he returns to the States he will go back to the hotel business. *[In 2007, George Kirkland, age 97, was still residing in Albany. A cofounder of Walden and Kirkland Realtors, he was honored as the Distinguished Senior Georgian in 2004 by the Georgia General Assembly for his outstanding career as a realtor and for his many other volunteer activities. Regretfully, Mr. Kirkland remembered neither Fred nor the suit.]*

Saturday, April 27, 1946—Early duty. Go to bed early. However, when I am in bed, I become very disturbed. I jump up, get dressed, and drive to the Mansions for no special reason. Meet Lamm, who invites me to DD's.

DD's was a restaurant on Avenue Joffre in the French Concession famous for its beautiful waitresses. The favorite dessert of young customers was "the best fresh mango ice cream in Shanghai." After the war, a slot machine was installed in the coffee shop. Winners received a free dessert. On the second floor of DD's was a lively nightclub that featured an excellent band and floor shows. One of the band members was a well-known Russian Jewish musician from the Shanghai Symphony named Bershadsky.

Tuesday, April 30, 1946—In the afternoon, go on duty to the Mansions. Very much to do, since ex-President Hoover has just arrived with his party on a worldwide inspection of the food situation. *[Fred learns he is to be transferred the next day to the Cathay Hotel.]*

Train my successor (Brandt). In the evening, go with Herbert
Braun to see Act 2 and 3 of the "Fledermaus" performance.

After World War II, famine threatened many countries, and President
Truman formed a Famine Emergency Commission with former President
Herbert Hoover as honorary chairman. In 1946, Truman sent Hoover on
a mission to study the food situation in various countries. Hoover traveled 351,000 miles and visited 22 countries in 57 days. Truman agreed to
Hoover's insistence to include the Far East in his itinerary, and allowed
him to make a stopover in China, a country for which Hoover felt much
affection. An expert mining engineer, Hoover had worked at various times
in China. In fact, he and his wife, Lou, spoke Chinese to each other when
they didn't want others to understand what they were saying.

Now, after years of struggle and deprivation, Fred was leading a different life—shopping at the PX, luxuriating in a bath, wearing new clothes
and shoes. Further happiness was derived from the forthcoming wedding
of Ted and Gerti; Fred was deeply involved in the extensive preparations
for that significant event. He continued to operate the button business on a
reduced scale. And when his schedule allowed, he spent peaceful moments
in the nearby Public Garden, relaxing, reading, and watching sampans and
junks sailing on the Whangpu River. Besides his stalwart companions, Ted
and Gerti, other devoted friends also continued to play an important role
in his life—the Gerendasis, Günther Looser, Fritz Juliusburger, and Heini
Meyer. New acquaintances, such as Mauri and Stephen Wu, and other
colleagues from work, were also mentioned frequently.

Wednesday, May 1, 1946—Day of Pappi's death. *[It is custom-
ary for Jews to observe the anniversary of the death of a family member by
lighting a memorial candle and saying prayers.]* Start duty at the Cathay
Hotel 10:00 a.m.–6:00 p.m.

Sunday, May 5, 1946—To the Jüdische Gemeinde to establish
an advance record of Ted–Gerti's marriage. Duty till 19:00. In the
evening with Burstein and Fritz to the Grand, "Casablanca." Very
good.

Thursday, May 9, 1946—Go to Wong about the samples from
Clark's. Duty. Evening: To Hongkew to try on my new linen suit
at Grynblatt and Balbin's. Ted tells me that his family has decided
to appoint me master of ceremonies. Of course, this gives me all
kinds of headaches, but nevertheless much joy.

Thursday, May 16, 1946 *[22nd birthday]* Morning: Public Garden. Duty. Congratulations from Burstein, Meyer, Uncle Martin,
Klaus, and the entire reception office at the Cathay. Evening Ted,

Gerti, and Günther come over. Beer, ice cream, coffee, coca-cola, and whiskey. Very nice pleasant evening. I get a briefcase from Ted and Gerti.

Saturday, May 18, 1946—Duty from 10:00–12:00. Then off. After lunch Klaus visits me with a fruit basket as post-birthday present. In the afternoon in Braun's bus to Lunghwa. Very beautiful temple *[the Temple of the King of Heaven]*, pagoda, CNAC airfield. Dinner in Cathay Hotel. Evening with Ted and Gerti to "Il Trovatore" at the Lyceum.

It was around this time that Fred began to plan and undertake delightful pleasure trips, at first to the environs of Shanghai, and later on to destinations further afield. He was fortunate to have these opportunities, which he worked at creating. Always adventurous, his desire to learn about and discover new places was insatiable. This passion for travel remained with him, and in his lifetime he visited 103 countries.

On May 18, Fred chose Lunghwa, about eight miles southwest of the Bund, for one of his early excursions. The pagoda he admired there was most likely built as part of an important temple in the ninth century, although some historians set the date of its construction about 600 years earlier. To admire a striking view of the surrounding countryside, tourists climbed to its top seventh story. (All pagodas have an odd number of stories, since such numbers are considered lucky by Buddhists.) East of the pagoda is the temple. Both are still standing. *[See Figure 18 for a photo taken by Fred of the pagoda at Lunghwa.]*

The airfield at Lunghwa was Shanghai's main airfield before and after the war. The once beautiful art deco (or art moderne) air terminal has been recently developed by a Taiwan businessman. Despite an outcry about the ruin of a historic site and the threat of a fine by the city government, the rather tacky conglomeration of bars, a restaurant, and massage parlors remain.

During the war, Lunghwa was also the site of one of the infamous camps in which nearly two thousand Allied civilians (British, U.S., and Dutch families) were held by the Japanese in a former middle school. The Lunghwa camp consisted of seven concrete buildings, three large wooden barracks, and numerous outbuildings. Life there was very difficult for the detainees, who nevertheless organized classes and various religious services. Poor food, lack of privacy, and unforeseeable actions by the Japanese filled the internees with constant dread.

China National Aviation Corporation was founded in 1929 in partnership with Curtiss-Wright. In 1933, Pan American Airways bought a

45 percent interest in the airline and essentially ran and largely funded it. (In 1949, Pan Am sold its remaining interest in CNAC.) During the war in the Pacific, when the Japanese cut off regular supply routes to China, CNAC's fearless pilots were the first to fly over the Himalayas (nicknamed "the Hump" and "the roof of the world"), with supplies for Nationalist troops. A number of pilots lost their lives during these highly dangerous missions that originated in Upper Assam (India).

>   **Sunday, May 19, 1946**—Go with the entire Alexander clan to the Kadoorie School to the Lag B'omer performance: Hours of humor. Partly excellent.

>   **Tuesday, May 21, 1946**—Mauri leaves the company today. He has obtained a job as "second in command" on Capt. Wagner's Liberty ship. I am getting Fritz Juliusburger as second man at the Reception.

>   **Friday, May 24, 1946**—Early duty. At 5:00 o'clock, go with Mr. Hendersen from UNRRA (who is spending the weekend at the Cathay Hotel) to Hungjao. With Burstein to the Capitol [*Bataan*].

UNRRA was the acronym for the United Nations Relief and Rehabilitation Administration, an agency set up by the Allies in 1943 to give aid to areas liberated from Axis power. Fifty-two countries contributed funds to this much needed endeavor. China became one of the chief beneficiaries. However, at the insistence of Chiang Kai-shek, the distribution of the enormous shipments of food, clothing, and medical supplies was turned over entirely to CNRRA (China National Relief and Rehabilitation Administration). This organization was run by T. V. Soong, Madame Chiang's brother, and H. H. Kung, their brother-in-law and Minister of Finance. Unfortunately, it soon became obvious that both men were gaining great personal wealth from their involvement in this operation. Moreover, many complaints were voiced that supplies were inequitably distributed, mainly reaching Nationalist supporters. In some cases, however, rations did reach the refugees in Hongkew, including the aforementioned olive-colored wool blankets and, among other foodstuffs, tins of tuna, butter, cheese, cookies, and cake. UNRRA discontinued its operations in Europe in 1947 and in China in 1949. Its functions were then transferred to other UN agencies.

Before the Japanese occupation, wealthy Shanghailanders built spacious villas in Hungjao, mostly in the style of British country lodges, like Sir Victor Sassoon's. Hungjao, a popular place for picnics, horseback riding, and hiking, was where Fred made his second foray into the Shanghai environs. Today, Hungjao is the site of the Shanghai Hongqiao (new Chinese spelling) International Airport. Located ten miles from the city center, it is the fifth busiest airport in China today.

Sunday, May 26, 1946—Morning: Public Garden. Then to the Hotel. Buy a new smoking suit *[British word for tuxedo]* for US $40.00. Want to sell Pappi's black suit to cover this. 12:00–15:00: duty.

Thursday, June 6, 1946—Evening: at the Alexanders. Great excitement because of differences of opinion in the family about some details of the wedding.

Friday, June 7, 1946—Meeting at the Promenaden Cafe with musicians: Sonnenschein and Krone *[a pianist and a violinist, who were to play during dinner.]* Get my Palm Beach suit from the tailor *[the one he received as a gift from George Kirkland]*. Buy the wedding present.

Sunday, June 9, 1946—Gerti and Ted's wedding day. Morning: Kadoorie School. Check preparations. Lunch at the Cathay. Take a bath. Put on my new smoking at the SACRA. Go to the Abramchiks and Wartenbergers in two taxis. Pick up the Alexanders *[Ted's parents]*, Ted, and Gerti.

The ceremony takes place in the Aula *[Latin word used in Europe for school or university assembly hall]* of the Kadoorie School. Rabbi Dr. Silberstein and Chief Cantor Wartenberger *[officiate]*. On the stage: family and witnesses: R. Salinas *[Renato Salinas, was the chief architect and CEO of the property department at E. D. Sassoon]* and ego *[I]*. After that Chinese wedding ceremony *[arranged]* through Günther Looser. *[Most Jewish couples who were married in Shanghai received both a ketubah, a Jewish wedding contract, and a Chinese certificate, which they jokingly called their Chinese ketubah. The latter were very ornate in design, and many former refugees, including Gerti and Ted, still proudly display theirs in a prominent spot in their home.]* Then photos taken. *[See Figure 19 for the wedding photo of Gerti and Ted.]* After that a festive meal for 35 persons in the (Liebling) school library. As master of ceremonies I translate speeches into English. Toasts: one from Gerda and one from me.

At 8 o'clock change to new Palm Beach suit. Then a big party for 80 people in the Aula. *[A dance band played during this reception.]* Badly organized. My big program, "GRTI," also a flop since it was not very good and the public was impatient. Broke off before the end. Go home feeling very dissatisfied. Drink up my stock of whiskey. Had the afternoon not been so successful, I would have had difficulty calming down. *[Due to his youthful enthusiasm, Fred's part of the program lasted for a seemingly endless length of time. Throughout the years, Ted and Gerti good-naturedly teased him about this fiasco.]*

Monday, June 17, 1946—Curfew lifted. *[There had been a midnight curfew, with violators subject to arrest.]*

19

Working Hard, Playing Hard

Anti-American demonstrations, such as the one mentioned in Fred's diary entry of June 23, were becoming more frequent. The war was finally over and most uniformed Americans were desperate to go home to the States, join their loved ones, and resume civilian lives. As their impatience grew, a number of American GIs became unruly and drank too much, which resulted in unpleasant confrontations—and sometimes violent brawls—with the Chinese. Cruising around town in their speeding jeeps, they caused frequent accidents and were responsible for many traffic casualties.

When he was stationed in Shanghai, Ed Diner *[see p. 136]* recalled an incident in a nightclub when a drunken Navy man slapped a Chinese woman who had rebuffed him. A riot ensued and the police were called. The man was arrested and immediately transferred out of the area. Luckily, a Chinese man pulled Ed from the fracas and led him out the back door.

Some months later, in Nanking, following a bachelor brawl on the eve of his wedding, a Corporal Frank Aldrich murdered two Chinese soldiers. After carousing around town, he and his friends accosted some Chinese youths sitting on the rail of the Chungho Bridge. Aldrich eventually pushed the two backward into the stream below. The Americans laughed, not realizing that the two Chinese could not swim. A court-martial took place in the auditorium of the Officers' Moral Endeavor Association. After four days of testimony, the court postponed its decision.

In addition to their disgust at the questionable behavior of American military, many Chinese were dismayed by America's staunch support of the corrupt Chiang Kai-shek regime. To this was added popular resentment that UNRRA aid was not reaching those who needed it most. The demonstrations to which Fred referred took place at the Race Course in Shanghai. American Embassy and State Department personnel were convinced that this particular protest was manipulated by the Communists. Contemporary scholars, however, assert that this influence, while present, was minimal.

Sunday, June 23, 1946—Off. Morning: Public Garden. Then to the Metropole. Lunch at the Cathay. Rest. Then play cards with Heini at the Metropole. Anti-American demonstrations.

Wednesday, June 26, 1946—Gert *[Fred's first cousin, the older son of Uncle Martin]* is engaged. *[Gert met Ruth Ronis in 1945 when she was 15 and a half and he was 23. They were married two years later, and left shortly thereafter for San Francisco.]*

While Fred and most Shanghai residents assimilated American ways and vocabulary, U.S. GIs, on their part, attempted to communicate with the Chinese population in *pidgin* English. *Pidgin* derives from the way the Chinese pronounced "business," i.e., *pidginess.* Everywhere, the word *chow* replaced "food," and any form of speech, be it a conversation, a lecture, an order, a poem, became *talkie.* "Good, better, best" are *goodie, mo' goodie, mo' mo' goodie.* Americans learned to state numbers in *pieces* like the Chinese. For example, a house boy announcing visitors would proclaim, *"Masta, two piecee Missee wantchee see you"* or *"Me go market buy one piecee big fishee."*

At times, Fred seemed somewhat dazed by his good fortune and the swirling events that affected not only residents of Shanghai, but all the world. His work in Shanghai's most prominent hotels afforded him the rare opportunity to come into direct contact with some of the most well-known players in World War II. These encounters made a great impression on the youthful Fred and filled him with a feeling of importance. He bragged about them to his diary—and most likely to friends and family as well.

Tuesday, July 2, 1946—Early duty. Evening: Hongkew. Published the 1st number of "Reception Office Speaking" *[a monthly newsletter he wrote for his colleagues].*

Thursday, July 4, 1946—Early duty. French. Then home. From the roof watched floodlights presentation on the occasion of the American national holiday.

Saturday, July 6, 1946—Work all day long. At 7:00 o'clock in the evening, Mr. *[James]* Forrestal, United States Secretary of the Navy, arrives. *[After viewing the atom bomb tests at Bikini Atoll, Marshall Islands, Forrestal visited China in an unsuccessful to attempt to help Gen. George Marshall's peace mission. Nevertheless, before leaving, Forrestal and his staff gave a party in Shanghai attended by both the Nationalists and the Communists. Truman later appointed Forrestal the first U.S. Secretary of Defense, but his erratic behavior finally led to his resignation. On March 1, 1949, he was hospitalized for psychiatric care, and on May 22, 1949, he committed suicide.]* Visitors: Shanghai Mayor Wu, Consul-General Davis, Alvin Gillem *[who replaced Gen. Wedemeyer as Commander of the*

China Theater], Admiral Cooke *[Adm. Charles M. Cooke, Jr., Commander of the 7th Fleet and Naval Forces, Western Pacific]*, and many others.

Saturday, July 13, 1946—Free. Have breakfast in the room. Visit the Metropole. When I return, find Julia Wong waiting for me in the lobby. Go with her to the room, although only for 10 minutes, which were properly made use of.

Wednesday, July 17, 1946—Today one year since the bombing *[in Hongkew]* occurred.

Tuesday, July 23, 1946—Planned to go home after duty, but our former guest, Capt. Wagner (Captain of the Merchant Marine on the *Chung Shan*—once a Liberty ship) invites me and Heini for dinner. We pick up Heini at the Metropole where we each drink a bottle. Then the three of us take a taxi to the Senet Restaurant. *[Senet was a high-class, Italian-style restaurant in the French Concession and the top restaurant in Shanghai. It was founded by homesick Italian seamen from the* Conte Verde *after they scuttled their ship to prevent it falling into Japanese hands.]*

Dinner for 3: $49,000. Then go back to the Cathay in a Navy Lieutenant's jeep. From there I call Juliusburger so that he takes the early duty for me. Then I close my books. Around 9:30 board a steam tug with Capt. Wagner and Heini. Take a 40-minute nighttime ride on the Whangpoo. Then board the SS Chung Shan. Inspect the ship thoroughly. Around midnight see a film *[Valley of Decision]* on the flight deck.

Tuesday, July 23, *[cont.]* and Wednesday, July 24, 1946—A nice snack of coffee and sandwiches, cold meat, cheese, doughnuts, etc. Then get alloted a cabin. Take a hot shower. Around 3:45 a.m. to bed. Get up at 7:00. Breakfast: grapefruit juice, 2 eggs, meat, hot cakes with syrup, coffee, bread, butter, jam, etc. Back to Shanghai in the steamer and in my office at 8:30. Almost collapse at lunchtime. Heat, sniffles, alcohol, cigarettes, and little sleep. Lay down without eating. Evening: early to bed.

Monday, July 29, 1946—Duty from 11:00–19:00. Work all evening. Finish the July issue of "Reception Office Speaking."

Saturday, August 10, 1946—With Burstein to the roof garden. One year since peace.

Monday, August 12, 1946—Rabbi Dr. Silberstein died. *[See p. 43.]*

Wednesday, August 14, 1946—Sell 500 bottles of penicillin *[probably acquired on the black market]* to Fürstenberg.

Thursday, August 22, 1946—Early duty. Evening: French. Then meeting on the roof garden of all the people renting space. Present: Charles Jordan, *[American Jewish]* Joint Delegate, Mrs. Van Teyn, UNRRA.

The arrival of Charles Jordan, a top official of the Joint Distribution Committee, caused a stir in Shanghai. Rumormongers whispered that he was a spy. The origin of these rumors is unknown. However, Jordan was found dead in 1967 in the Vltava River near the Charles Bridge in Prague, four days after disappearing from the Esplanade Hotel in the city center. His mysterious death has still not been explained. The Czech secret police file on the suspected murder (code name "River") was destroyed in 1987. The Czechs described this as a "normal 20-year cleaning operation."

Saturday, August 24, 1946—Evening: with a group of friends to a concert *[Municipal Orchestra]* at the Canidrome *[This dog-racing course where huge sums of money were gambled away is today the main flower market of Shanghai.]* After that, go for a beer.

Saturday, September 7, 1946—Free. In the morning Lipsmann calls the entire Executive Staff. He says good-bye to us, since he is flying tomorrow to America. He is to return in around 8 weeks from the States, on November 12. In the evening Heini and Brandt give an open-air concert with records from the USIS *[United States Information Service]* that replace the orchestra. Very enjoyable.

Monday, September 9, 1946—Duty: 9:00–12:00 and 15:00–19:00. Lipsmann leaves for the U.S. Mahler becomes Assistant General Manager. Have a date in the evening. By chance met Carol, a saleswoman at Whiteaway's *[a high class English department store]*. Invited her once but she turned me down. I invited her again on Friday, and we are meeting this evening. She appears exactly on time. Go together to the Victoria *[café/restaurant owned by Russian Jews]* on Avenue Joffre. Then to the Cathay cinema *[The Rake's Progress]*.

Sunday, September 15, 1946—Plan a motorboat ride. Since it is raining in the morning, first change our plans. In the end, we decide to go anyway. Pick up Gerendasis and Carol in Hongkew by car. Board at 11:45. Arrive at Minghong *[about eight miles from Shanghai]* at 4 o'clock. Swim in the river above the village. Then return, arriving at the Bund at 9:15.

Saturday, September 21, 1946—Free. Carol does not come because of heavy rain. Go with Fritz to the Chocolate Shop. Then together to the Roxy [*Random Harvest*].

The Chocolate Shop was a very popular place for breakfast, snacks, dessert, and milkshakes. After the war, Shanghailanders from all classes of society enjoyed its informality and simple, tasty food, and its air conditioning. A sign in front boasted, "Air conditioning is one of our features." Among others, local radicals, including Agnes Smedley, Edgar Snow, and Harold Isaacs were frequent patrons.

Smedley, a leftist journalist, reported on the Chinese revolution and the war against Japan for British, German, and U.S. papers. Snow was known for his interviews of leaders of the revolutionary Red Army and for his many books, including his most famous, *Red Star over China*. Senator Joseph McCarthy later accused both Smedley and Snow of being communists. Isaacs, likewise a journalist and at one time a Trotskyite, subsequently became disenchanted with the communist philosophy.

Emily Hahn, the free-spirited Shanghai celebrity, who worked as a reporter for the British *North China Daily News*, also enjoyed the informality of the Chocolate Shop and was a frequent guest, possibly with her well-dressed gibbon, Mr. Mills, from whom she was seldom separated. (Mr. Mill's beautiful jackets were made in the children's salon of the toy store Peter Pan Shop, owned by Aida Rabinovich, mother of author Rena Krasno.) The gibbon wore nappies (diapers), which according to Hahn in a 1994 letter to Rena Krasno, "outraged certain Shanghai residents." "How angry they would have been if he didn't," she went on to say. Besides being a regular companion of Sir Victor Sassoon, Hahn had close relations with Chinese friends, which was very unusual in colonial-minded Shanghai.

Fred was very attuned to weather conditions, and commented about them regularly in his diaries. The Whangpoo River, a tributary of the Yangtze, would occasionally overflow as a result of prolonged heavy rains. Shanghai's inadequate drainage system worsened the problem, and the streets and lanes became flooded. Often, the rain lasted many days and water inevitably seeped into the bottom floors of apartment houses, shops, and hotels. Rickshawmen floundered in water up to their knees, and the "Wellies" (Wellingtons, or rubber boots) residents wore offered little protection. Garbage and litter of every description floated in the water, and diseases proliferated. During the typhoon season, between July and September, the situation was exacerbated by strong tropical storms. The flooding in late September 1946 was caused by the tail end of a typhoon that had hit Guam.

Thursday, September 26, 1946—Free. First day of Rosh Hashanah. In the morning go to services at the Alexanders in a Sassoon station wagon. Ted preaches. Stay there for lunch. In the afternoon set off in the pouring rain with Ted, Gerti, her parents, and Mrs. Alexander for a New Year visit to the Loewenthals. Coffee and cake. Back to the Alexanders for evening services, then to the Langers for supper.

Friday, September 27, 1946—Second day of Rosh Hashanah. In spite of pouring rain go to services at the Alexanders. Lane flooded. Lunch at the Langers. Home by bus. Most of the streets under water, since the Whangpoo flowed over the shore. Duty: 15:00–19:00. Go again to the Langers for dinner.

Saturday, September 28, 1946—All day duty. In the evening meet guest Carl Dies Andersen. Go for a walk with him. Discuss possible business.

Fred engaged in an intensive week of negotiation (and socializing) with hotel guest Carl Dies Andersen. An executive with Pacific Overseas Airways, Andersen claimed to be the sole representative for a frozen fruit company. *[This airline must have been in the formative stages at that time, as it began operations on May 25, 1947 and then operated a service from Siam—now Thailand—to the United States. American shareholders owned 44 percent of the company.]* Even though legal papers had been drawn up by Fred's roommate, Günther Looser, nothing seems to have come from this prospective deal.

Thursday, October, 3, 1946—Early duty. Evening: with Andersen to the Arcadia. *[The Arcadia was a classy—and quite expensive—dinner/dance place in an old villa in the French Concession. The women usually wore long dresses and most men dressed in tuxedos as they enjoyed the excellent food and the grand dance floor.]*

Friday, October 4, 1946—Early duty. Luncheon in Palace Hotel with Andersen and people from Cathay Export. *[The Palace, across from the Cathay Hotel, was a favorite spot of Fred and his friends for tiffin. Both hotels were famous throughout the Far East as first class hotels are still in operation. Today they are overshadowed by newly constructed, ultramodern hotels.]* Discuss the frozen fruits deal. To Alexanders for supper. Then by taxi to Hongkew for the Kol Nidre prayers at Ted's parents' place. Sleep overnight at SACRA *[in his room in the Designated Area that he had once shared with Günther Looser].*

Saturday, October 5, 1946—Yom Kippur. Pray at Alexanders. Have Break the Fast there in the evening.

Sunday, October 6, 1946—All day duty. Evening play gin rummy at Ted's. Gerda Abramchik gives birth this afternoon to a healthy boy.

Gerda Abramchik, Ted's sister, and her husband Mechuel, observant Jews, wasted no time in starting a family. Their first boy, named Elchonon Shraga Leib, was born in Shanghai. (He was given the name Charles in the U.S., but is called Chuna by his family and Chuckie by close associates, and became the principal of a Jewish school in Florida.) Mechuel was offered a lifetime contract as Rosh Yeshiva (head teacher of the Jewish college) in Shanghai. However, because of the looming threat of a Communist takeover, Gerda's mother urged the couple to leave China while it was still possible to do so. On January 7, 1947, the Abramchiks left Shanghai for New York, where Mechuel obtained a similar position. The family eventually settled in Chicago, and grew to include two other boys, Joseph (a businessman) and David (also a school principal), 14 grandchildren, and dozens of great-grandchildren. Mechuel passed away in 2003 and is buried in Israel.

Saturday, October 12, 1946—All day duty. Evening: go to see Andersen, who has a room for one night at the Metropole Hotel. He will leave Shanghai tomorrow. Then with Lola and Heini to the Roxy *[Rio Rita]*. Andersen of Pacific Overseas claims, by the way, that he is the sole representative for Pelar Frozen Fruits. After long negotiations, I find the local agent (Cathay Export) and, this evening, Andersen signs over to me all the powers of attorney prepared by Looser. Now I must wait for further notice from Andersen. Will I ever hear anything from him again? *[Apparently, he did not.]*

Sunday, October 13, 1946—Afternoon: go together with Ted and Gerti to the Brit Milah *[ritual circumcision]* of Gerda's son. Then to the sukkah at Ward Rd. Synagogue.

Saturday, October 19, 1946—Go to the Alexanders in Hong-kew to bring a present for the baby *[Gerda and Mechuel's son]*. Meet Gerti and Ted there. *[See Figure 20 for photo of the Alexander family.]* Together to the city to Seventh Heaven. *[This was on the roof of one of the big department stores and was considered a prime spot to pick up girls. Taxi dancers, accompanied by their private amahs, "made deals" with customers.]*

Regardless of his seemingly carefree existence, this was a period of great uncertainty for Fred. He partied, drank more than necessary, dressed like a dandy, and attempted to impress women as a *bon vivant*. The handwriting in his diary became unclear and untidy, a reflection of his restlessness, mood changes, insecurity, and drinking. Yet, at the same time, another aspect of his character emerged. He was more and more drawn to nature, to excursions, hikes, and boat rides down the river.

Like many Shanghailanders at the time, Fred seemed to be almost unaware of the Communists' advances in China. Mao Tse-Tung's earlier prediction that cities would fall indirectly after villages had been taken over materialized. Communist forces began infiltrating larger centers of population. Wherever Nationalist troops established a front, Communists fighters moved behind them, harassing them and gaining new recruits. Carrying with them their arms and equipment, more and more Nationalists defected to the Communists.

> **Tuesday, November 5, 1946**—Early duty. Pick up new dark
> blue suit with silver stripes from the tailor. Tomorrow is Ted's
> birthday. In the evening go by taxi with Ted, Gerti, and Günther
> to Sun Ya. Cold mixed meat, omelette, curry beef, sweet and sour
> pork, walnut chicken, and fried chicken livers. Also, Shaohsing *[a
> grainy Chinese wine, made of glutinous rice and served warm]*. Finally to
> the apartment in Hamilton House. Coffee and cakes, drinks and
> sandwiches, stewed fruit. All very plentiful. At midnight, congrat-
> ulate Ted. 1:30: go home.

Sun Ya was considered the best Chinese restaurant at the time, and a favorite of foreigners, including Fred, and also Helene Degroodt (see p. 183), who described the experience of eating in one of its private dining rooms in one of her columns for *The Enquirer and News* in Battle Creek, Michigan:

> Its three floors are always filled and it's a wise idea to reserve
> one's private dining room in advance. Its small curtained area is
> then posted impressively with your name and you are assured
> of excellent service. The guests are seated around a large table,
> centered with a bowl of candied watermelon seed or some other
> delicacy to eat while studying the menu. . . .While waiting for
> the food, an attendant is summoned by a buzzer on the wall. He
> brings a tray of individual hot towels, which are used by the guests
> to wipe face and hands before and after the meal. Napkins are
> never used. Steaming pots of fragrant tea follow. . . . Each (dish)
> is carried in on a hot-water plate and set in the center of the
> table. More and more dishes keep arriving until the table is loaded

down. . . . Peking duck, chicken and bamboo shoots, sweet and sour pork, Cantonese rice, beef and peppers, shrimp balls and chicken with chestnuts or almonds are some of our favorites. All are so rich and filling that often one is too full to enjoy the rice that is served at the end of the meal. All during the repast, hot Chinese wine flows freely from the quaint silver wine pots.

Sunday, November 10, 1946—Free. At 11:00 go with Klaus by ship to Woosung *[Woosung Village, with its old forts, was once a popular tourist destination. It had been almost wiped out in 1932 during the Sino-Japanese conflict.]* Back to Kiaochao. Go for a 2-hour walk there. Return by bus and boat.

Sunday, November 24, 1946—Free. Sleep a long time. Walk with Heini to Hongkew. *[See Figure 21 for a photo of Fred and Heini.]*

Fred enjoyed going for walks, taking in the fascinating sights of Shanghai. The traffic-jammed streets had changed radically since the Allied victory.

During the war, most private vehicles had been requisitioned by the Japanese military, and gasoline was unavailable to most civilians. A very limited number of civilian trucks and cars ran on substitute fuel, heavily polluting the air. Now, jeeps, weapons carriers, U.S. army trucks, as well as up-to-date cars and sleek black limousines congested the streets. Bicycles, rickshaws, pedicabs, and wheelbarrows snarled the heavy traffic as they attempted to wend their way. Adding to the general confusion, hawkers selling black-market goods from PXs, shouted their list of wares and blocked sidewalks, forcing pedestrians into the already overcrowded streets.

Sunday, December 1, 1946—All day duty. Yesterday and today RIOTS by Chinese vendors in Hongkew. Shooting in the streets and broken windowpanes. In the evening go with guests Cooper and *[Ralph A.]* Watkins *[of]* Senator McFarland's party to Zum Weissen Roessl and Kavkaz.

Senator Ernest W. McFarland was a Democratic Senator from Arizona who became majority leader of the U.S. Senate after being reelected to a second term in 1946. In November and December, McFarland led an international communications inspection tour to the Pacific Theater, meeting with Chiang Kai-shek, Special Ambassador General George Marshall, and General Douglas MacArthur, among others. McFarland was the only senator on this tour, which included visits to Korea, the Philippines, and Australia. Ralph Watkins, McFarland's good friend and campaign manager, accompanied the senator. An auto dealer, Watkins was an active Democrat who was a delegate from Arizona to the 1948 Democratic National Convention. Hoping that Watkins might help him come to the U.S., Fred wrote to him a few days after the evening they spent together. In his entry of September 28, 1947, Fred mentioned a letter from Watkins, so it seems likely that several letters were exchanged between the two in the intervening months.

The Kavkaz was an outstanding Armenian restaurant. It was very popular with the Flying Tigers and members of the U.S. Air Force, and top-ranking businessmen also were loyal patrons. A favorite dish was called Sedlo (literally, saddle), Armenian rack of lamb. Eventually, after the Communist takeover, Yervand Makarian, the Russian-Armenian owner of the Kavkaz, emigrated to Brazil in 1951, and finally to Los Angeles where he opened a restaurant of the same name on Sunset Boulevard. Many old China hands, who had also resettled in the U.S., became regular customers. Some did not recognize each other after many years of separation. One oldtimer referring to the owner asked: "Who is that guy?" The reply: "Don't you remember? We used to play marbles together at school in Shanghai!"

Wednesday, December 4, 1946—Early duty. When I return to the office in the afternoon after a visit to Ted, find a letter for me from Mahler. From Monday 9th, I am transferred back to the Cathay Mansions, where I will take Burstein's place *[as chief receptionist]*—as well as his room. Bolt of lightning from a clear sky! Till late in the night write a letter to Watkins, who might possibly help me with emigration to the United States.

Sunday, December 8, 1946—My things are loaded and taken to the Mansions. I go back to my old room 126. I quickly unpack and barely have time to take a bath and get dressed. Today we are having a staff farewell party for Mahler.

Tuesday, December 10, 1946—Early duty. 7:00–15:00. In the afternoon move to a different room, which is colder, but bigger and lighter. It is the nicest room I have lived in up to now. Besides, I have taken the best furniture from my old room.

Thursday, December 12, 1946—We get a pair of petroleum stoves for the public rooms such as the Reception, the dining room, etc., since our electric generator cannot be completed and installed before the New Year. Thanks to the kindness of our house engineer Kretzky, I manage to borrow one of these stoves so that I can finally stay at home and put my things in order.

Monday, December 16, 1946—Duty: 12:00–20:00. Get a half-month salary and Christmas bonus (one month's salary). In the evening, talk till late in the night about Germany and the Jews with Frosty *[Fürstenberg]* and Milly Hartig *[colleagues at the hotels with whom Fred became good friends]*.

Wednesday, December 18, 1946—Meet Capt. Wagner early in the morning at the Cathay. Go with him in a Cheesebox *[apparently some sort of military vehicle]* to Chenju, where there is a big CNRRA *[see p. 156]* camp, of which the captain is now in charge. He takes me through the offices, and then lets me visit the grounds by myself. The mud is incredible. Although I borrowed rubber boots from Heini for this purpose, my trousers and coat become filthy. On the grounds are machines worth billions. I am trying to get a half-day job with the help of Capt. Wagner. At 12:00, we drive back to the Cathay, where I have lunch. Then on duty till 20:00 at the Mansions. Evening: listen to the radio, fiddle around, take a bath and read.

Saturday, December 21, 1946—To a football game at the Race Course. Glen Line *[shipping line]* against the Army. 18-6. Our billeting officer, Frank DeGroodt, is on the Army team. *[Thanks to this connection, Fred watched the game from officers' boxes.]* Then to Whashing Rd. to the Marcuses. The whole family is gathered there. Vodka. Much joy. Then home in Günter Matzdorff's "taxi." *[The taxi was a 9-passenger Fiat that Günther (now Gary) Matzdorff rented after the war for US $10 a day from a Chinese friend. He took two loads of refugees to work from Hongkew to downtown, then freelanced in front of the Cathay Hotel until it was time to take them back. In the evening, his fares were often sailors who wanted to have a good time in the bars and meet young women. Matzdorff also worked in leather factories, and later, in the U.S., became a manufacturer of leather goods.]*

Franklin T. DeGroodt, a captain in the U.S. army, was sent with a small field team to China in August of 1946 as part of the American Graves Registration Service (AGRS). Their assignment was to gather information in the interior of China about downed pilots and to collect remains and process them for return to the states for proper burial. This was an extremely difficult task because the interior was ruled by various warlords and bandits who had, in many cases, already stripped the bodies and planes. They also often attacked the field teams, stealing whatever they could lay their hands on.

Frank was also the billeting officer for the Hotel Metropole, where Fred was working at the time, and also for Shanghai Mansions and Broadway Mansions. At six feet tall, 160 pounds, he was a star on the Army E.M. Club team, which won the China Bowl on New Year's Day in 1948. He introduced Fred to American football at the Race Course, and once he understood the rules, Fred became a lifelong, ardent fan of the game.

Frank's wife Helene and their young son joined him in November of that year. Among the first Americans to arrive in Shanghai, they were warmly welcomed by the foreign and U.S. embassies and their staffs and led a fascinating, glamorous, and very social life. While in Shanghai, Helene was a correspondent for a chain of Michigan newspapers. Some of the delightful and informative columns she wrote during her stay in Shanghai are quoted herein. She later worked for the *Orlando Sentinel. [See figure 22 for a photo of Frank and Helene at a cocktail party at Broadway Mansions.)*

The AGRS was pulled out of China beause of the Communist threat, and Frank was sent to Saipan. He and Helene lived in a variety of places, eventually settling in Florida, where Frank worked in the space industry. After a stint as chief of police of Palm Bay, he served three terms as mayor of the city. After his death, a public library was named in his memory.

The Race Course and Recreation Grounds offered a variety of sports facilities to Shanghailanders, including swimming, cricket, golf (regular and mini), baseball and soccer (as well as, after the war, American football fields). However, the most exciting events that took place there were the horse (actually Mongolian pony) races. Racing days were traditional holidays in Shanghai. Banks and offices were closed as both foreigners and Chinese rushed to gamble. Each pony was famous, its attributes well-known and analyzed. Shanghai's entire Who's Who never failed to attend racing events, the highlight of the year. Women wore fancy hats, as at the Ascot in England. People looked discreetly at others, gossiped, and won or lost huge sums of money.

Tuesday, December 24, 1946—Buy Christmas gifts. Order a tombstone for Pappi from Ernst Berlin *[a German refugee tombstone manufacturer who later immigrated to San Francisco where he worked for the Jewish Cemetery in Colma]*. 8th day of Chanukah.

Wednesday, December 25, 1946—Lunchtime: Christmas party for staff. Hors d'oeuvres, cream of tomato soup, stuffed chicken with French fries, and mixed vegetables. Plum pudding. A huge Christmas cake, and beer ad lib *[flowing freely]*.

Tuesday, December 31, 1946—Morning: Go to Sun Sun *[a big department store on Nanking Road]* to buy a black bow tie. Then to the barber at the Cathay Hotel. Duty till 18:30. Then change to smoking, black bow tie, and soft shirt. By taxi to the Marcuses. Dinner: "Eisbein" *[ham shank]* with sauerkraut and beer. Then to the first floor which is decorated *[for New Year's Eve]* in a charming way. Coca Cola and gin, Gin and Coke, plain gin, and then start again from the beginning. At 12:00 pancakes and toasts.

20

Loneliness and Introspection

The first months of 1947 marked the start of the emigration of the Shanghai Jewish refugees to other countries, particularly the USA, Canada, Australia, and Israel. (About 20 percent of the refugees went to Israel.) Additionally, the troup transport ship *Marine Lynx* carried over 600 German and Austrian refugees to Naples, Italy, in July 1947, 295 of whom returned to Berlin. The tiny minority who accepted repatriation to Germany and Austria under a right established by the United Nations and UNRRA were resented by some of the other refugees for returning to countries that had treated the Jews in such an inhuman fashion. A number of these repatriates were communist sympathizers who wished to reside in territory under Soviet control. Some, however, had to decide where to live while waiting for their quota number to come up because of U.S. immigration laws. In 1921, the U.S. Congress had passed emergency legislation imposing a quota system based on the 1910 census. The National Origins Act was implemented in 1924, further limiting the number of immigrants admitted, and using the 1890 census as the base. This law favored immigrants from Northwestern Europe and discriminated against Asians and Eastern Europeans.

As Fred's friends and family members began to depart from Shanghai, he was left with an aching loneliness that was reminiscent of his last year in Berlin when so many classmates at his Jewish school emigrated or were taken away. To overcome this sadness, he threw himself ever more obsessively into work and social life. Nonetheless, it is clear that these partings affected him deeply. What steps should he now take? Would he be trapped forever in China? He agonized for hours on end over his future with Ted and those friends who remained.

Wednesday, January 1, 1947—In the lobby, meet Capt. DeGroodt. Drive with him and some other officers to the Canidrome where a big football game is taking place today between the 11th Airborne vs. the 7th Fleet All Stars.

All Americans are "warned off" Ave. Joffre, since there are
again anti-American demonstrations of Chinese students because
of a rape in Peking.

The demonstration to which Fred referred on this date was a response
to the alleged rape of a Peking (Beijing) University student, Shen Chong, by
two U.S. marines, William Pierson and Warren Pritchard. The crime, which
resulted in protests by thousands of students in major cities all over China,
was viewed as more than simply an offense against an individual; rather,
it was considered to be a crime against the entire Chinese nation. Feeding
into this was the already existing sentiment against the presence of U.S.
military personnel and a growing view of American policy as imperialistic.
Pierson was sentenced to life imprisonment, and Pritchard, who was ruled
innocent of the rape, received ten months. Citing inconclusive evidence,
Secretary of the Navy James Forrestal later reversed both sentences.

Thursday, January 2, 1947—Get up rather late. Then to
Hongkew to Uncle Martin. Again, buy a suit (for $30, payable in
16 cartons of cigarettes) which cost me only $9.60.

Friday, January 3, 1947—To the tailor, to have him alter my
newly bought suit. Go to the Jüdische Gemeinde to register for
Australia. Just in case. Duty till 19:00. For supper to Alexanders.

Sunday, January 5, 1947—Go with Uncle Martin to Mc-
Gregor Rd. Synagogue. *[Cousin]* Gert is getting married today to
Ruth Schapiro. I hold one of the *chupah* posts. *[The chupah is a wedding canopy held up by four posts that symbolizes the Jewish home. The honor
of holding one of the posts is given to family members or close friends.]* Dr.
Kantorowski officiates. Then go with the wedded couple to the
photographer. Then to the reception at 818 Tongshan Rd. Eat a
lot, drink a lot. Many speeches, and I also make a short one. Then
together to Gert's flat, where he changes his clothes. Then Gert
and Ruth and Hedy (Ruth's sister who is around 14) go to the
girls' mother's flat (Mrs. Ronis). There is a fantastic dinner. Soup,
roast goose with red cabbage, and stewed apples with whipped
cream. Then I take a taxi together with the bride and groom and
we go to the Mansions where I have reserved a room for them.
They come to me for a drink, then I give them a couple of extra
blankets, which I bring to the bed in their room. Since yesterday,
we have no heating, because Standard Oil did not deliver any heating oil.

Monday, January 6, 1947—Duty: 7:00–12:00; 16:00–19:00.
Ruth and Gert's room is complimentary from Negri. In the eve-
ning, in spite of horrible rainy weather, go to Hongkew to the old
Alexanders. Farewell party for Gerda *[Abramchik]*, who is leav-
ing the day after tomorrow with Mechuel and their baby for the
States.

Tuesday, January 7, 1947—Morning: French. Duty till 20:00.
Evening: at home. Hot water again available. Read, took a bath,
listened to the radio. Go through an old diary and do some
thinking.

Wednesday, January 8, 1947—Secretary of State Byrnes
resigned. General Marshall, who is leaving China today, is taking
over his post.

General George C. Marshall's mission to China was doomed from the
start. Despite a dizzying schedule of meetings with Generalissimo Chiang
Kai-shek and Chou Enlai and other representatives of the Nationalists and
the Communists, as well as journalists, ambassadors, and other embassy
staff, military personnel, and visiting Congressmen, Marshall was unable
to effect a rapprochement between the warring factions. His initial success
in brokering a truce on January 10, 1946 was undermined by both sides,
and the civil war between them resumed shortly thereafter, and Marshall
returned to the U.S.

Shortly after his return, Marshall was sworn in as Secretary of State.
It was in this capacity that he masterminded the Marshall Plan, a unique
and very successful aid program that fostered the recovery of free Europe.
Until it ended in 1952, the Plan provided more than $13 billion dollars for
economic, agricultural, and technical assistance. In 1953, in recognition of
his world leadership, Marshall was awarded the Nobel Peace Prize.

Thursday, January 16, 1947—Duty till 20:00. Evening play
cassino with Frank DeGroodt. Today, around 900 Austrians were
repatriated on the Marine Falcon by the UNRRA.

Thursday, January 23, 1947—Register for America at the
German Refugee Association. Visit Uncle Martin and firm up text
for inscription on Pappi's gravestone and deliver it to Ernst Berlin.

Friday, January 24, 1947—To the American Consulate to
register for immigration. Am supposed to do it in writing.

Even as he enjoyed the frenzied pace of his life, Fred often experienced an aching sense of loneliness. The following amusing and poignant
poem, written in English, was found on a separate sheet of yellowing

paper in the diary. It indicates plainly his sexual longings and his strong attraction to an unnamed woman, either real or imaginary.

Contemplations on a Wintry Afternoon
Dedicated to an Old Maid

I wish I were your nice black belt
And rest around your hips all day.
I'd like to feel what he has felt
When you go wild and dance and sway.
I wish I were your nice warm coat
And snuggled close around your throat.
And always when you're feeling cold,
I'd keep you warm in my strong hold.
Oh, could I be there on your back
The zip that goes up to your neck
And holds your dress up firm and tight
All day and sometimes too all night.
Stop running wild imagination!
Methinks, you do forget your station.
Calm down, my mind, and stop to rove,
You better rest near a warm stove.

Saturday, January 25, 1947—Straighten up a little and throw out old junk. Have to slowly prepare to liquidate the SACRA apartment because Looser is probably leaving on February 10th. Grand Cinema. A little snow.

Sunday, January 26, 1947—Duty 7–12, 16:00–17:30. Evening to the Roxie with Ted and Gertie for "Ziegfield Follies." Later the conversation turns to plans for the future and finances. Great economy is decided on. Decide to save at least US $30.00 per month.

Thursday, January 30, 1947—The Americans are now publicizing that their Peace Team is pulling back. They will fully adopt a "wait and see policy." What effect will this have on me? Will the army leave the hotel? Will mainly Chinese live in the hotel then?

Wednesday, February 5, 1947—In the evening, farewell party for Günter at Alexanders. Gerti prepares a very nice cold buffet.

Thursday, February 6, 1947—Morning: Hongkew. Start the liquidation of my room there. Go to the KF at Alcock Rd. to offer furniture [for sale].

Friday, February 7, 1947—Write a poem: "Lonely Evening" [this poem has not been found].

Monday, February 10, 1947—Morning: take the hotel truck to Hongkew, pick up my belongings. Completely liquidate the Hongkew flat and send everything to the Mansions. Then go with Günther to his ship, the Marine Adder. It is anchored on the D.K.K. wharf. Then back to the Cathay. Eat lunch. Then back to the wharf with Ted and Gerti *[and others]*. Almost everyone else leaves since it is beginning to pour. I stay there. Finally, at 3:00, the ship sails away. I start back home with mixed feelings and, at 4:30, come to the office wet through and through. Duty till 19:00. Return home at 11:00 with a bad cold. Take aspirin. Hot bath. U.S. $ reached $13,600 *[the exchange rate for one U.S. dollar]*.

Quite often, Fred referred to the daily decline in the value of Shanghai currency against U.S. dollars. The Nationalist government had issued this money after the war and, although it was plunging in value, they continued to print it with abandon. As prices for essentials soared, people now had to carry huge quantities of bills in sacks. When Ted and Gerti purchased their ship tickets, they exchanged about $700 that morning in U.S. currency for Shanghai money (it was illegal to pay in dollars). As a result, they had to hire a pedicab to transport the huge number of bundles of Shanghai dollars to the shipping company. By the time they arrived to pay for the tickets, the value of the money had further decreased to such an extent in a couple of hours that they had to exchange another $30 in U.S. dollars to cover the difference.

Tuesday, February 11, 1947—Argument with cashier regarding profit on exchange rate. US $ at 16,000. With money from sale of furniture order a pair of shoes. Down payment of half the sum. They are to be ready in 6 days, and by then the balance of the payment will have depreciated a lot.

Wednesday, February 12, 1947—Duty: 12:00–19:00. Frank calls me. He must move to the Race Course in spite of the fact that his wife and baby son are arriving this weekend. Go with him to the Mansions where I help him pack his things till late at night—strengthened with coke and whiskey.

Wednesday, February 19, 1947—Frank's wife *[Helene]* and son Jeff arriving on the Admiral Benson today. Before lunch go with Hallberg, Al Lee to the Race Cource to decorate Frank's flat. I had a cake baked for him. Duty from 12:00–20:00. Evening: at home. Wen Weih arrives around 9:45 and stays till 11:30.

Prostitution ran rife in Shanghai, due to widespread poverty among the Chinese population and families' preference for sons. "Business cards" of the kind found in Figures 23 and 24 were distributed by brothel owners to potential clients.

Sunday, February 23, 1947—Pappi's birthday. Duty 7:00–11:00 and 15:00–18:00. Morning: with Uncle Martin to the cemetery. Martin stays for lunch and dinner at my place. Then go by taxi to the Marcuses in Hongkew for little cousin Gaby's birthday. Very pleasant.

In March 1947, Fred engaged for the first time in self-analysis in his diary: Was he applying the ethical principles taught him by his father? Could he fit in again into normal society with its set rules of behavior? He also pondered his deep friendship with Ted, expressing the hope that it would always remain a strong bond. *[See Figure 25 for photo of Ted, and Figures 26 and 27 for his identification card from the International Committee for Granting Relief to European Refugees.]*

As the future of Nationalist China became more and more dismal, pressure increased on European refugees to seek a new haven. The obstacles were many. As yet, Israel had not won independence, so Jews had no special sanctuary, and most other countries imposed severe entry restrictions that were hard to overcome. Refugees enclosed prepared cards in letters to their nearest relatives begging them to help those stranded in Shanghai. A special sticker affixed to the envelope called attention to their desperation. *[See Figures 28 and 29 for photos of a card and a sticker.]* They were aided in this endeavor by HIAS, which forwarded the letters for them. Thus, in Shanghai, the fight to obtain a visa became the focus of most refugees' lives.

Monday, March 3, 1947—Hand in Quota Registration at the American Consulate. Duty from 12:20. Then alone to the Cathay Cinema.

Wednesday, March 5, 1947—Morning: Hongkew. China Merchants Lower Wharf. Hoffmans leaving on the General Gordon. Unfortunately, could not speak to them again. Duty: from 12:20. Evening sat at home and read.

Saturday, March 8, 1947—Home alone, write the following: Where am I today? An independent young bachelor of 23. Dark blond, well built (as long as I don't show the weak upper part of my body when wearing a bathing suit). When I am conscious of it, I walk straight. Otherwise my shoulders slope slightly. The prominent nose I inherited from my mother is not too beautiful, but distinctive and, alas, almost German, combined with my blue eyes. My father's eyes. My ears are also from him, as is my rather high forehead. My strong mouth with the rather heavy lips is too big when I laugh. The hair is combed back and nicely waved when I use enough oil.

On the whole, I don't look 23 years old, rather 19 or 20, maybe 21 but, in any case, I certainly don't look older. This is how, I think, a well meaning observer, would see me today: FWM is a clerk in a 350-room hotel, which was very luxurious before the war. He doesn't do his job the way he used to. At the beginning he had no experience, but then he learned his job. He learned that he must look away from many of the irregularities carried out by the native workers if he wished to keep his position. He learned that he must measure honesty and decency by standards other than those his father had taught him. He is not dishonest, definitely not. He is trying not to lose his decent ways, but also tries not to lose his livelihood, while surrounded by corruption and bribery. (A paradox! I believe the whole life in Shanghai is a paradox. How will I be able to fit again into an orderly society? How to earn lots of money but use it as a means and not an end in itself? Money should not be an obsession.)

He is a hotel employee and is fulfilling his duties. The guests are fond of him and he gets along with almost everyone. He is often very nervous and loses his temper, but as soon as he realizes it, he tries to control himself. He has his relatives (who all like him) and friends. On Mondays he meets Milly Hartig and Frosty, colleagues and friends, with whom he can discuss business matters regarding the hotel.

On Saturdays, he goes to Hongkew to the Marcuses—who are dear relatives—and their family circle. There, he is the "smart" young city guy. He flirts with the ladies, tells jokes, drinks a lot, and enjoys it all. "Fredel, do tell us something. You live in quite another world!" Gaby, his little cousin, is very much in love with him and he with her! During the week, when Klaus comes over, the conversations mainly center on girls. He respects Klaus's father, Uncle Martin, as the brother of his father even though he is not a help, or a support. Uncle Martin always seeks advice from me. Frank DeGroodt: openhearted and friendly. Ready to help but somewhat flaky. Heinz Meyer is leaving soon. Burstein is a good soul, but turned inward to himself. So, that leaves Ted and Gerti.

I love Gerti and value her as Ted's wife. Still, there is some kind of barrier between her and me. But, Ted has always been there in my hardest hours and also there in my happiest experiences. Where would I have been without Ted? What would I have been without Ted? Unfortunately, today that good fellow is also over- burdened with private worries. But, when we are together, then we feel a spiritual bond, that we are not alone, and that together we will be able to overcome all obstacles. We have no secrets from each other. We keep silent on nothing. We find strength and trust. We discuss the future, our worries and problems. May good for- tune always keep us together, and may fate always lead our paths together. In short, we can say about ourselves: we are friends.

But then, when I come home, I am alone within my four walls. God, I am used to being alone. But then, one sits in one's arm- chair and thinks. One looks around and sees a lovely, pretty, and well heated room. Clean. When I ring, the boy comes in, asking what I wish. The pinnacle of comfort. I had to suffer to reach this. And then, cold and cruel fear suddenly hits me—before a film in a dark cinema, in the middle of work. What is going to happen if, God forbid, this job . . . No, I cannot express this thought. Work, reach out, hope, and pray. Be a decent, honest man. Bring honor to the memory of my parents. Do good and help other people. Don't show youthful pride and conceit when someone approaches me. Have only one thought: how can I help him? In all cases, big and small. Only then can I quiet my edgy nerves and wild thoughts. Only one thing remains: loneliness. Friends, acquaintances, even Ted, can do nothing for this. There is the need for a female person with whom I can talk, at whom I can look, whom I can stroke, with whom I can share my feelings! No stormy longing for carnal ecstasy. Eroticism? Yes, but no planned raging orgasms, only deep intimate love. Wen Weih satisfies such uncontrolled feelings and gives the body its balance, but love and tenderness are withheld from my life when I am in my room and dream of this . . . alone.

Yes, the so self-assured, friendly, and cheerful Fred appears quite different on the inside. Yes, when it comes to it, I am actu- ally shy and, therefore, turn gladly to drink. I know that alcohol helps me overcome my limitations and inhibitions. When I am sober, I attempt to force myself to conquer my inhibitions.

Admit that I am the victim of too proper an upbringing. Yes, I was taught to be quiet and modest. Yes, I must do my duty in all matters. I blush easily! So what! I should not be ashamed that I am sensitive. Don't forget who I am and what I can accomplish. Rid myself of neurotic inhibitions and fears. If I remain decent and honest, I will make my way in life. I try to better myself. I am studying French. I already correspond with hotel magazines and the American Hotel Association. Some day I will succeed in going to the U.S.A., and if I continue to learn and persevere, and live and behave according to the values of my parents, then with the help of God who helped me during all these years of horror and misery, then I will find my way as a successful and happy man in a free, happy world. Amen.

In the evening: read at home. Then alone to the Lyceum.

Sunday, March 9, 1947—Duty: 7:00–12:00; 16:00–17:00. Go with Ted to the Nanking Theatre. On the way from the Nanking to the HH *[Hamilton House]* have a long, personal discussion. (Theme: the notes I wrote yesterday.) Then have supper and talk till midnight.

Friday, March 14, 1947—Visit Ted. Am promised a Sassoon station wagon by Mr. See *[Leo See, a friend and an executive at Sassoon's]* for Sunday. Duty: 12:00–19:00. Have a drink with Lt. Agnew. Then with him and his friends to the German School. *[Shanghai's German school was called Kaiser Wilhelm Schule. After the war it became a chic officers club where the opening theme song was "On the Sunny Side of the Street," and the closing song "Goodnight Irene." The orchestra, among the best in Shanghai, played for uniformed officers ranging from lieutenants to generals, who danced with elegantly dressed women—both foreign and Chinese.]*

Saturday, March 15, 1947—Duty: 12:00–19:00. When I start duty, Negri tells me that Stahly wants to speak to me at 5:00 o'clock. Stahly comes and asks me if I want to go back to the Cathay Hotel. (Meyer is leaving next Thursday for the U.S.A.) I reply: if you wish to have me. He says yes, but on condition that I treat Juliusburger better than before. I agree to that. Nonetheless, in spite of the good side earnings, a better room and better food, I am convinced that the Cathay Mansions *[where he was then working]* is better for me, both in terms of my career and my personal comfort.

Sunday, March 16, 1947—Klaus picks me up early in the morning *[for the dedication of Pappi's tombstone]*. The Sassoon station wagon is waiting for us at the entrance. We drive to Hongkew and pick up the following: Ted, Knoche, Loewenthal, Uncle Martin,

Sammy, Abraham Beck, and Weissmann *[Meyer David Weissman was either a relative of the Marcus cousins or an employee of their business, Elite Fashion]*, as well as Alexander Sr. On Ward Rd. we are questioned by several overzealous Special Policemen, then we go on without being bothered any more, and finally arrive at 11:00 at the Columbia Road Cemetery. *[See Figure 30 for a photo of Semmy's gravestone.]* Ted officiates and makes a wonderful speech.

In his talk Ted spoke of his own closeness to Fred's father and to Fred, whom he considered as more than a friend, but rather as a brother. Following are some other thoughts he expressed that morning:

> During one of my last conversations with the deceased, he told me among other things that he knew only one aim in life for his child: Judaism and all-encompassing love of humanity. Both indivisible ideas, both completely interwoven. One without the other is unimaginable because Judaism equals humanity, and humanity is on a par with Judaism. If you, dear Fred, continue to take to heart this teaching, the ideas that were at the core of your dear deceased father, you are building him a monument longer lasting than granite and steel.

Fred concludes this diary entry: "At the end of this beautiful service, I recite Kaddish."

Monday, March 17, 1947—Pack in the morning. Then go to duty at the Cathay. Nearly everything is the same as before. Even many old guests are still there. Except that Stahly now sits on the 2nd floor and comes down only 3 times a day. Back to the Mansions. Pack the rest of the stuff. My suitcases are still full of old things from Hongkew (and even from Germany) and I stuff everything I really need into wash *[laundry]* baskets.

Tuesday, March 18, 1947—Duty from 12:00–19:00. In the evening arrange a farewell party for Heini. Negri puts a private dining room at the Cathay Mansions at my disposal. Coffee and cakes from Cafe Louis. Fruit and sweets. Make a short farewell speech.

Thursday, March 20, 1947—In the morning go to the Hongkew and Shanghai Wharf. Gert and wife *[Ruth]* and Klaus are sailing on the Marine Lynx. *[Also]* Werner, Heini, and the Brandts. After the young people board, go to the Ronis's apartment where we eat a good snack. Then we go back to the wharf. It's raining. Finally, around 14:00, the ship leaves, and once again I feel terribly sad.

21

In Limbo

Constant farewell parties were the order of the day as more and more individuals and families left Shanghai behind and set off for another new beginning. During May and June, Fred spent considerably more time with Uncle Martin and the rest of his family, who were also preparing to depart. Fred was torn between a desire to remain in his good job and comfortable circumstances and the realization that action was imperative. Yet, he continued to take on new responsibilities, and aside from sporadic attempts to obtain an affidavit, he seemed to fall into a state of inertia about the urgency for action.

Many of those who left, including Fred's family members, traveled to San Francisco on former troop ships. Two that Fred mentioned specifically were the USS *General M.C. Meigs* and the USS *General Gordon*. Both ships were launched in March 1944. During the war, the *Meigs* ferried troops to Italy from the U.S. and Brazil, and could carry 5,000 troops at a time. The *Gordon* made some 12 voyages to European and African ports, later brought replacement troops for the Pacific campaign, and then carried occupation forces. Its troop capacity was 5,650. After the war, both ships were transferred to the American President Lines as passenger ships, but were again reactivated for active military duty when the Korean War broke out.

> **Sunday, April 6, 1947**—Meet Charlie and Kay early in the morning. Go by steamer to Kiaochao. Then to a garden cafe. Order coffee and eat our rolls. Then sunbathe in deck chairs. Charlie takes our photographs. *[See Figure 31 for a photo of Fred and Kay at Kiaochao.]*

Kiaochao was a popular spot on the bank of the Yangtze River. Buses waited on its jetty for visitors coming by boat from Shanghai and drove them to the nearby Kiaochao village, where there was a foreign style hotel. From there, an hour's hike led to a sandy beach on the banks of the river. Fred and his friends made frequent trips to this agreeable destination.

Saturday, April 12, 1947—Free. 8th day of Pesach. Pick up Ted and Gerti with See from Sassoon. Go in the Plymouth to the Eastern for the Maskir *[Yizkor]* service. Lunch at Alexanders. In the evening, Chinese dinner party at the Sun Ya, given by a Chinese guest for the reception staff. After that to Hongkew to the Marcuses.

Sunday, April 13, 1947—Duty: 7:30–18:30. Two American CID *[Criminal Investigation Division of the army]* agents call me to the office to receive 2 quilts that had been stolen from the hotel.

Monday, April 14, 1947—French. Duty: 12:00–18:00. Burstein picks me up. We get a lift in the Cathay laundry truck to the Race Course for supper at the DeGroodts. Frank cooks excellent macaroni. We eat huge portions. Of course, before and after that we get a lot to drink. With full stomachs and slightly tipsy, we walk home after a charming evening.

Helene and Frank DeGroodt were warmhearted friends with whom Fred felt completely at ease. *[See Figure 22 for a photo of the DeGroodts.]* He looked forward to his visits to their apartment, often with his friend Harry Burstein, where they were able to relax and enjoy stimulating conversation, good food and drink, and a loving family atmosphere. In a letter to author Audrey Friedman Marcus dated November 26, 2004, Helene DeGroodt wrote about their friendship with Fred, and also commented on the existing political situation that made it necessary for her and Frank to leave Shanghai in January 1948:

> They *[Fred and his friend Harry Burstein]* were such nice kids, very polite in the old European manner, clicking their heels, bowing from the waist, kissing ladies' hands. . . . Fred never talked about his own life, just wanted to know all about the States. We hated to leave him there in Shanghai when we were ordered out because of the approaching revolution. Mao had taken the northern cities and was moving down toward Shanghai. One had the feeling Shanghai had already been taken politically, *[but]* underground. The wealthy Chinese and all the foreigners were beginning to transfer their assets out of China and make plans to leave. Those who had survived the Japanese occupation didn't want to be caught again.

Although Fred was having problems in arranging his own papers, he did not miss an opportunity to help family members and friends who had similar problems.

Thursday, April 17, 1947—Early duty. Then go with Uncle

Martin to the police regarding his Letter of Conduct. *[This document was required when applying for a U.S. visa to prove that one had no
criminal record.]*

Friday, April 25, 1947—Dr. Gerendasi pulls out a molar. *[Dr.
Gerendasi's extensive and expert dental work lasted until Fred's death.]*
Evening: at the Alexanders.

Friday, May 2, 1947—Early duty. At noon with Uncle Martin
to the American Consulate.

Monday, May 12, 1947—Early duty. Go with Meyer Weissmann to the "English Circle" *[also called "Success Circle"]* of Mr.
Hamburger at the Promenaden Cafe. Am asked to speak and do
so for 15 minutes, extemporaneously, with clear success. Since
Hamburger is leaving next month, I am thinking about taking
over the Circle.

The English Circle met once a week for 30 to 40 minutes in a café,
which closed to other business at 8 p.m. that evening. The students were
able to buy coffee. Fred was well qualified for the task of leading the
English Circle. He had learned English in Germany at the Grosse Hamburgerstrasse Schule in Berlin. When he first transferred there, he had
wanted to join the French class. It turned out to be fortuitous that the
class was full, as E. D. Sassoon Company would never have hired him
had he not been fluent in English, nor would he have had the opportunity
to lead the English Circle. This new undertaking improved his financial
situation, and also facilitated the saving of funds for his eventual emigration from Shanghai.

The English Circle serves as an example of the cultural activities in
which refugees continued to engage, and which enabled them to develop
academic knowledge while socializing.

It was uncharacteristic of Fred not to make reference in his diary to
a strike of rice dealers. However, in a letter dated May 11, 1947 to Heini
Meyer, who was then in the U.S. (and called Henry), Fred related in considerable detail the tense labor situation in Shanghai and the looting of
rice stores during the previous week.

The following day the rice dealers joined their employees in
demonstrations before the Municipal Building and, on their way
home, vengefully destroyed several stores, a radio station, and a
theatre because of some disparaging remarks against the rice dealers. Finally, the police and MPs arrived, arrested several people,
and sent the rest home. The French tramcars are on strike (2,000

persons) and, since yesterday, the cable messengers (1,600 persons), too. A general strike has been declared for tomorrow.

In 1947, a number of small merchants (mainly British) who had left Shanghai directly after the war, returned with the hope of reestablishing their businesses, but they were bitterly disappointed and soon left in disgust. In fact, by simply claiming the rights of victory, the Nationalist government had taken over all municipal properties, disregarding the title deeds of the rightful owners. Only the Central Bank of China was now allowed to transfer foreign funds at the set official rate of exchange. There was a vast difference between the official rates and those on the black market. Nazis, who had cultivated commercial ties with powerful Chinese industrialists and merchants (and often secretly entered investment deals with them), escaped arrest. Many had long before transferred their fortunes to Swiss banks and lived comfortably on their spoils in Europe, Latin America, and even the U.S. Anti-U.S. slogans began to appear on the walls of American military buildings.

Friday, May 16, 1947—23rd birthday. Early duty. In the afternoon get tipsy with Ted at the Palace. In the evening go with Uncle Martin and the Alexanders to the Senet. Hors d'oeuvres, beef tea, Tournedos Rossini, mixed salad, Braziliano *[a robust and aromatic expresso]*. Then all go by taxi to Hongkew to the Marcuses where everyone is already gathered. I had taken care of the cakes and coffee. Presents: a leather briefcase from the Alexanders, a silver cigarette holder from the Marcuses.

Saturday, May 17, 1947—In the evening, Ted and Gerti pick me up and we go to the Grand *[Carnival in Mexico]* Feel hungry after the show and go to the Hamilton House. Gerti surprises us by wearing an evening dress, and we spend a pleasant time together till 2:00 a.m.

Now that he was on a more sound financial footing, Fred was able to frequent restaurants more often than in the past. In addition to favorite places already mentioned, such as the Palace Hotel, the Chocolate Shop, and Senet, he wrote about a number of other venues that were new to him. He visited nightclubs somewhat less often, but later in the month he thoroughly enjoyed a big night on the town, during which he and his friends—"the Shanghai sophisticates"—introduced an American guest to Shanghai nightlife. Nevertheless, in spite of these pleasures, Fred was at a low point, full of trepidation about the future, which he attempted to erase with alcohol.

Monday, May 19, 1947—French. Afternoon duty. To the English Circle. Hamburger appoints me to be his successor as of June 1. Speak again with much success. Hope that it will be possible to continue leading the Circle effectively, and to make a nice additional income.

Thursday, May 22, 1947—French. Meyer David has a cousin, Ernest Lee (Liebmann), who went to America when he was a child. He is now a bandleader in the USO in Shanghai. This evening, we show him Shanghai's night life. I wear a new suit from Freundlich *[tailor]*, with black and white (also new) shoes. Meyer picks me up by taxi with a Mrs. Eisenstadt, and we go to the Park Hotel where we meet his cousin, as well as Charlie and Kay. On the 14th floor have several drinks. Around 11:00 take a taxi to the Silk Hat. Beef Stroganoff and plenty of Cuba Libre. Break up at 12:00 and meet Bill Honby (Lt. USAAF) there, whom I know from the Cathay Mansions. He joins us with his jeep. The Arizona *[night club]* is already closed and we go on to Yu Yuen Rd., and finally find the Merry Widow, a nightclub with singing gypsies, which is still open. Whiskey and coffee. Before we leave, a fight takes place over a girl. *[The Merry Widow, a nightspot where the gypsies sang soulful Russian songs in throaty, heart-rending voices, was especially popular with Russian clientele. The performers wore multi-colored costumes embellished with loose floating ribbons and flashy costume jewelry. They encouraged the patrons to drink vodka, and approached the tables singing passionately, "Pei do Dna" [drink to the bottom, or bottoms up].* Then home in Honby's jeep. To bed at 3:00 a.m. after a wonderful evening.

Tuesday, May 27, 1947—Early duty. Have a photo taken *[see Figure 32]* at the Josepho Studio.

Monday, June 2, 1947—Evening: English Circle. Farewell party for Hamburger *[former leader of the Circle]*. Very nice. Give a speech. Then with Meyer and Uncle Martin to Cafe Europe to have a beer.

Saturday, June 7, 1947—Farewell party for Uncle Martin and Goldman. Hot dogs and plenty of beer.

Monday, June 9, 1947—Typhoon. Early duty. For the first time, lead the English Circle. 16 people. Think I was successful. Yesterday there was a big advertisement *[for the Success Circle]* in the *Shanghai Echo*. Today a smaller advertisement. A lady asks me about private lessons.

Sunday, June 15, 1947—Duty from 7:30–13:00. Go by steamer to Kiaochao and back. Evening: at the Marcuses. Ernest Lee is also there, as well as a lady from his band, Miriam Stiglitz. On the way home by taxi, Miriam promises to obtain an affidavit for me.

Monday, June 16, 1947—In the morning go to the Navy Y *[Y.M.C.A.)* to give Miriam all the information about me. Then duty (opening of the UNO Conference). Evening: Hongkew, Success Circle. Again a number of new students. Very nice and successful evening. *[See Figure 33 for a photo of Fred and his students.]*

In March of 1947, ESCAP (United Nations Economic and Social Commission for Asia and the Pacific) was founded in Shanghai. Originally called ECAFE (Economic Commission for Asia and the Far East), it was headquartered in Shanghai. In June of that year, the first Commission Session was held with the goal of helping the region recover after the war. It is probable that the UNO Conference to which Fred alludes several times is that Commission Session. The delegates undoubtedly stayed at the Cathay Hotel, which is probably why he was able to attend some of the sessions.

During the ensuing years, ESCAP, now based in Bangkok, has been the only inter-governmental economic and social development organization of the UN in the Asia-Pacific region. Today, there are 53 member countries and 9 associate members, and it continues to promote the economic and social development through regional and sub-regional cooperation and integration.

Thursday, June 19, 1947—In the morning take Mrs. Franken-busch *[a member of the]* Success Circle to the UNO meeting. Then to Dr. Reines and to bed. Inflammation of the throat.

Sunday, June 22, 1947—All day duty. Evening to the Marcuses in Hongkew. Charlie and Kay are leaving next week for the States on the SS General Meigs.

Monday, June 23, 1947—Early duty. Evening: Hongkew. 3rd meeting Success Circle. Over 30 people. Very good success.

Tuesday, June 24, 1947—Early duty. In the evening, a group of 24 American newspaper publishers are arriving, flown by PAA *[Pan American Airlines]*.

In the 1930s and '40s, Shanghai was a mecca for foreign journalists. In fact, the top six floors of Broadway Mansions were taken over by foreign correspondents, who even operated their own club on the seventeenth floor. The international press was much in evidence in Chungking as well, where Chiang Kai-shek had moved the Nationalist headquarters in 1938. Living conditions there were much less luxurious than in Shanghai. The weather was mostly foggy, and rats roamed the streets. Reporters lived in a hastily built government building called the Press Hostel (which at one time was bombed and rebuilt), and were forced to take refuge from the recurrent Japanese air raids in damp caves built into the rock hillsides. These raids became less frequent after Pearl Harbor when the Japanese concentrated on bombing other sites. Some women were among the foreign journalists, including Betty Graham, who represented Reuters, United Press, Associated Press, and Havas. Later, she worked for Hollington Tong, spokesman for Chiang and head of the Nationalist (KMT) Government Information Office, who became a supporter of the Chinese revolution. She died under mysterious circumstances.

It is not surprising that foreign newspapers were interested in developments in China. The ascendancy of Chiang Kai-shek after the death of Sun Yat-sen, the Sino-Japanese War, World War II, the Allied victory, General Marshall's failed mission, and the escalating civil war are but a few of the significant events that attracted world interest. A number of the foreign journalists were fiercely critical of Chiang Kai-shek and the corrupt Nationalist regime. However, Henry Luce, editor-in-chief of *Time* and an ardent anti-Communist, remained a close friend and supporter of Chiang. *[Luce was born in China, the son of an American missionary educator.]* Luce's prestige in the U.S. and the articles he wrote greatly influenced American public opinion on China. He traveled there twice, and other newspaper publishers and editors also made the journey. Fred mentioned such a junket in his entry of June 24, 1947. No doubt the publishers were guests at the hotel where he was working.

During this period, journalists also journeyed to Yenan to interview Mao Tse-tung, Chou Enlai, and other Communist leaders, and many wrote favorable reports about the simple lifestyle and goals that were in evidence there. They were particularly captivated by the very charming and highly intelligent Chou, and erroneously dubbed the Communists "agrarian reformers." Some later analysts have asserted that the reporting of these journalists strongly favored the Communists. In fact, one correspondent, Mark Gayn, who grew up in Harbin and was a reporter for *The Washington Post* and *China Press*, was eventually accused of obtaining secret documents from the Office of Strategic Services. Although the charges against him were dropped, FBI files indicate that he was a spy for the Soviet Union. (Gayn's brother, Sam Ginsburg, who lived in Shanghai, left his Russian Jewish family behind and joined the Chinese Communists.

He later married a Chinese woman, with whom he had two children, and taught Russian at a university.)

Wednesday, June 25, 1947—Early duty. Get cholera and typhus shots. *[Because both diseases were endemic in Shanghai, shots were compulsory three times a year. During serious epidemics additional shots were given.]*

Thursday, June 26, 1947—Early duty. Evening: Farewell party for Charlie and Kay. Cakes and coffee. Beer. Charlie's parents are now being left behind all alone, and only Meyer and I can take care of them.

Saturday, June 28, 1947—Ted and Gerti get their visas.

Sunday, June 29, 1947—Feel very weak. After lunch go to the China Merchants Lower Wharf where Charlie and Kay are leaving on the General Gordon. All the family and friends have gathered. After the ship sails, we all go to the Waldmann's flat (above Cafe Louis) and have coffee and cake. Then go by pedicab to the Victoria, where I meet Ted and Gerti.

The situation in Shanghai grew grim as Communist forces gained power in China and Nationalist soldiers showed signs of lethargy and disenchantment. Huge numbers now simply crossed over with their weapons to the enemy. Conversations among the worried European refugees centered on emigration, affidavits, and visas. Fred's anxiety mounted. His financial situation worsened, since the value of "the [U.S.] dollar was always climbing higher." Moreover, his health continued to worsen, and he was personally unhappy, longing increasingly for a loving girlfriend with whom he could really bond, and who would love him in return. At last, he made the decision to go to the U.S., although he remained pessimistic about his chances.

Tuesday, July 1, 1947—The biggest problem in life now is further immigration. All immigrants find themselves in a sort of psychosis, which, naturally, grips one when one sees one's beloved friends and relatives leave one after another. In addition to this, the present conditions here are so unsettled and disorderly that one does not know what the next day will bring. Financially, I now earn less every month since the dollar is always climbing higher.

I have basically decided to go to the United States for the following reasons: 1) My entire family is moving their residence there. a) Already there: Uncle Martin, Klaus, and Gert (with Ruth), Gerhardt and Pueppi with Gaby, Charlie and Kay. b) Will be leaving soon: Ted and Gerti. Will leave as soon as their quota comes up: Uncle Sammy and Lieschen, as well as my friends Günther Looser, Heini Meyer, Milly Hartig, Frosty (?) *[the question mark is Fred's]*, Meyer Weissmann, etc. 2) I believe that in the U.S.A. there is the possibility of great business developments, although I am aware from reports that I would have to start from the bottom. 3) I want to live in a civilization where I have equal rights and am respected. 4) I don't want to be a stateless refugee any longer.

My chances to emigrate are at present nil. Nevertheless, I hope that I will get an affidavit through a) Miriam Stiglitz, or b) Gerhardt Abraham, or c) Uncle Martin, or when nothing else works, through d) the Joint *[American Jewish Joint Distribution Committee]*. Julius Tuchler may provide a collective affidavit, but in spite of this I would prefer to get an individual affidavit, because with God's help, I have been able to become independent from mass actions and I want to continue being so. *[A collective affidavit guaranteed that refugees would not become "public charges," and was provided by the U.S. Jewish community. Such affidavits were available from organizations like the American Jewish Joint Distribution Committee and HICEM.]*

However, at the moment, I have taken the position of waiting because a) I have planned to save in 1947 $300 (a maximum of $500), b) I hope to reach at least the minimum sum by July, and therefore my objective is to leave Shanghai for the U.S. with at least $1,000. For that reason, I am making an effort to save every cent in order to reach this goal. I may get a call any time from the Consulate, and then, most probably, I will not be able to delay my departure as I might like to do. I will speed up my departure only if I cannot save any more money.

The Success Circle has, of course, been a help. I have had to give up my private tutoring this month (which could have given me a very nice income) since my state of health prevented me from making this extra effort. I have not really recovered from my flu at the end of April. Although I have been drinking so much for so long, I should not feel as bad as I do. Of course, I don't show anything on the outside. Nevertheless, I am swallowing lots of vitamins and live more quietly, smoke and drink less, and take care to get enough sleep. Hope that if things continue like this, I won't have any problems at the Consulate—should things get that far—when I have a medical checkup. In the meantime, I am still lonely without the right girlfriend, and get quickly irritated.

Thursday, July 3, 1947—Afternoon duty. Stahly calls me in. He is in an excellent mood. Says that during the hot season we should lighten the burden of our work. Besides, this year, I have the right to one week's vacation, and next year I get 2 weeks. Am very happy.

Fred sought solace, if only temporary, in the Chinese countryside, traveling with friends by car, bus, and ferry. Fortunately, Shanghai's ferry boats, which ran on set schedules back and forth to picturesque villages, were well maintained and comfortable. Fred and his buddies enjoyed hiking through fields, tanning themselves on small beaches, and swimming in the river. They brought picnic lunches and stopped at simple inns or hotels for additional refreshment. In spite of his stated intentions to cut down on alcohol, he nonetheless continued to drink far too much. It is clear that concern about obtaining a U.S. visa remained deeply troubling.

Sunday, July 13, 1947—Free. At 10:30 take a full day trip in a rented motor boat: Ted and Gerti, Gerendasis, Loewenthals, Armando Salinas and his wife, Mannheim, and I. At 1:30 land in Dong Koe, a village on a creek off the Whangpoo. Visit the village. Leave around 2:00 and reach Ming Hong at 16:30. (*Ming Hong, 18 miles from Shanghai was a popular destination for day trips. One could get there by boat, ferry, or—after the construction of a new road—by car.*) Of course, I myself swim in the river. Back again in Shanghai at 8:30 in the evening.

Tuesday July 15, 1947—Morning: Migration Office, Herr Kaiser: Report from New York about Julius Tuchler. He is not in a position to give an affidavit, but will take full responsibility for my board and lodging. I am deeply touched by Julius's proposal. Kaiser thinks that I should go in December–January on a collective affidavit. Afternoon duty. Evening: with Milly to the Roxy [*National Velvet*].

Thursday, July 24, 1947—Start early duty, but must soon leave because of 40 degree temperature. Go to bed. Inflammation of the throat. In the evening still fever: 101.1 degrees. Hottest day in 7 years.

Friday, July 25, 1947—No fever, but still in bed. Cancel my date to go to Mahler's dinner party.

Sunday, July 27, 1947—All day duty. In the evening visit the Marcuses, who are suffering very much from the heat. They received a lot of mail from their children in the U.S.

Wednesday, August 6, 1947—Early duty. Apply for a visa to travel inland to Mokanshan. In the afternoon go swimming at the Race Course. Evening: got a girl to the room. OK.

Sunday, August 10, 1947—Free. Morning: to Rio Rita *[a modest river resort, most likely named after the 1929 Hollywood musical of that name, starring Bebe Daniels and John Boles]*. Swim. Stay there for lunch. Lots of beer.

Friday, August 15, 1947—Evening: farewell party for Frosty and Milly at Resi's: Beefsteak a la Tartar and plenty of beer. Then more drinking at my place and take flash photos. Get $200,000 advance for my holiday.

Saturday, August 16, 1947—Free. In the morning run around for Max's visa. Ride with Gerti in a pedicab to do errands. In the afternoon buy suitcases *[for his forthcoming vacation to Mokanshan]*. Then go swimming at the Race Course. Evening: to the Marcuses in Hongkew.

Monday, August 18, 1947—Morning duty. Pack in the afternoon. Evening: 11th English Circle meeting. Regular attendance.

22

Mokanshan—First Vacation

Fred was elated to be going on his first holiday, to a mountain resort called Mokanshan *[literally, "Isolated Peak"—2,500 feet high]* some 120 miles south of Shanghai. This heavenly spot was discovered for outsiders by a missionary in 1890. Enchanted with its exquisite nature and cool summers, many missions built mountain resorts so their members could find respite from the noise, dirt, and unpleasant climate of Chinese cities. Soon the word spread, and the "hill station" of Mokanshan became the destination of both Shanghailanders and Shanghainese who enjoyed the shady bamboo groves, pine forests, orange and yellow tiger lilies, unusually large, velvety butterflies, and sunrises that cast pastel colors on low floating clouds.

At the foot of the mountain, sedan carriers waited with simple straw sedan chairs *[see figure 41 for a similar sedan chair ride up a different mountain.]* to carry luggage and visitors up the steep slope. *[Carriers would look over each individual and decide if he or she were a three-person or a four-person load. Two carried the sedan chair and the other ran alongside. The switch was effortlessly done: first one, then the other extra man would duck between the poles and take the weight. Then the other one ducked out. Today, there is a road to Mokanshan, and the mountaintop can be easily reached by motor vehicles].*

At the summit, comfortable stone villas and pleasant hotels offered hospitality. In 1947, there was no electricity, and only simple oil lamps for light. This resulted in an early bedtime for most. During the day, visitors swam in icy mountain water, and enjoyed hikes in the bamboo groves. Chiang Kai-shek owned a summer home in Mokanshan *[today an upscale hotel]*, and Du Yuesheng *[Shanghai's notorious Green Gang boss, known as "Big Ears Du"]* also had a heavily guarded villa there.

With time on his hands to relax, Fred wrote extensively in his diary about his very delightful days in Mokanshan.

Tuesday, August 19, 1947—Got up at 5:15. Take a taxi to the North Station, and the 6:45 Express *[train]* to Hangchow *[Hangzhou, which Marco Polo called "the greatest city in the world," located on the shore of the celebrated West Lake.].* Arrive at 11:30. Grand Hotel. Meet

the Manager, Fung. He invites me for lunch. Meet the ladies Duld-
ner and Dr. Landau. Take a car together to Mokanshan. After a 2-
hour ride, arrive at 4:15 to the foot of the mountains. Get a sedan
chair, and start the 2-hour upward climb. Check in at the Ao Lin
Hotel, and with the help of Dr. Gerendasi who has already been
there for several days, get a nice room. After supper, walk a little
in the darkness. Then drink two bottles of beer with the doctor.
Sleep wonderfully in a real Chinese bed *[a large, high wooden platform
with bed posts and curtains]*.

Wednesday, August 20, 1947—After breakfast, go with Dr.
Gerendasi, Mrs. Alt, and engineer Steiner on a hike along the ridge
to the grotto—and the Dah Wha Hotel. *[See Figure 34 for photo of
Fred and Dr. Gerendasi on hike.]* Around 12:00 go to the swimming
pool (Pacific Pool). The water is ice cold and I can remain in it
only a few minutes. At 1:00 have lunch. Then sleep till 4:00. After
coffee and cake go on a hike with Mrs. Alt to the Waterfall Swimming Pool and then to the waterfall itself.

Thursday, August 21, 1947—After a breakfast go swimming.
After lunch: take a nap. After coffee and cake, go to the market
with the doctor. Then to his favorite excursion spot behind the
Sports Place. The scenery, the air, the mountains, and woods are
of dream-like beauty and I enjoy everything completely. After
supper, Max Weissmann arrives and we walk through dark paths
with a flashlight to the Dah Wha Hotel, where we visit the Duld-
ner ladies, then return to the Ao Lin.

Friday, August 22, 1947—After breakfast go for a hike with
Max to the waterfall through wildly overgrown land, until we
finally reach the main path. Go swimming. Sleep after lunch and
after a snack go with the doctor and Max for a walk After supper,
go to the terrace to take some flash photos. Then I am asked by
the so-called "younger set" to join them. I do so.

Saturday, August 23, 1947—Get up at 5:00. Meet Max and go
up Mt. Taishan to see the sunrise. It was one of the most beautiful
sights I have ever experienced. Then back to the hotel for breakfast. Then go to the waterfall and its surroundings to take photos.
In the evening, we tell jokes at a big party on the terrace.

Sunday, August 24, 1947—In spite of cool cloudy day, go
swimming. Take more photographs. *[See Figure 35 for photo of Fred
relaxing in a pagoda.]* Around 10:00, pack my things and go to bed.

Monday, August 25, 1947—Get up early at 4:30. Have breakfast on the terrace. Then take off at 5:46. A baggage carrier takes the luggage and walks down the mountain at a lively pace. At 7:00 I arrive at the bus station and find place on a crate. There, tightly squeezed between luggage and Chinese, I cannot relax at all. Only fifteen minutes pass before I leave, but I feel that I might faint any moment. Then, when the bus starts moving, a wind blows in fresh air, and I begin to enjoy it. I reach Hangchow at 10:00 o'clock and take a pedicab to the Grand Hotel, where I am once again met by Manager Fung in the most welcoming way.

Monday, August 25, 1947—I take an excursion boat and sail around the lake. This is one of those moments—a gift to man—when one feels completely happy, wishing for nothing more. I return to the hotel, take a pedicab to the train station, where the hotel had already sent my luggage. They also reserved a good place for me. *[The railway service was government-owned, comfortable, and reliable.]* The ride back is pleasant.

On the way to the Cathay, I am suddenly terribly lonely. I feel like a stranger in the city, since nobody is waiting for me. In this state of mind, I get dressed and drive to the 12th Meeting of the Success Circle (regular attendance), where I tell them that they are my family, since they had waited for me. Several ladies burst into tears. Fall into bed dead tired.

The holiday was a complete success. It cost me $1,800,000, or US $45.00. I have recovered exceptionally well, and I discovered again the meaning of nature. By the way, Milly Hartig left for the U.S.A. on August 24th.

Thursday, August 28, 1947—Afternoon duty. In the evening go to the Marcuses to show them photos of my trip.

Saturday, August 30, 1947—Free. In the morning go with Stephen, the Winters, and Stephen's relative to Rio Rita. Eat Chinese lunch outside. Return at 6:00. Change. Go to Hongkew to Epstein, where the entire Alexander family is gathered to see the film of Ted's and Gerti's wedding. I can be seen often and well in the film.

23

Living It Up

September 7th was indeed a sad day for Fred, as his dearest friends and constant companions, Ted and Gerti, left for America. While Fred's heavy drinking had previously taken place mostly in the evenings, he admitted in his diary to imbibing heavily in the daytime for several days before his friends' departure. In the ensuing weeks when he felt forlorn, he found some small comfort in frequent visits to his friends' parents, the Alexanders and the Langers, and in visits to the two remaining Marcuses. Nonetheless, his life was seemingly aimless, and he darted from one group of acquaintances to another, and from one activity to the next. To assuage his loneliness, he invited Mei Ing to his room more often, but he did not reflect any pleasure in her visits.

Even as he was about to receive the coveted collective affidavit, Fred stubbornly wavered about accepting it, continuing in his vain hope that Gerda Alexander (through one of her Orthodox friends), or one of his own other contacts, would be able to sponsor him as an individual.

Friday, September 5, 1947—Early duty. In the afternoon to the Race Course for the murder trial of Cpl. Malloy. Then visit the DeGroodts. Shopping. Evening at Ted and Gerti's. Together to the Palace Hotel for supper.

Cpl. Thomas A. Malloy of Chicago was tried in a U.S. army court-martial for the robbery and murder of Yu Shen-chao, a Chinese black-market gold dealer. Yu was alleged to have had five ten-ounce gold bars in his possession when he was shot in a speeding car and thrown out onto the road. Helene DeGroodt remembers attending this lurid trial, which had all the elements of a B movie: "White Russians, Chinese lowlifers, a woman nursing her baby on the stand, wily New York lawyers for the defense, and Malloy himself, not the least cowed by his predicament." All Shanghai followed the trial avidly. Malloy was found guilty and sentenced to life imprisonment but, according to DeGroodt, was released after a successful appeal that determined that the ranking officer at the trial had not served as president of the court. Charles Archer, a Briton, apparently the driver of the car, was tried later that month in a Chinese court.

Sunday, September 7, 1947—Have breakfast at Jimmy's *[Jimmy's Kitchen, a very popular American-style restaurant owned by an American]*. Then to the Alexanders where all the family is gathered. I accompany Ted and Gerti to friends while they say good-bye. At 11:00, we take the Sassoon station wagon and go to the Hongkew and Shanghai Wharf, where Ted and Gerti board the Marine Adder sailing to San Francisco. The ship sails at 2:00. The older Alexanders return home. The Langers, the Epsteins, Braun, and I ride in a private motor boat that follows. However, we are unable to reach the Marine Adder. We get off at Kiaochiao and have lunch around 4:00. Then we go for a walk and take the 6:40 boat back.

Tuesday, September 9, 1947—In the morning go with Mrs. Frankenbusch to Malloy trial at the Race Course.

Wednesday, September 10, 1947—Morning: to Malloy trial. Afternoon duty till 9:30 p.m. since the night clerk is off.

Saturday, September 13, 1947—Free. In the morning went with Stephen to the Race Course. Swam. Since the weather is comparatively "cool" for Shanghai, we had the swimming pool all to ourselves.

Sunday, September 14, 1947—All day duty. However, am replaced early at 4:00, since it is Erev Rosh Hashanah. Go to the Eastern *[Theatre]* for services. Cantor Glass faints during the Kiddush, but recovers quickly. *[Rudolph Glass was originally an actor in a provincial German town, then a part-time cantor in Charlottenburg. In Shanghai, in addition to cantorial duties, he was an actor in the Shanghai Jewish Theatre.]* After the services go to the Marcuses for supper.

Monday, September 15, 1947—1st day of Rosh Hashanah. To the services at the Eastern. Then for lunch at the Langers. Afternoon: visit the Gerendasis. Evening: with Fritz J. to Hongkew to his parents who invite me for dinner. After dinner to the Marcuses. Gin.

Wednesday, September 17, 1947—Early duty. After lunch go to Hongkew to the Migration Office. Have my call in to the American Consulate. They are ready to give me a collective affidavit, but I prefer to wait and see if I can get one through Gerda Alexander.

Tuesday, September 23, 1947—Duty: 7:30–12:30. Rest in the afternoon. At 4:00 o'clock eat a "Kalte Platte" *["cold plate," usually cold cuts and cheeses]* with Fritz. Supper at the Alexanders in Hongkew. Kol Nidre at the Eastern at 18:30. Sleep over at the Alexanders.

Wednesday, September 24, 1947—Yom Kippur. The whole day at the Eastern. Recite Maftir Yonah. Have a bite at the Langers' home in the evening.

Thursday, September 25, 1947—Duty: 7:30–12:30. In the afternoon get another call from the U.S. Consulate. They must move me back since no affidavit has yet arrived.

Sunday, September 28, 1947—Duty: 7:30–16:30. Get a letter from Ralph A. Watkins.

Thursday, October 2, 1947—Go with Gerti's and Ted's parents to the Roof Garden. They read aloud letters from their children.

Monday, October 6, 1947—Duty: 10:30–6:30. Am just about to leave the staff dining room, when the boy comes up and tells me that a big fire can be seen. Go to the roof. See bright flames coming from a roof in the direction of Nanking-Kiangse Rd. I rush to my room, put on my rubber boots and run along Nanking Rd. to the site of the fire, a Chinese Bank (No. 200). The firemen are very willing but inexperienced. There are too few officers. So, I spontaneously start giving them orders which, to my great surprise, they immediately follow. Since the Chinese realize that I understand something *[about the equipment]* they spare no efforts.

By then the fire is almost out. I suddenly feel wet through, glance at my watch and realize that it is time to hurry to the 17th Success meeting. After that, since it is Simchas Torah, go with others to Zernik and have a few drinks.

Although Fred didn't mention it specifically in 1947, October 10 was the holiday called Double 10, the tenth day of the tenth month, which celebrated the establishment of the Chinese Republic in 1912. Helene DeGroodt, in one of her columns for *The Enquirer and News*, described the excitement surrounding this observance:

> People streamed from homes, shops and offices. Children happily deserted their school rooms to join in joyous celebration with their elders. Holiday trappings cloaked the dusty reaches of the city with gaiety. The flags of China lined the streets with brilliant

red, the color of courage. There were parades and demonstrations, staged by the military for all to see. All this seemed to renew the hope cherished in the hearts of China's millions that perhaps next year Double 10 may bring them peace, a peace that can be shared by all.

Saturday, October 11. 1947—Slept late. The Knoches visited me. They have just received their U.S. visa at the American Consulate.

Sunday, October 19, 1947—At 7:30 in the morning go with Max and Trude in the Ely personnel carrier to the Shanghai Hills. Have breakfast at the Zao-seh Cottage. Then climb up *[to the observatory on]* the Calvary hill. After lunch drive to the Creek, singing, and go for a walk. Around 6:30 turn back. Visit the Marcuses in Hongkew. Cosy get-together.

Shanghai Hills are located some 15 km. from Shanghai. In pre-war days, well-to-do foreigners used modern houseboats (manned by sailors and servants) for excursions to the Hills, which rise 200 to 300 feet above sea level and are covered with cool, shady, bamboo groves. An astronomical station was maintained by the Jesuits in nearby Zoseh. This was part of the world-famous Shanghai Jesuit Siccawei Observatory, linked to a network of 70 stations. By monitoring of typhoons and storms, and warning of their advance, the observatory helped provide safety for the entire China coast, as well as for navigation in other countries. Its weather forecasts were remarkably precise.

Thursday, October 30, 1947—Duty from 7:30–12:30. Buy a bike. Cheap for $1400 = US $95.

Those who knew Fred in Shanghai maintain that he always had an innate sense of style. Women sought his advice on the design of custom-made clothing that was sewn by talented Chinese tailors. He went out often with his friends, but they found that the atmosphere in bars and nightclubs had undergone a drastic change. Patrons could no longer use chits; only U.S. dollars were accepted, even though that currency was officially illegal in Shanghai except in PXs and other U.S. military establishments. The friendly personal welcome extended to longtime patrons became a thing of the past. Most customers were U.S. military personnel on short-term duty in Shanghai, not loyal regulars. The owners of new night spots had only one obvious objective: to make as much money as possible, as soon as possible, before the fluid political situation deteriorated further.

Saturday, November 1, 1947—Duty: 7:30–16:30. Chief Ac-

countant Devicha's 35th birthday. Invited to a cocktail party at
12:00 noon in our Silver Bar (8th floor). Later, big Chinese dinner
party with lots of wine. After dinner the Chinese begin to gamble.
A group of us goes to "West Point" in Love Lane *[lane of ill repute]*
where things are really interesting. Then return home by pedicab.

Tuesday, November 4, 1947—Duty: 7:30–10:30. Then self-
taught Spanish lesson with Kurt Hirsch. Supper at the Alexanders,
then to the Austrian Center for first beginners course (32 participants): 7:30–9:00. Home by bicycle.

Wednesday, November 5, 1947—After lunch, play wee golf
[miniature golf] at the Race Course. Register to play in a tourna-
ment. Duty: 14:30–21:30. Evening: Mei Ing at my place till 11:30.
Semper idem *[always the same]*.

Wednesday, November 12, 1947—Duty: 7:30–14:30. Evening:
meeting of the Success Theatre Committee. Preparations for operetta to be presented during Chanukah: "The Grand Dukes."

Sunday, November 16, 1947—Wedding of bookkeeper Kung.
Dinner party started at 6:00. Drink a lot. After the dinner, go with
Bookkeeper Smith-Chu's daughter "I Poo" to the Carlton Cinema.
*[With Ted no longer around to chastise him, Fred must have felt perfectly free
to date the daughter of a subordinate.]* Leave during the show and go
by pedicab to the Venus Ballroom. Dance very nicely.

Wednesday, November 26, 1947—Duty: 7:30–14:30. Then
to Wing On to buy a silver wedding gift from Ted and Gerti for
the Langers. Then to the Langers. Big group of people. Give a
speech. Stay till 10:00 o'clock.

Sunday, November 30, 1947—After lunch, go with Stephen and Lehrer to the Roxy for "The Beginning of the End,"
which refers to the atomic bomb. After the cinema, go to the
Race Course for coffee. United Nations vote for the partition of
Palestine.

On November 29, 1947, the UN General Assembly declared that the
Mandate Power in Palestine (Great Britain) had announced its decision to
evacuate Palestine by August 1, 1948. A partition plan, dividing Palestine
between Jews and Arabs had also been approved. The Mandate Power
agreed to do its utmost to ensure that the Jewish State would have a sea-
port (Tel Aviv was the objective), as well as sufficient inland territory to
enable substantial immigration. Both the Jewish state and the Arab state
would be independent, while the city of Jerusalem would obtain special
international status.

Tuesday, December 2, 1947—Duty: 7:30–12:30. Order a suit: (CN $8.500.000; $1:00 = 130,000) *[total: $65.38]*. Uncle Sammy brings me news from the Heim, and an enquiry from Kowalewski from Berlin. *[Kowalewski was the maiden name of Fred's mother. This letter, inquiring as to the well-being of their relatives in Shanghai, is most likely the first to be received from family members in Germany since the end of the war.]* I am very happy. Will write immediately. After the course visit the Maerishchels and the Gelbards. *[Sylvia Maehrischel had been in Mokanshan when Fred was there. Her husband Karl, or Karli, was a well-known and very popular soccer player. The Maehrischels later emigrated to Australia. Trude Gelbard, whose husband at the time was also named Karl, was Sylvia's very close friend. She and her present husband, Cantor Zachary Kutner, reside in Denver, Colorado.]* Long discussion with Karl M. about the Palestine question. The Jews have declared tomorrow to be a victory holiday.

Wednesday December 3, 1947—After lunch ride the bicycle to Goldschmidt's operetta rehearsal. After duty write a long letter to Ted and Gertrude.

Sunday, December 7, 1947—Duty: 7:30–16:30. Get dressed and go to the Marcuses by taxi. First day (eve) of Chanukah. Big dinner. I light the candles and say the brachot *[blessings]*. Then we eat and drink. A lot. Then we sing.

Monday, December 8, 1947—Duty: 10:30–18:30. Then to Goldschmidt. All operetta participants there. Go together to the Promenaden Cafe. 26th Success meeting. Very good attendance and mood. Perform the 2nd part of "The Grand Dukes." After the meeting ends, all the participants and others go together to Goldschmidts where we tell jokes, drink, and have a very merry time.

Saturday, December 13, 1947—Duty: 7:30–16:30. In the afternoon take Gert Edward Seissar, who is having problems with his exit visa, to Dr. Reines at the Country Hospital.

Sunday, December 14, 1947—Visit Sassoon *[Sir Victor]* at the Country Hospital. At 6:00 with Max and Trude to the Majestic: "Jolson Story," an outstanding film. *[This film was very popular in Shanghai, and was especially loved by the Jewish residents who flocked to see it.]* Then to Greenland for a Chinese meal. Then to Ciro's for dancing. (Things are going well—I am sober.)

Tuesday, December 16, 1947—Sir Victor Sassoon arrives at the hotel *[after being discharged from the hospital]*.

Monday, December 22, 1947—Duty: 10:30–18:30. Lehrers give a cocktail party for the officers of the China Bear and I am also invited. In no time, take many drinks and discuss with Captain McBride a possible free passage to the U.S. as a "workaway." Feeling very tipsy, go to the 28th meeting of the English Circle. Since I am under the strong influence of alcohol, the course naturally suffers, which I very much regret.

Monday, December 29, 1947—Cable news: Cousins Charles and Kay had a baby in San Francisco (June Dolly).

Tuesday, December 30, 1947—Alexanders receive a cable that Gerda and Mechuel (Abramchik) had a second son.

Wednesday, December 31, 1947—Duty: 14:30–19:00. Mohoff relieves me early. Shave and dress. Smoking, black tie, boiled shirt. By car to the Marcuses in Hongkew. Big New Year's eve dinner, drinks, and a little dancing.

24

First Love

Another year had passed, and Fred celebrated the usual long and exciting New Year's Eve with his friends. The year 1948 was to be momentous for him. Not only did his plans for emigration crystallize, but—at last—he found the girlfriend he had longed for. Between them, there was an instant attraction. They saw each other almost every day throughout 1948, enjoying an active social life with their large circle of friends. They went to frequent parties and balls, rode their bikes to the environs of Shanghai and, of course, saw many American movies. Later in the year, they embarked together on an ambitious trip to the inland of China.

All of these events occurred against the backdrop of continuing Communist victories over the Nationalists. In March, the Communists captured Yan'an, in April, Lyoyang. In May, 200,000 Nationalist troops were trapped by Communist forces in Mukden, Manchuria. Mukden fell to the Communists on November 1. Fred must surely have been aware of the deteriorating military and political situation. However, preoccupied by his new love and complex arrangements for leaving Shanghai, in addition to organizing two major trips, he never mentioned the civil war in his diaries. Yet, unquestionably, it was these events that spurred his plans to depart.

> **Thursday, January 1, 1948**—At 12:00 we all raise our glasses, etc. . . . I think: I don't want to have any year in my life worse than 1947. Of course, it would be good if it were to be better. On to Route Pichon to the Shanghai Jewish Club. Big ball in a huge hall. All the ladies are wearing exceptionally attractive evening gowns. Trude (Gelbard) comes in looking lovely in a dress inspired by me: an open shouldered, one strap evening dress. The mood and atmosphere are excellent. The band is good, perhaps a little overheated.
>
> Around 3:30 we finally end up in Zernik's Kunstlerklause where we meet the rich tailor, German, with his party and join

them. German is accompanied by a young immigrant *[Thea Gel-lert]* whom I had met as a kid at the Chaoufoong Heim. I get her address and promptly invite her out next Tuesday. Around 5:30 we decide to go to Gelbards' flat where a big bottle of vodka is passed around. Someone puts on the gramophone and in spite of the very narrow space, we begin to dance.

German, Thea, and I ride to Cafe Roy for breakfast. Since it is late for me *[his duty begins at 7:30 a.m.]*, I excuse myself, leave them, and take a rickshaw to the hotel. I reach the hotel feeling very tipsy. Take off my coat and start working. Mohoff tells me that he is afraid that a "walkout" is taking place since no Chinese have appeared to work. As I begin to go through my books, which I find very hard to do, Stahly comes over. I wish him a happy New Year and he says somewhat confusedly, "But Marcus, you are still in evening dress." I realize he is right and go to my room to change.

When I return Mahler is also there and we discuss how to keep the most important services running. I state that I can run the lift and am given this important duty. Sir Victor *[Sassoon]* is my passenger many times. After the end of my duty, I take a hot bath and begin to read in bed. However, after five minutes my eyelids droop and I begin the New Year by going to sleep at 8:45.

That Fred was instantly smitten by Thea, whom he had met only the night before, is indicated by the following letter he wrote on January 2 and which he had hand-delivered to her by a messenger:

Hello, Thea Darling,

I hope that everything is all right with you after that pleasant New Year's night. I, too, have recovered from all aftereffects and want to take this opportunity to remind you of our date. As I mentioned before, I want you to come with me to the Charity Gala-Premier at the Metropole Theater on Tuesday, January 6. It starts at 9 p.m. As I will be busy in the Austrian Center until 8:30 p.m., I suggest that you meet me right there at that time. I will have a car ready to take us to town then. (Or shall I pick you up someplace?)

I surely hope that you will come. So please confirm by giving the bearer a message or call me this afternoon until 6 p.m. under number 11340, ask for Reception Office, and then my name.

Hoping to be in your very pleasant company very soon I am

Yours

Fred W. Marcus

Monday, January 5, 1948—Duty: 10:30–18:30. Evening: 30th Success meeting. Good attendance. Somewhat nervous because the police come to check our Residence Certificates. Then everything goes on its usual way. Several nervous members go home to their families.

Tuesday, January 6, 1948—Had arranged to meet Thea Gellert at her door after the Circle. She is already standing there, all dressed up in a hat with a veil. The car I ordered is also there. We pick up Karl and Trude and all go together to the gala charity premier of "Sinbad the Sailor" at the Metropole cinema. The film is very colorful but rather bad. Thea lets me hold her hand from time to time. After the film we go to my place where we drink the better part of a bottle of whiskey. Make a date for the following afternoon.

When Fred met Thea Gellert, she was just 17 years old. He was a much "older man" of 23. Thea, her parents, and her sister had sailed to Shanghai in 1938 on the *Conte Biancamano*, the same ship on which Fred and his father traveled in 1939. She lived with her family in the Chaoufoong Heim until in 1948, with Fred's help, she moved out into a small room of her own. Thea was a beautician, having trained in Shanghai under Kurt Mosberg, a Viennese hairdresser. She had originally wanted to attend pharmacy school, which was outside the Designated Area, but Ghoya refused to grant her the necessary pass.

Reflecting on her years in Shanghai, Thea (changed to Dorothy on her first American papers because she felt the name "Thea" would be too difficult to pronounce for Americans) recalled that Fred, who was her first boyfriend, was fun-loving, polite, intellectual, smart, and a real gentleman. He wanted her to look her best and desired to show her off, which is why he sometimes designed dresses for her. Her happiest times in Shanghai were when she was bicycling with Fred in the country. At first, he would rent a bike for her and turn up at the door saying, "Let's take a trip into the blue" (a German expression for a trip to a surprise destination). Later, when one of the refugees left Shanghai, she got his bike and no longer had to hire one. *[See Figure 39 for photo of Fred on a bike ride.]*

Wednesday January 7, 1948—Duty: 7:30–14:30. Thea comes to visit me at 5:30. We go to my room, chat a while, then she is suddenly in my arms and as we kiss our conversation stops completely. We take a car and drive to Resi where we have a good dinner. *[Resi Seitz was similar to a German beer hall, and a favorite of Fred and his crowd.]*

Sunday, January 11, 1948—Go with Thea to Jimmy's for lunch. Then back to my room. We have a lot to tell each other between kisses and are getting closer every day. Thea tells me often how much in love with me she is. Finally, dead tired, I take her home and return at once in the same pedicab.

Saturday, January 17, 1948—Yesterday, in a protest against the eviction of squatters in Kowloon (Hong Kong), the British Consulate in Canton was set afire. Today there are also demonstrations here in Shanghai. Thea comes after lunch. We go to the Chocolate Shop for coffee. Then shopping to Wing On and other department stores. As we return to the hotel around 6:00, a demonstration in front of the British Consulate has just been scattered. Police in full force are occupying the hotel entrance, which has a very calming effect. We go to my room where we have supper. Then I take Thea home and ride my bicycle to the Marcuses.

Tuesday, January 20, 1948—Duty: 7:30–12:30. Ride my bicycle to the Race Course. Pay my club fees and pick up an application form for Thea.

Thursday, January 22, 1948—Duty: 7:30–12:30. Then Thea comes over and we go together to the Race Course, where we play wee golf and drink coffee. *[See Figure 36 for photo of Fred having fun at the Race Course and Figure 37 for one of Thea playing wee golf there.]* Back to my place. Thea washes my hair.

Sunday, January 25, 1948—Free. 39 degrees fever *[102.2 Fahrenheit.]*. Stay in bed. Dr. Reines: inflammation of the throat. Thea takes care of me in a very touching way. We have supper together. She leaves me around 10:00.

Saturday, January 31, 1948—Free. Sleep late. Then to the IRO *[International Refugee Organization]*. Apply for a visa to Brazil.

Fred's first big trip since Mokanshan in 1947 was to Nanking with Stephen Wu, a friend who was a night clerk at the hotel and a student at Great China University. Stephen's uncle, with whom they planned to stay, was a wealthy commissioner with the Examination Yuan (a branch of the government that validated the qualification of civil servants). This was the first time that Fred enjoyed the hospitality of a Chinese family.

In a popular English language pre-war guidebook to Nanking, the city was described as the ancient capital of China, about 200 miles from Shanghai on the left bank of the Yangtze River. To get there from Shanghai, one could take a Nanking-Shanghai Railway train or a river

steamer. The most important historic site at the time was the Sun Yat-Sen
Mausoleum, a gigantic structure on Purple Mountain, where the decisive
battle of the 1911 revolution took place. Fred and Stephen went to this
world famous temple, visiting both of its two chambers—the memorial
ceremony chamber and the coffin chamber. Sun Yat-Sen was venerated
as the father of modern China,

Friday, February 6, 1948—With great difficulty manage to
get train tickets. Duty: 10:30–18:30. Go to the Langers for supper.
Then to the Circle at the Austrian Center. Thea picks me up and
we go to my place. We prepare underwear for my trip and Thea
puts everything in order and also sews on buttons.

Sunday, February 8, 1948—Get up at 5:00. Thea arrives before 6:00 and we have breakfast together. Then Stephen's cousin
Wei-Ming arrives. We take a taxi and pick up Stephen from the
Metropole and drive to North Station. There we take the Triumph
Express to Nanking. Thea stays behind. We reach Nanking after a
very pleasant trip. After 1:00 o'clock we take a taxi to the residence of Stephen's uncle, Commissioner Liu. The three of us are
very warmly received and I get to know the entire family. Besides
the uncle and his wife, there is a concubine, Stephen's mother,
Stephen's grandmother, Stephen's brother, and the children: Wei-
Ching, Ih-Miang, Lou-Mei, Hsiao-Men. We get the comparatively
warmest room in the unheated house.

After a hot noodle dish, we visit a Japanese temple, which has
been turned into a war trophy museum. We photograph. Feeling very tired, we go back *[to the house]* at 5:00 and lie down to
sleep. Get up again around 8:00 and have supper. Then I go with
Stephen's brother to a Chinese cinema, where we see a modern
Chinese film. When we return, find the entire family assembled in
our room and I get to know the uncle personally.

Monday, February 9, 1948—Louise, Stephen's married sister,
comes after lunch to pick us up in a jeep. We visit the Chin Min
Temple and then the Hsuan Wu Park, where we have a snack. In
the evening, there is a big *[Chinese]* New Year's dinner for the entire family. After that we light firecrackers and play poker. Around
midnight we go to sleep. *[Fred related in later years that at one point
there was a big hullabaloo in the house, as the commissioner was going to sleep
with the concubine, although it was actually the wife's turn.]*

Tuesday, February 10, 1948—Sleep a very long time. Then
we go into the garden to take family photos. After lunch we rent

a horse and buggy to go the Du Tze Miao, a famous shopping district. Back by rickshaw.

Wednesday, February 11, 1948—We visit the OMEA *[Officers' Moral Endeavor Association, now the Zongshan Hotel]* building, in which there is a stone with the blood of a Ming dynasty governor who committed suicide. We have dinner and much wine in Louise's house. Then gamble seriously

Thursday, February 12, 1948—Early in the morning, the grandmother prepares hot noodles for us to take along in a thermos. We go by horse and buggy to the Purple Mountain and during the day visit the Ming and Tang Tomb, the Sun Yat-Sen Mausoleum, the Memorial of the Unknown Soldier, etc. *[The road to the mausoleum of Hung-wu, the founder of the Ming dynasty, who ruled 1368–1398, is lined with impressive pairs of stone animals and statues, which are supposed to guard the tomb. On a repeat visit to the Ming Tombs in 1983, Fred climbed onto the back of one of the stone camels as he had in 1948. See Figure 38 for a photo of Fred on his first visit to the tombs.]*

I write every day to Thea, and every day in the morning, I get a wonderful letter from her. I think about her and speak about her, more than I ever thought possible, more than I want to admit to myself. Especially during quiet moments, but also when I look at wonderful sights, I wish she was by my side. I try subsequently to have her come to Nanking—she would like nothing better—but is prevented from doing so by the opposition of her parents.

Now, on the way back from these wonderful excursions, with the weather turning bad, and my feeling that I had visited all the important sights of Nanking, it suddenly occurs to me that I had originally wanted to take 4 days off and had promised Stahly that I would be back on duty if possible by Friday. A feeling of agitation overwhelms me and I tell Stephen that I must return as soon as possible to Shanghai. He and his family try and convince me to stay longer. But I don't want to spend a rainy weekend in Nanking, but rather save my time off for sunny days.

Since it is hard to get train tickets for sleeping compartments, I go by pedicab to the station. There I go to the China Travel Service where they help me get a ticket. The visiting card of Stephen's uncle proves to be very helpful in this case. I call Stephen to inform him, send a telegram to Thea, and take a taxi back to the house. There I pack, eat soup with meat dumplings, drink Shaohsing wine, and say my good-byes. A taxi takes me to the train that is leaving at 11:00. The sleeper is fantastic, as good as a pre-war German train. It is warm, clean, and the service is excellent. I share my 4-bed compartment with a Chinese general and a Chinese colonel, and soon after we leave go to sleep. The beds have 2 pillows and a down cover, which is too warm. I sleep very well, but wake up every time the train stops.

Shanghai, Friday, February 13, 1948—At 8 o'clock in the morning we reach Shanghai. I take a taxi to the hotel where I have breakfast, shave, and go on duty from 10:30–18:30. After lunch, to my great joy, Thea phones, and later she comes over for a short visit. In the evening she comes again and we have supper in my room.

25

Mounting Pressure

Now that Fred was involved in the close relationship with a girlfriend for which he had hungered, he seemed, on the surface at least, to be happier than he had been in a long time. Still, he profoundly missed his family members and dear friends who had departed Shanghai. Seeking companionship and moral support, and realizing he needed to make new friends, he decided to apply for membership in the Independent Order of Odd Fellows (IOOF). This connection was to become extremely significant to him during his last year in Shanghai.

Monday, February 16, 1948—Duty: 12:00–18:30. Thea comes over. Stephen returns from Nanking. I invite him to my room and the three of us have supper. Then I take him to the Promenaden Cafe to the 35th Success meeting, where I give a report about my trip.

Sunday, February 22, 1948—Free. Get a letter from Ursula Finke in Berlin (also 2 days ago from Aunt Ella): Günter, Erich, Ida, Elli, Hans, Lieschen are all still alive. *[Ursula Finke was a childhood friend of Fred's; their mothers had worked together in a bank before they married. Ursula remained in Berlin during the war, living in hiding with a Christian family and working in private lending libraries they owned. When she was captured by the Gestapo in a subway station, she threw herself under a train. Miraculously, she survived, and was hospitalized until the war's end. In the 1980s, Fred reconnected with Ursula, and he and Audrey visited with her in Berlin a number of times. The others mentioned were all relatives on Fred's mother's side.]* After lunch ride my bike to the Columbia Road Cemetery, since tomorrow is Pappi's birthday.

Wednesday, March 3, 1948—To Hongkew to the barber and to the Joint to ascertain an address. Then spoke to Frau Dr. Edith Lavrik at SACRA, Muirhead Rd. She is in charge of collective affidavits. Go back to the hotel for lunch and then duty: 14:30–21:30. Since I have a sore throat that has bothered me for the last three days, I ask Thea not to come over.

Friday, March 5, 1948—Sleep late. Duty: 10:30–18:30. Go
to Dr. Reines in the morning. My throat is not at all better. Need
penicillin shots. They cost 4,500,000. ($15.00). I go to Mahler to
see if the company will pay for that and get his OK. In spite of
101 degree fever, still go to the Austrian Center. Thea picks me up
and takes me to the tram. Go home to bed.

Wednesday, March 24, 1948—Duty: 7:30–14:30. Put in an
application at the Odd Fellows Lodge. A certain Mr. Dombrower
comes over for coffee to investigate me and we converse a long
time.

The Independent Order of Odd Fellows first began in England at an
undetermined date perhaps two centuries ago, then spread throughout the
United States and many other countries. It is not clear why it was named
"Odd Fellows," but some historians assume that this may reflect its very
diverse membership: laborers, craftsmen, businessmen, and intellectuals.
Basically, the Odd Fellows is a benevolent society with no religious orienta-
tion that has as its chief concern the welfare of its members.

After supper take a taxi to Hongkew. Pick up Thea and her
parents and take them to the Grand cinema. Have a snack at the
Rose Marie [a restaurant next door to the Grand movie house], then see
"Rainbow Island."

Saturday, March 27, 1948—Free. Thea comes over. She is
wearing her new black dress that I designed and has a new hair-
style, and she looks very sophisticated. We go to the Kadoorie
School where a Purim ball is taking place. Thea creates much
excitement with her appearance and I am busy with eye to eye
skirmishes. We down lots of drinks and meet many friends. We
have a good time. The ball ends much too early at one o'clock.

As Shanghai was assailed by political and social unrest, Chinese
antagonism toward foreigners was growing. At least one of Japan's war
policies was successful: the reduction of Western prestige in Asia. In
China, Communist propaganda ceaselessly attacked "outer barbarians,"
whose presence was resented.

Reflecting the mounting psychological pressure, Fred's nervousness
kept increasing. He drank frequently and sometimes heavily. He often
complained about being tired. Once he even admitted to weeping. Nevertheless, he still attempted to maintain a cheerful outward appearance
and a balance in his life. He spent most of his time with Thea and his few
remaining friends, and his application to the Odd Fellows was accepted.

Saturday, April 10, 1948—Since there is glorious sunshine, get on my bike and ride to Nantao. Back at the hotel at noon.

Nantao (Southern Market), to which Fred rode his bike, was part of the Chinese municipality of Greater Shanghai. The most famous tourist site at Nantao was—and still is—the Willow Pattern House (Doo Sing Ding). It is thought that this is the tea house pictured on China's very popular willow pattern dishes. The tea house, reached by walking across a zig-zag bridge, is built on stone pillars in a pool.

Thursday, April 15, 1948—Duty: 7:30–12:30. Festive opening at the Austrian Center of Franklin D. Roosevelt Lodge No. 1 of the Order of Odd Fellows. After the introduction and a break I also give a short speech (with great success).

Monday, April 19, 1948—44th Success meeting. Weak attendance (because of many departures).

Many Shanghailanders besides refugees were also leaving, among them those British, American, and Dutch nationals who had been evacuated and later returned to Shanghai. Finding that it was not the Shanghai they remembered, they urgently sought passage back to their home countries.

Friday, April 23, 1948—Get up somewhat earlier than usual, take a bath and make a bit of order. Duty: 10:30–18:30. Dressed and arranged for flowers to be delivered to the Marcuses. I lead my first Seder honorably and everything goes smoothly.

Sunday, April 25, 1948—Duty 7:30–16:30. Afternoon with Thea, Stephen, and Jimmy *[a friend of Stephen's]*. Play poker. Go together to Sun Ya for dinner. This time I pay. As the evening passes I feel terrible and we break up shortly after 10:00. In spite of feeling weak in the heart take Thea home.

Wednesday, April 28, 1948—Duty: 7:30–14:30. Lodge meeting. Appointment of several new board members and then a lecture by Dr. Schnittkin about hypnosis and suggestion as healing measures.

The situation in Shanghai continued to deteriorate. The value of the Chinese currency dropped daily. The following notice was published in the Russian Jewish cultural magazine *Our Life:*

From the Editorial Board

In view of the sharp devaluation of local currency, the Editorial Board requests that payment of membership fees be made THE FIRST TIME THE COLLECTOR ARRIVES.

Saturday, May 8, 1948—After lunch ride my bicycle to pick up Thea. She also rides her bicycle. Take a boat at the Bund to Chingminghsieh. From there over fields to Fungkou. It is very adventurous to ride our bicycles over canals and rice fields. The weather is beautiful. The sky is a brilliant blue. In Fungkou we snack and take a one-hour break in the park. Then we ride in a small sampan over a little river and ride—this time using the main street—saving almost an hour's time to get back to Chingminghsieh. Then we go by motorboat over the Whangpoo to Yangtzepoo. There, I have to have some repairs made on my wheel, after which we ride to the Marcuses. We have supper there followed by many drinks. Both of us are nicely tight and feel very tired. We ride hurriedly back to the hotel, where we arrive covered with perspiration in spite of the cool air.

Saturday, May 15, 1948—Duty: 7:30–16:30. Go by taxi to Hongkew to the Marcuses, where I am giving a birthday party *[his twenty-fourth birthday was the next day]*. There is wine and schnitzel with potato salad. Beer and stewed fruit. Egg brandy and coffee brandy. I ordered the society photographer Bobby. We dance a lot, drink a lot, do a lot of nonsense. At 12:00 everyone congratulates me and gives me presents. When I get a letter from Columbus, Ohio, I suddenly become very sentimental and weep—only possible because of the strong influence of alcohol. *[The name of the sender of this letter was not revealed.]*

At 1:00 a taxi picks us up and we all go to the Kadoorie School where a Zionist celebration on the occasion of the Proclamation of Israel's Independence is about to end. When I get home, I find Thea's presents on my desk. A big, long silver cigarette case with my initials and an inscription from her, an extravagant fine tie, a bottle of Palmolive After Shave lotion, and a very sweet congratulations card. Finally I go to bed at 3:45 a.m.

On May 14, 1948, a very moving ceremony had taken place at the Tel Aviv Museum. At 2:00 p.m. the Philharmonic played "Hatikvah," the Jewish national anthem, followed by David Ben Gurion's proclamation on the formation of a new state to be named Israel. Paragraph #3 of Israel's charter announced the Law of Return, opening the doors of the newly formed state to all Jews who wished to come. In mid-June, an Israeli representative arrived in Shanghai and set up an office to register those who wish to emigrate to Israel. Approximately 900 Jewish refugees applied in Hongkew.

It was not until December of that year when the first representative of Israel in China, Moshe Yuval, arrived in Shanghai. Although Israel and China had no official relations at that time, Yuval was able to issue Israeli visas to Jews wishing to make *aliyah* (to emigrate to Israel). In 1949, he was appointed Israeli Honorary Consul. Yuval left Shanghai in 1951.

Fixed on emigrating to the U.S., Fred never considered the option of making Israel his home. In later life, however, he traveled there enthusiastically, and took university courses, mainly in archaeology.

Sunday, May 16, 1948—24 years old. I get up around 9:00, drink a glass of milk, and take a bath. I get dressed and with the boy and coolie begin to put the room in order. Stahly put the adjoining room #3 at my disposal today. We plan to dance in that room, and Thea and I decorate it accordingly. We dash back and forth to prepare the birthday table. We have a really big buffet in my room: hors d'oeuvres, cakes, stewed fruit, whiskey, egg brandy, coffee brandy, light and dark beer, soda, Coke, etc. At 8:30 the guests start to arrive. After a few drinks, we begin to eat. The hors d'oeuvres are really good and the drinks are merrily gulped down. Thus the mood reaches a high point very quickly. In the adjoining room, people dance under red lights, or with all lights switched off, smooch. Later we make coffee, eat cream cakes, and dance and kiss again. A few people go peu a peu *[little by little]* home. We break up at 3:00 a.m. *[See Figure 40 for photo of the party guests. Thea is wearing a dress designed by Fred.]*

Monday, May 17, 1948—At 8:00 get up. It looks like the aftermath of the Battle of Waterloo. I put away the most important things and leave the rest to Lung Doo and Hsiao Mao who put the room in beautiful order. Duty: 10:30–18:30.

Wednesday, May 26, 1948—In the morning to Hongkew. To the Migration office to meet Mrs. Lavrik. Discuss the application for a collective affidavit. Next step: medical examination through a Joint doctor.

Fred no longer resisted applying for a collective affidavit, realizing that because of the worsening political situation it represented his best—and perhaps only—chance to emigrate. By mid-1948, the great majority of Shanghailanders had lost all confidence in the capacity of Chinese Nationalist armies to withstand Communist advances. The general belief was that should U.S. forces eventually be withdrawn, the fall of Shanghai would rapidly follow. And then what? Riots? Looting? Attacks on foreigners?

Delays in obtaining exit permits? Crowds of Displaced Persons, as well as Chinese gathered in the outer office of the U.S. Consulate desperately seeking to obtain a visa. For many, the outlook was dim.

Friday, May 28, 1948—*[After two days of fever]* talk to Dr. Reines about combined vitamin injections. Have to get 24. Will cost me $15. Will start tomorrow. Duty: 12:00–18:30. For supper to the Langers.

Tuesday, June 1, 1948—Duty: 7:30–12:30. Go to the National City Bank, to discuss with Gordon Bell the transfer of my savings to the U.S.

Wednesday, June 2, 1948—Duty: 7:30–14:30. Then to the National City Bank, where I have an appointment with Vice-President Standt. With his assistance, I will open an account in San Francisco. *[Fred later revealed his anxiety about whether his savings, amounting to around a thousand dollars, would actually be there at his disposal when he arrived. It was.]* Meet Thea at the Uptown cinema. We eat supper at Resi's. After that go to the Lyceum for the opening of Gruehling's production of "The Play's the Thing" by Molnar. Excellent performance. Most of the audience is dressed in evening clothes, and Shanghai High Society is represented: Sir Victor *[Sassoon]*, Ellis Hayim, the Ezras, etc. *[all prominent Shanghai Sephardi Jews]*.

Saturday, June 5, 1948—Anti-American student demonstrations held in check by strong police forces.

Friday, June 11, 1948—Morning: Hongkew. To the barber. Then to the Ward Rd. Heim for a checkup by the Joint doctor for the purpose of a collective affidavit. Duty: 14:30–21:30.

Thursday, June 24, 1948—Duty: 7:30–12:30. Get permission from Thea's parents to take her along during my vacation. Then to a short Lodge meeting.

Sunday, June 27, 1948—Free. At 8:45, Lilly, Karl, and her parents, the Schlochauers, the Gelbs and, of course, Thea, come over in a weapons carrier. We go to Chapei where we rent a tent on the beach and swim in the sea. Then we eat and chat and after two hours we go back into the sea, in spite of stones and shells that cut us. We start on our way back at 4:00, which is a very exciting drive since we overtake other cars as in a car race.

Tuesday, June 29, 1948—Duty: 7:30–12:30. Meet Thea at 3:00 and we go together to the IRO to apply for our Inland

Travel Visas. We must however take our applications back at once, since they require letters from the Joint and the S.R. Hospital. *[The Shanghai Refugee Hospital was located at 138 Ward Road near the Ward Road Heim. Patients with non-contagious diseases were treated there, operations were performed, and babies delivered. People with communicable diseases, such as smallpox and scarlet fever, were treated in a separate isolation hospital, located in the Chauofoong Heim.]*

Wednesday, June 30, 1948—Get up early and go to Jimmy's for hot cakes and coffee. Then to Hongkew to the Joint and S.R. Hospital, where I get the letters for the IRO. Duty: 10:30–18:30.

26

Inland China Adventure

Fred's anxiety continued in the months to follow. For a time, he questioned his relationship with Thea, thinking at one point that he had fallen in love with someone else. The IOOF Lodge became a solace, and the members chose him for greater responsibilities. Even in the midst of the endless task of discovering some way to leave Shanghai, he found time to complete arrangements for his departure and embark with Thea on the extensive 13-day trip to the interior of China.

Thursday, July 1, 1948—Duty: 7:30–12:30. Since I have very much to do cannot leave the office before 2:00. Meet Thea again and go to the IRO, where we hand in our visa applications *[necessary for the inland China trip]*. In the evening to Hongkew. I go to a Lodge meeting at the Austrian Center.

Tuesday, July 6, 1948—Duty: 7:30–16:00. Dreadful weather before noon announcing a typhoon. In the foyer, pieces of windowpane are flying to one side, so that the rain comes in and later there is an electric short circuit. In the afternoon, I put on rubber boots and a raincoat and go over to Thea's. Stay there for supper. After that, play gin rummy till 4:00. Then go home and do some work. The storm has almost completely ended.

Wednesday, July 7, 1948—Duty: 7:30–15:30. In the evening, pick up Thea and we go to the Mascot roof garden. Go home at 1:00. The streets are flooded as a result of the heavy rains, and we can hardly get through by pedicab.

Thursday, July 8, 1948—Duty: 7:30–15:15. Then go to the China Travel Service *[CTS]* to buy train tickets. In the evening to a Lodge meeting. Celebration in honor of the 70th birthday of a Lodge Brother. After the meeting, festive table with many speeches and cabaret skits. I recite my own poem with great success.

Tuesday, July 20, 1948—Duty: 7:00–14:40. China Travel Service hopes that we still will be able to travel *[despite the flooding]*.

In the afternoon, go to Seppi, who pulls out another of my teeth. Then home. Visit Thea's parents. Dr. Langer also there since his wife is in the hospital with pneumonia.

Undaunted, the couple set out by train for Hangchow (Hangzhou), 110 miles southwest of Shanghai, and the first stop on their ambitious trip. For hundreds of years a prime tourist attraction, the city is still famous primarily for its picturesque beauty and the magnificent West Lake, with gardens and temples on its banks and bordered by graceful hilly peaks on three of its sides.

Shanghai to Hangchow, Thursday, July 22, 1948—Get up very early and go on duty from 6:30–12:30. Max and Trude, who are taking us to the train station, arrive with Thea. *[Max Eisenstadt seems to have accompanied Fred and Thea as a chaperone for at least part of the trip, no doubt at the insistence Thea's parents.]* Take a taxi to North Station around 15:30. Go to Hangchow on the 16:00 o'clock express. At Passport Control, our visas are checked and found in order. Arrive in Hangchow at 20:30. Go to the Grand Hotel, where I had asked Tung to make 2 reservations. Eat on the terrace. Then by boat across the lake to the Island of the Three Pools and Moon's Reflection, which we visit in moonlight. Super romantic from the water, which looks silvery in the moonlight. Back to the hotel. We take a bath, sit on the balcony, then sleep.

The Grand Hotel was right on the lakeside near the center of the city. The tireless young couple wasted no time. Right after dinner, they took a boat to the lovely Island of Three Pools and Moon's Reflection where, at night, candles were lit in stone lanterns jutting out of the water, appearing like the reflections of three moons. Fortunately, they had arrived in July, a time when lotuses on the lake were in full bloom, adding to the splendor.

Hangchow, Friday, July 23, 1948—Have breakfast on the terrace. Then hire a rickshaw for the whole day for 2 millions (30 cents). In the morning to the Jade Emperor's Mountain, then climb to the Taoist monastery on the mountain peak, then to the heavenly viewing platform. Visit the entire temple and mountain peak. Also a deep ice-cold cave. Back to the Grand Hotel for lunch. Then rest. At 3:00 continue with the rickshaw. Pick up tickets to Kiukiang *[Jiujiang]* at the China Travel Service. Go around the lake. Visit Yue Fei. Then on to Ling Yin Temple and take a carriage to Dancing Fish. Back to the Grand via Imperial Island

and the *[he uses a Chinese character here]* Gardens. After supper shop
a little. Then on the lake with a boat.

The next leg of the trip required an overnight train ride to Nanchang,
capital city of Jiangxi Province, the jumping off point for the subsequent
stop, Kiukiang. From there, they went first by car and then were carried
up Mt. Lushan for two hours in sedan chairs *[see Figure 41]* to reach their
destination, Kuling (Guling). Many foreigners fled the brutal heat of
Shanghai and Tiensin to relax in this cool, charming hill resort. There were
fresh streams and pools in which to dip, small pensions, and grandiose
hotels. Visitors often claimed that the top of Lushan (4,500 feet) was clearly
shaped like a water buffalo. Generalissimo Chiang Kai-shek and his wife
occupied a fine stone house there in the 1930s and Kuling became the
summer capital of the Kuomintang government. Later, China's post-1949
revolutionaries held party conferences in Kuling.

Hangchow, Saturday, July 24, 1948—Get up early. Pack. To
the train station after breakfast. Obtain a sleeping compartment
for the 8:30 Hangchow-Nanchang train. An American missionary
is in our compartment. The trip is interesting, the food average.
We go to bed after 10:00 in the evening. During the night, I get up
several times, while the train rattles deep into China's inland.

Nanchang, Sunday, July 25, 1948—Arrive at 7:00 in the
morning. Hurry through the city by rickshaw to the station to
catch the 9:00 o'clock train to Kiukiang. There is no locomotive
[yet], and I am now sitting in the train and writing. We have been
standing in the station for 1½ hours. Finally, a locomotive arrives
after 4 hours delay and we leave Nanchang at 10:50 a.m. During
the first stop, I get permission from the engineer to ride in the
locomotive. This is a first-class experience for me. The locomotive is coupled in an opposite position with the train, so that a
breakage could only occur in front. *[Fred's avid love of trains probably
dated from his childhood in Germany. During train journeys in later years,
he always stood on the platform at the back of the train to get a better view.
He loved to go on narrow gauge and old steam trains, and always wore his
engineer's cap on such trips.]*

Nanchang-Kuling, Sunday, July 25, 1948—I climb on the
tender and enjoy the wonderful stretch ahead of me without
smoke and heat. The scenery is the most beautiful part of the
trip so far. The rails wind around the mountains of the Kushan
Range, climbing upwards all the time. 16 kms. before the end, the
descent to Kiukiang along the Yangtze River begins. At the last

station before Kiukiang, the locomotive is changed since the large Espey machine is too heavy for the flooded earth on which the rails have been laid. I return to my compartment. The last part of the way leads over the badly flooded area around Kiukiang. Groups of workers are attempting to keep the rails out of the water. We reach Kiukiang at 4:00. We ride rickshaws over flooded streets to China Travel Service to arrange the continuation of our journey. Then we have a light lunch and continue by rickshaw through flooded Kiukiang until we reach the place where we get a CTS car. There we negotiate for sedan chairs and start our way upwards, a grandiose climb that surpasses the beauty of the one in Mokanshan. We reach our hotel at dusk, around 9:00. Our room has only one Chinese bed. Max is staying next door.

Kuling, Tuesday, July 27, 1948—Go on a gorgeous hike to Yellow Dragon Temple, Three Trees, Emerald Grotto, and a natural basin in a mountain stream, where we swim. Then climb to Dragon Pool, where we swim again. Get back to the hotel at 1:30, eat well and then sleep. Go with Thea in the afternoon to the Post Office and to the market for small purchases. After that dinner and bath.

Kuling, Wednesday, July 28, 1948—Get up early and go for a hike to the Three Waterfalls. We cross the second highest path, 4,600 ft., then turn on a mountaintop path leading to the valley and reached our goal after five hours. Rest for an hour and eat a snack. Then start on our way home, which is very difficult for us. I have a bad sunburn (in spite of rubbing myself with oil) and am not only exhausted but reach the hotel trembling with fever. Thea puts me to bed, gave me pills to *[make me]* sweat, and rubs oil on my sunburn. After I am through sweating, fall fast asleep.

S/S Kiang Tai, Saturday, July 31, 1948—Get up early. The luggage handlers arrive at 7:30. Go to the police where we get our travel chops *[seals]*. Then, in streaming rain, we go down the mountains to Linhuatung. From there we go by car to Kiukiang, where the flooding has already subsided. Then to China Travel Service and China Merchants where we can get only First Class tickets (not Salon Class). Reach the wharf, get into a launch, wait a while, then meet the Kiang Tai in midstream. We board the boat where we share an airy cabin with 3 Chinese. Everything is very plain and simple. After a Chinese dinner, we stay on the deck till 10:00, then lie down to sleep in our berth.

The final stop on the trip was Nanking, which Fred had visited previously with Stephen. The couple stayed for two nights with Stephen's relatives, Commissioner Liu and his family, and enjoyed visits to some of the interesting sights. Although Fred had visited the Ming Tombs and the tomb of Sun Yat-sen on his previous trip to Nanking, he willingly returned to both for Thea's sake. Today in Nanjing a memorial commemorates the massacre there of over 300,000 Chinese by the Japanese in 1937.

Nanking, Tuesday, August 3, 1948—At 3:00 go to the station by carriage, where we take the very fast Triumph Express to Shanghai. Arrive there at 10:30. Take Thea home by taxi and ego ditto.

Wednesday, August 11, 1948—Breakfast at Jimmy's Kitchen. Duty: 10:30–18:00. Then a short conversation with Laura Mayer (Joint), who lives in our hotel. She tells me in confidence to try, as urgently as possible, to be included in the collective affidavit. Thea waits for me in the room. We go to the Grand, 6:45 show of "13 Rue Madeleine." Very thrilling.

Thursday, August 12, 1948—Lodge meeting. New Obermeister Dombrower appoints me to the Culture Committee.

Friday, August 13, 1948—Shop for Thea's birthday. Buy her a gold wrist watch.

Wednesday, August 18, 1948—Visit Hugo and Kaethe Alexander who are both bedridden, he with a kidney attack and she with sciatica. We celebrate Thea's birthday.

Tuesday, August 24, 1948—Duty: 14:30–21.30. Missie Frankenbusch comes over and reports she had heard from the U.S.A. that Kurt Seligsohn has been drafted into the army. This news, of course, upsets me. So, since I am also thirsty, drink a bottle of beer with my supper.

Wednesday, August 25, 1948—Duty: 7:30–14:30. With Thea to the Cathay (free tickets) to see "My Favorite Brunette." Then to my place where we eat. I feel somehow estranged from Thea and soon take her home. Go to bed feeling disturbed.

Friday, August 27, 1948—Duty: 7:30–14:30. Thea comes over in the evening. We have a long discussion. I make clear to her that I feel absolutely nothing but friendship for her. Then take her home. *[Despite this bump in the road, Fred and Thea continued to see each other. However, it was not until September 18 that they actually make up, and in the months that followed, the relationship was never quite the same.]*

Tuesday, August 31, 1948—Duty: 7:30–12:30. To the Austrian Center for a meeting of the Lodge's new Cultural Committee. Together with Erwin Schlesinger, I am named Cultural Manager of the Lodge. Also take the minutes of the meeting, since the Cultural Secretary does not feel well.

Tuesday, September 7, 1948—Strong rain accompanying typhoon trough *[this time of low pressure occurs when a typhoon bottoms out]*. Duty: 7:30–14:30.

Thursday, September 16, 1948—Duty: 7:30–12:30. Rest in the afternoon. Evening: Lodge meeting (speaker Dr. Salomon). Apply for membership at the J.R.C. *[Jewish Recreation Club, which featured sports opportunities and events, as well as and dramatic performances]*.

Saturday, September 18, 1948—Duty: 7:30–16:30. Write Thea to come over. We make up somehow.

Thursday, September 23, 1948—Get a written request to appear at the U.S. Consulate to be there at 1:10. In the morning to Hongkew to Frau Dr. Lavritz and Miss *[Laura]* Mayer. Then take passport photos. Duty: 10.00–19:00. Then to a Lodge meeting and finally to the Roy, where we sit for awhile outside.

Shanghai, Monday, September 27, 1948—Get a letter of recommendation for the U.S. Consulate. Then duty from 10:45–4:00. For supper to the Alexanders. Then meet Thea at my place.

27

Trapped Again?

The Communists were close at hand. Unrest and fear increased sharply in the refugee community. Now that Fred had given in and made the decision to accept a collective affidavit, he quickly submitted to the necessary medical tests and began to complete the many other arrangements required for departure.

Friday, October 1, 1948—Appointment at the U.S. Consulate after getting the collective affidavit. Everything goes smoothly. After that go to the Chung Mei Laboratory to take a blood test. Then to Ave. Haig to get an X-ray. However, have to go again tomorrow. Lunch at the hotel. Then duty from 14:30–21:30. Thea comes by late in the evening but I am already in bed.

Saturday, October 2, 1948—In the morning to Ave. Haig for an X-ray. Then to settle hotel business. Duty: 11:00–19:00.

Sunday, October 3, 1948—Duty: 7:30–16:30. Erev Rosh Hashanah. To services at the Eastern. Then supper at Alexanders.

Monday, October 4, 1948—First day of Rosh Hashanah. To services in Hongkew. Then for lunch to the Langers. Return home at 3:00. To supper to the Alexanders.

Tuesday, October 5, 1948—Duty: 7:30–12:30. After lunch go with Stephen to Avenue Haig to pick up the X-ray report: Both lungs clear. Heart and diaphragm normal. Then to the tailor in Bubbling Well Rd. for a fitting.

Wednesday, October 6, 1948—In the morning for a medical checkup at the U.S. Consulate. Everything is going smoothly. Then a visit and long second breakfast at the Gerendasis. Duty: 11:00–19:00. In the evening to Erwin Schlesinger to prepare a Lodge quiz.

Sunday, October 10, 1948—Free. Beautiful weather. In the morning, go by bicycle with Thea to Pappi's grave. At 1:00 o'clock back at the hotel. I have to go to a tea party (with vodka) at the

Maehrischels. Then to Trude Gelbard's birthday party at her parents' home. Around 1:00 very drunk home.

Tuesday, October 12, 1948—Duty: 7:30–12:30. Kol Nidre. Services stopped because of disturbance caused by Chinese coming too early to the cinema. In pouring rain, I hurry to Wayside Theatre where Hugo Alexander is leading the prayers, and continue praying there.

Wednesday, October 13, 1948—Yom Kippur. At 10:00 to the Eastern to chant Maftir Yonah. Pray till 18:04. Then to the Langers for Break the Fast.

Thursday, October 14, 1948—Duty: 6:30–12:30. Go home with throat ache. Find out that my temperature is over 100.4 degrees. Take sulfa pills and go to bed. *[This is the first time Fred mentioned taking sulfa. Perhaps he benefited from the sulfa Ed Diner brought to Jewish doctors from his ship. See p. 136.]*

Saturday, October 16, 1948—Free. Pick up Lilly from the office and go to the Chocolate Shop for lunch. One has to wait for a long time for service now, and because since August 19th price increases are not permitted, the food portions have become decidedly smaller.

Saturday, October 23, 1948—Duty 7:30–16:30. Then to the Austrian Center where the Lodge has an afternoon coffee with music, organized by Paul Weiss. Then to a Cultural Committee meeting. We plan "The Resurrection," a comedy by Felix Salten. *[Salten was an Austrian writer of witty comedies, as well as the book* Bambi.*]* Then to the Alexander parents.

Thursday, October 28, 1948—Duty: 7:30–13:30. At 2:30 go to the Langers to make some translations for the U. S. Consulate.

Tuesday, November 2, 1948—Duty: 7:30–12:30. With Thea eat a cold supper, just what I like. Then chat a while. *[In this conversation, he made it clear to Thea that he was going alone to the U. S.]*

Sunday, November 7, 1948—After breakfast go for a short bicycle ride in the city. Everywhere long lines of people in front of rice stores. Dress at home and go to Sun Ya with Mahler and Smith for a farewell party for Stahly. We eat and drink a great deal together.

Monday, November 8, 1948—Duty: 11:00–19:00. In the evening the police are taking a census of all the Chinese, and because of that nobody is allowed on the streets after 7:00 p.m.

Saturday, November 13, 1948—We have reached a difficult situation. The compulsory price control, which made all goods disappear from the market, has been lifted, and once again goods begin to appear, especially rice. To help in this serious food supply situation, the official exchange rate has been raised from GY4 *[yuan]* to 20. Martial Law has been proclaimed and an 11:00 o'clock curfew imposed. So, of course, social life is completely out. "Nu, schoen!" *[How nice!]*.

Tuesday, November 16, 1948—Drive to the Lodge where the installation of officers will take place today. Among others, Harry Burstein also installed in office. In the evening, at the election of the Brothers, give a speech in English re "Peace and IOOF" that is repeatedly interrupted by applause.

Friday, November 19, 1948—Duty: 14:30–21:30. Prince Axel of East Asiatic Co. is giving a cocktail party for 300 people. Since Mahler is busy negotiating with the Labor Union, I quickly change into evening clothes and supervise the event. Also, drink a lot. *[His Royal Highness Prince Axel of Denmark was the Chairman of the Board of the East Asiatic Company, initially established in 1897 to operate ships between Copenhagen, Bangkok, and the Far East. Today EAC is a multinational company that produces processed meat, distributes industrial ingredients, and operates moving and relocation services in Asia.]*

Tuesday, November 23, 1948—Duty: 7:30–12:30. In preparation for my possibly hurried departure, take out suitcases and put them in order.

Sunday, November 28, 1948—Duty: 7:30–14:00. To the Kadoorie School. Dr. Kantorowski officiates at the wedding of Lilly and Karl Epstein. I am a witness to the marriage. Then by car to Café Louis. Sit with Karl and Lilly and the honored guests at one table.

Tuesday, November 30, 1948—Duty: 7:30–12:30. Thea comes over with her sister. I choose two evening dresses, which she orders for herself. Then to Peking Rd. where I buy a large suitcase. Go to a Cultural Committee meeting. Dr. Salomon bursts in with his wife and announces: "The Communists broke through!" However, this is incorrect. We slowly find out that the IRO is considering the evacuation of all DPs *[displaced persons]*, and two ships with 1,700 persons will leave for Palestine. I am now faced with the worry whether I can leave in time for the U.S.A., or whether I should let myself be evacuated in the meantime.

The IRO was founded in 1947 with headquarters in Geneva, Switzerland. In Shanghai, it became officially "the successor agency of UNRRA," the United Nations Relief and Rehabilitation Administration, which assisted Jewish refugees, as well as DPs and Chinese, in very troubled times.

In the autumn of 1948, the IRO was overwhelmed by the number of people desperate to flee from China. They arrived in Shanghai from Tientsin, Harbin, and other Chinese cities pleading for IRO help. Among those trying to escape Mao Tse-tung's advancing armies were thousands of White Russians terrified of Communist retaliation. The I.R.O. negotiated a sanctuary for them and other stateless people in the island of Tubabao (Philippines). The face of Shanghai changed once again as the foreign population declined sharply and Chinese refugees from the provinces thronged the streets. Caught up in the dread of being trapped, Fred frantically pursued his objective to leave Shanghai without delay.

> **Wednesday, December 1, 1948**—Duty: 11:00–19:00. Speak to Laura Mayer. She says the consulate will make a decision on Friday regarding the collective affidavit.
>
> **Friday, December 3, 1948**—Can't find my bicycle in the Arcade *[the Cathay Hotel Arcade]*. Assume it has been stolen.
>
> **Wednesday, December 8, 1948**—Duty: 11:00–18:00. Get a cable from Charlie in San Francisco *[probably telling Fred he could stay with him and Kay upon arrival in the U.S.]*.
>
> **Thursday, December 9, 1948**—Duty: 7:30–12:30. In view of the heavy workload facing the IRO in preparation of the evacuation of 1772 refugees to Palestine, I spontaneously write a letter to IRO Director Jennings Wong offering to help on a voluntary basis. After that, get a letter from Shanghai IRO Director, G. Finchlay Andrew. Today I get a call to go there around noon. Am very well received and start work immediately with the help of two secretaries. At 6:00, eat together with all the secretaries. Then back to the hotel, send Charlie a telegram. To the Lodge. After the meeting, give a lecture to the Brothers and Sisters: "2,000 Miles through China's Interior." *[Such travelogs became a specialty of Fred's in later life. He often gave lectures on Jewish history that were illustrated by slides taken by Audrey on their overseas trips.]*

Even as he worked each day for the IRO, Fred continued in his regular job as receptionist at the hotel. His writings about his IRO experiences capture the excitement and turmoil that accompanied the almost daily departure of hundreds of refugees.

Sunday, December 12, 1948—Picked up by the IRO people. Go together to the Kadoorie School where we begin the distribution of the ship tickets. Then back to the hotel. Duty: 12:00–16:00. Then to Hongkew for the theatre rehearsal.

Tuesday, December 14, 1948—Duty: 7:30–12:30. After lunch, to the IRO. Distribution of tickets. Then pick up Vati Alexander and take him to the American Consulate. He cannot get a visitor's visa.

Hugo Alexander, Ted's father, fell under the Polish quota. (He had come from the province of Posen, which was given to Poland under the Versailles Treaty following World War I.) Because the Polish quota was very small and filled rapidly, he and his wife Kaethe, anxious to leave Shanghai before the Communists took over, decided to return to Germany and wait there until their number came up. They were housed in Föhrenwald, one of the largest DP camps in the American zone, and were finally able to enter the U.S. after Congress passed a bill in 1948 allowing 400,000 DPs into the country. Nearly 80,000 of these DPs were Jewish.

Similarly, Gerti's parents, the Langers, went to Montreal to await their quota number. Dr. Langer fell under the Romanian quota, although the Austrian town where he was born, Chernowitz, became Romanian long after he had left.

[At the American Consulate] I don't get a satisfactory answer regarding my own matters. So I go back to the IRO and telephone Consul Hannah, who assures me that I will be contacted in the near future.

Thursday, December 16, 1948—Duty: 7:30–12:00. Then work at the IRO till 4:30. Then to the Lodge. After the meeting, performance of the "Resurrection" of Felix Salter by the Cultural Committee.

Friday, December 17, 1948—In the morning, to the IRO Duty: 14:30–21:30. By taxi to Hongkew. Today Laura Mayer calls me to say that I have an appointment for fingerprinting at the U.S. Consulate on January 7.

Monday, December 20, 1948—At the IRO from 8:30–12:00. Then duty: 12:00–18:00. In the evening, Haas gives a farewell party at my place for Frosty and me.

Wednesday, December 22, 1948—At 8:30 to the IRO. Get

news that the Wooster Victory has laid anchor at the Hongkew and Shanghai Wharf. In pouring rain, ride the Cheesebox to the wharf. After completing all the administrative requirements, visit the ship. At 1:00 back to the IRO. Then duty: 13:00–17:00. Go with Thea to the ship. Dinner (with Chianti) on board. Then to the J.R.C. where a farewell dance is taking place. At 12:00 go down to the office to prepare the books for tomorrow. Outside, on the street it is not at all quiet. Full of police and people who, in spite of the curfew, want to withdraw money from government banks. Police with clubs charge into the people and I watch the unrest for a very long time.

Thursday, December 23, 1948—Duty: 7:30–12:40. Then, at once, to the Hongkew and Shanghai Wharf, where the boarding of the ship is taking place. I work very hard for the I.R.O. till 6:00 o'clock.

Friday, December 24, 1948—The Wooster Victory is due to sail at 8:00. I am the last visitor to leave the ship. Then to the I.R.O. office. Have breakfast and work. Then to the hotel. Duty: 12:00–18:00.

Sunday, December 26, 1948—To the IRO. Then with Thea to Chanukah eve services. Few people there because of pouring rain. Afterward, we go to a birthday party for Lieschen *[Sammy's wife]* at the Marcuses. First I light *[the candles]* and we sing "Maoz Tzur" *["Rock of Ages," a Chanukah song]*. Then a big dinner, lots of drinks and dancing.

Monday, December 27, 1948—In the morning to the I.R.O. Receive the news that the Castel Bianco is arriving on Wednesday and advise the staff who are still on holiday that the lists must be prepared. *[The ship was actually delayed, and did not arrive until Thursday.]* Lunch at the hotel. Duty: 12:00–19:00. Supper at the Alexanders. Then to the PALAMT *[a committee that arranged immigration to Palestine]*. Work at the I.R.O. till 10:45.

Tuesday, December 28, 1948—Duty: 7:30–12:30. To the I.R.O. Worked till 8:45 in the evening. Then to the typists for the preparation of the Passengers' Manifest of the Castel Bianco.

Thursday, December 30, 1948—Duty: 7:30–12:30. Then to the I.R.O. Get information that the Castel Bianco will arrive at 2:00. Go by weapons carrier to Hongkew and Shanghai Wharf. Have to wait 2 hours in pouring rain till the ship finally comes and anchors. I go on board and sit together with the Chief Purser to discuss the embarkation of passengers on the ship. Half an hour later we begin to receive the first passengers. I sit by the Chief Purser and do practically all the assignments of passengers. By 7:30 we have disposed of the first half of the passengers on the list and stop our work.

The Chief Paymaster asks us to come to his office where he sticks a microphone into my hand and orders me to make some announcements in German. I am fascinated as I hear my voice echoing throughout the entire ship. Then we eat in the officers' mess and drink Chianti. I get an idea, which I carry out. While the passengers eat their first meal on board ship, I make a short, calming, encouraging speech, which is greeted by applause (for the invisible speaker). Then I announce through the microphone that the distribution of hand-carried luggage will be completed by midnight.

All the while I drink a big quantity of Chianti. Go to sleep in an empty dormitory. Because of all the wine, cannot rest quietly, so I get up and check the guards at the gangways.

Friday, December 31, 1948—After a restless night in unfamiliar surroundings, rise at 5:30. At 7:00 to the passengers' breakfast after a short announcement on the microphone. Then from 8:00–1:00 register the rest of the passengers. At 2:00 return exhausted to the hotel, shave, and go on duty from 14:30–21:30.

Saturday, January 1, 1949—At midnight we clink champagne glasses and the dancing, eating, drinking, and flirting start. This goes on till 6:30 in the morning. An IRO car comes to take us home.

The passing of another year was observed once again in the usual long and lively manner. But, for Fred, this New Year's Eve was unlike any other. After nearly ten years, his time in Shanghai was nearing its end. The boy of 15 who had fled Nazi Europe and came by boat to China in 1939 was now a man of nearly 25. The Fred of 1949 was a mature, self-assured individual, well read and self-educated. He had proven himself successful in a job steadily held since October 1945. He was a leader among his friends, as well as in his Lodge, and his recent performance as an IRO employee was exemplary. He—as well as the other refugees in his age group—knew that Shanghai had prepared them to succeed in life, whatever obstacles they faced. He was ready to leave behind his harrowing past and move on as soon as possible to a new phase as an American citizen.

28

The Frenzied Last Month

During the frantic days of his last month in Shanghai, Fred flew from one activity to another—completing the usual hotel duty, continuing his work for IRO, packing all his belongings, finalizing the myriad details related to his departure, enjoying last visits to friends, and attending several farewell parties that were given for him. Thea was also making preparations to leave Shanghai, which added to the hectic pace. Characteristically, amidst all of this turmoil, Fred still found time to go to the occasional movie, as well as to plays, lectures, and Lodge meetings. Although only a short time remained before his departure, he even accepted a new appointment from his Lodge.

> **Monday, January 3, 1949**—Morning at the IRO. (Since December 18 have been awaiting Actual Employment Status, and am *[now]* getting paid for my work.) Then duty: 12:00–21:00. In between go to the Alexanders for supper.
>
> **Thursday, January 6, 1949**—Duty: 7:30–12:30. Then till 4:30 at the IRO. Then go to the Lodge. Appointed First Assistant to the U.M. *[Übermeister]*. After the meeting hold a "Quiz" with Erwin Schlesinger, which pleases the Lodge very much. Then short visit to Thea. (Today get IRO Travel Document.)
>
> **Friday, January 7, 1949**—To U.S. Consulate for fingerprints.
>
> **Saturday, January 8, 1949**—8:30–16:30 at the IRO. Then home. Thea there. Am really excited because I may get the post of Escort Officer at the IRO. Evening: Hongkew. First to the shirtmaker and then to the parents. Nice evening.
>
> **Monday, January 10, 1949**—In the morning: IRO Then duty: 12:00–18:00. With Thea, who has received her first O.K. from the U.S. Consulate, to the Roxy to see "The Search." Then take her straight home since she suffers from frostbite and can hardly walk. *[This condition was caused by chilblains, as there were holes in Thea's shoes. In the winter, her hands were also afflicted because she had no gloves.*

Mrs. Schwartz, Trude Gelbard's mother, who was like an aunt to her, eventually knitted mittens for Thea.]

Tuesday, January 11, 1949—Duty: 7:30–12:30. Then to the IRO. Work there until 6:30. Then in a weapons carrier to the CMSN wharf on the French Bund, to pick up 10 Russian refugees from Hongkew and take them to the French barracks on Rte. Frelupt to await the delayed arrival of an evacuation ship which was to take them to Tubabao, Philippines.

Thursday, January 13, 1949—Duty: 7:30–12:00. Then to the IRO ship Hwa Lien that is sailing to the Philippines. Work till 4:30, then home. After supper to Hongkew for some chores, then to the Lodge. After the meeting, a lecture by Dr. Cohn. Numbers, stars, and other occult things. After that a short visit to Thea.

The SS *Hwa Lien* sailed to Shanghai in January 1949 to evacuate some 500 passengers. Six thousand refugees from Shanghai lived in the Tubabao camp in the Philippines from 1949 to 1951 under very difficult conditions. Eventually, 3,000 of them emigrated to the U.S. Subsequently, a large group was permitted to enter Australia and, later, smaller groups were sent to countries in South America. A limited number received visas to France.

Friday, January 14, 1949—Morning: IRO. Lunch at the hotel. Then rest a little. At 3:30 to the *[U.S.]* Consulate. Get an immigration visa after being sworn in. Then to the hotel. Duty 16:00–21:00.

Monday, January 17, 1949—Morning: IRO. By jeep to the Russian Emigrants' Association, then to the Lunghwa Airport. Sent back an IRO flight to Guiuan at 1:00 o'clock.

Evacuated U.S. forces had left surplus military equipment in the city of Guiuan which was connected with a bridge to Tubabao. In 1949, some 50 Russians, led by a Russian engineer were flown from Shanghai to Guiuan to prepare a camp for Russian refugees and to keep an eye on the unsupervised U.S. equipment. An abandoned wooden church was eventually turned into a Russian Orthodox church.

Thursday, January 20, 1949—Duty: 7:30–13:00. Then to the IRO. Book passsage provisionally for February 13th on the U.S. Lines. Go to the fire station to get confirmation for the time I served as a volunteer.

Monday, January 24, 1949—Morning at the IRO. Duty at the hotel: 14:30–21:00. Am worried about the entire situation. Call the U.S. Line and book for February 13 on the Liberty ship Joplin Victory. Then go to Mahler *[the General Manager of Cathay Hotels, Ltd.]* and give him notice. He promises me to do his utmost to get me a settlement from the firm.

January 24 was the first time Fred expressed his grave concern about the political situation, and with good reason. The decisive Huai Hai Campaign of the Communists against the Nationalists that ended on January 10, 1949, just two weeks before, was the second most significant victory for the Communists (the first was the Liaoshen Campaign, beginning on September 12, 1948, during which they routed the Nationalists in Manchuria). The strategic Huai Hai Campaign, in which more than half a million Nationalist troops were defeated by the Peoples Liberation Army, was fought and won in the northern Jiangsu province on the east coast of China. The victory provided the Communists access to cross the Yangtze and conquer Nanking in April of 1949. (Among the leaders of this campaign was Deng Xiaoping, then secretary of the General Front Committee, and later the individual most responsible for the opening up of China.) The third consecutive triumph for the Communists, the Pingjin Campaign, was raging at the time of the following diary entry, and just six days later resulted in the Communist conquest of northern China, including Peking, which they took without a fight on January 31. These three campaigns are called in China the Great Decisive Wars.

Now that a complete Communist victory was inevitable, Fred hurriedly changed his departure date from February 13 to February 3. *[He actually sailed on February 6.]*

The SS *Joplin Victory* on which Fred sailed to San Francisco was one of 534 Victory ships, cargo ships that were mass produced quickly in North American shipyards during World War II. These ships, a refinement of the Liberty ships, were designed to be slightly larger, stronger, and faster in order to carry more supplies and to outmaneuver German submarines. There were 2,710 Liberty ships produced and 534 Victory ships. The SS *Joplin Victory* later saw service in the Korean War.

Wednesday, January 26, 1949—After breakfast at Jimmy's, go to the IRO. Take a jeep and drive to the Mansions to Negri *[Lipsmann's successor as manager of the hotel]*. Get my testimonial and whiskey. Then to U.S. Lines. Clarify some details. Back to the IRO. Eat there. Hotel. To Dr. Weitzmann, to take care of my teeth. *[Seppi had left Shanghai some time before on the* Capt. Marcos *to Palestine. It appears that Missie did not accompany her husband and that they*

were either divorced in Shanghai or at some point afterward.] Then duty:
14:30–21:00. Get the compensation (equivalent of 200.).

The testimonial to which Fred referred was dated January 26, 1949,
and signed by the manager of the Cathay Mansions. It certified that Fred
was employed as assistant manager from 1945 to 1947 when he was
transferred to the Cathay Hotel. The letter states, "we have found him to
be a very capable man, with a reputation for efficiency, honesty and hard
work. He rendered us a valuable service by his efficient handling of his
Dept. We do not hesitate in recommending him highly to anyone requiring
his services." This reference, along with one from his old friend Harry
Burstein, who was still Manager of the Metropole Hotel, and another from
1st Lt. Robert C. Walker of the U. S. Army Forces in Shanghai, Mess and
Billeting Officer, Cathay Mansions, were treasured by Fred as mementos
of his achievements in his first real job and kept among his records. His
membership card from the IOOF Lodge, stamped when he left Shanghai,
was also retained with those letters. *[The stamp certifies that F.W. Marcus is
leaving the Lodge on February 2, 1949 due to his departure from Shanghai. It also
says, "It gives us great pleasure to record his good standing, and we heartily recommend
him to our Brothers abroad."]*

Thursday, January 27, 1949—Duty: 7:30–14:30. To the
AJJDC *[American Jewish Joint Distribution Committee]*. Pay for the
U.S. Lines passage. Then to the IRO. Before that buy some gifts
for *[people in]* the U.S. and go to the Quarantine Service regarding
vaccination book. After finishing with IRO go to Laura Mayer's
office regarding the Alexanders. Thea just got a fingerprinting appointment for tomorrow morning. Take it along and give it to her.
Visit the Langers and Alexanders.

Saturday, January 29, 1949—Did some pre-packing. Visit
Missie Gerandasi. Duty: 14:30–21:00. Mahler comes down around
8:00, so that I can leave earlier. By taxi with Thea to the Marcuses
where I am giving myself a farewell party. *[The next afternoon, Thea
came over and she and Fred worked a long time on his papers. On the following day, he completed the few remaining procedures necessary for emigration
and served his last duty at the hotel.]*

Tuesday, February 1, 1949—Visit the doctor appointed by
U.S. Lines and complete other formalities. Max comes over in
the afternoon and we pack the big trunk together. In the evening
Trude and Thea come over.

Shanghai, Wednesday, February 2, 1949—In the morning

to the IRO. Farewell visit. *[When he left his service with IRO, Fred was given another splendid recommendation, this time from Jennings Wong, the Chief of IRO in the Far East. "Mr. Marcus has had considerable experience with IRO," Wong wrote, "especially with the operational details of mass movements. He has always been most hardworking and conscientious, and has shown considerable initiative and understanding in his work."]* Go in the Cheesebox to Hongkew for some errands. To Hongkew for farewell party at Maehrischels'. Then to the Lodge. Festive farewell from Brothers and Sisters, for U.M. Weiner, Rosen, and me. Of course, say a few words. Finally, after that a "Bunter Abend" *[a jolly—literally, colorful—evening]*.

Shanghai, Thursday, February 3, 1949—Do some errands in the morning and in the afternoon. Also some farewell visits. Then to the Capitol to see "St. Francis of Assissi." Thea comes in the evening and we go to the Metropole for supper.

Shanghai, Friday, February 4, 1949—In the morning, farewell visit to Pappi's grave. Then with IRO car to Hongkew and Shanghai Wharf. Board the General Gordon on which Thea is sailing for the U.S. Then for coffee to Dr. Salomon's. To services at the Broadway. Then visit the Langers and Alexanders and for supper to the Marcuses. Say good-bye and back home at 10:00.

It is hard to imagine that Fred slept that night as he prepared to bid farewell to Shanghai the next morning. Doubtless, he spent a good part of the night looking back at the last ten years—the hard times he had experienced, the good times after the war, the close friends he had made, the strange city that had become his home—and looking ahead to the unknown new life that was in store for him.

PART III:

HOME AT LAST

29

The Golden Gate

On the day he embarked for the U.S., a new life had begun for Fred. Significantly, he made the switch from German to English in all future diary entries. He continued keeping a diary until August 21, 1955, when the entries abruptly stopped.

Shanghai, Saturday, February 5, 1949—In the morning pack with Max. A quick visit to the barber and then to the Customs Jetty for Baggage Examination. Max and Trude then go with me to the Nantao Wharf to board the SS Joplin Victory together with 8 other passengers. Due to good connections, get a three-bed cabin which I share with only one American (Scott Randall). The others sleep 6 to a cabin. Since we are given the chance to go back on land, I take the opportunity to have supper with the Marcuses in Hongkew. Great joy. Max and Trude also come along. We drink a whole bottle of rum, then return by taxi to the ship and go to sleep.

Aboard the SS Joplin Victory, Shanghai, Sunday, February 6, 1949—Get up early to observe the departure at 6:20. Sail down the Whangpoo past the Bund, seeing the Cathay Hotel for the last time. Reach Woosung at 9:10 a.m. and drop anchor in the Yangtze to await Pilot and final quarantine inspection. Heave anchor at 10:00. Write a short letter to Thea and to cousin Charlie in San Francisco.

At last, Fred's longtime dream was about to come true, and he was on the way to his promised land, America. The voyage aboard the SS *Joplin Victory* was rough and uncomfortable, and he suffered from seasickness for much of the trip. When he finally reappeared in the dining room after a several day hiatus, the captain greeted him and teasingly said, "Welcome back, Mr. Marcus. We thought you had gotten off!"

Aboard the SS Joplin Victory, Sunday, February 6, 1949— Reach the open sea about 12:00 noon. Lay down after lunch. Sea is quite choppy and the boat, with very little cargo, starts to roll heavily. Get up at dinnertime, but cannot eat anything. Feeling quite bad, lay down early, read a little and sleep.

Aboard the SS Joplin Victory, Monday, February 7, 1949— Sleep late. Boat still rolling heavily, but feeling a little better. Have only some fruit for lunch. However, during the afternoon we reach the Japanese Coast and the sea becomes calmer. Have a full dinner. At 8 p.m. to bed.

Aboard the SS Joplin Victory, Tuesday, February 8, 1949—Up at 7:30. Breakfast. Reach Kobe at 11:00 a.m. After a long wait am finally able to go ashore with a few fellow passengers. Two hours through the quiet streets, looking half-heartedly for debauchery. Have a cup of coffee in a "teahouse," then return to the ship, which is discharging cotton bales. Am a little worried because boat will be even lighter after that unloading. Write and read a little, take a hot shower and go to bed.

Aboard the SS Joplin Victory, Wednesday, February 9, 1949—During the night still very noisy because of loading cargo and drinking of fellow passengers in the cabin near the hall. After breakfast go to town. Kobe consists at present mostly of small new buildings. The old big ones have been destroyed by bombing. The population seems very impoverished. All the stevedores and longshoremen who come aboard the ship ask especially for soap. Cannot help feeling a certain satisfaction to see all the former bullying Master Race of the Far East as a vanquished nation. Back to the boat for lunch and sleep after that. Have nice chat at dinner with Captain Johnson, our skipper. Cut loose at 7:30 and clear the Kobe Harbor at 18:45. Sea most calm. Go to mess and do some writing.

Aboard the SS Joplin Victory, Thursday, February 10, 1949—After quiet trip with a sudden hailstorm during the morning, reach Yokohama at 11:30 a.m. Finally secure passes and go ashore for dinner. Walk around a bit and go to the Seamen's Club where a boxing match between Japanese boxers is being held. Have a beer and return to the ship at 9:30 p.m.

Aboard the SS Joplin Victory, Friday, February 11, 1949— Go ashore after breakfast and take the electric elevated train to Tokyo. Along the elevated, small, recently constructed wooden houses did not conceal the debris of bombed out industrial establishments. During lunchtime we find a nice place where we have

sukiyaki and afterward go shopping and stroll down the Ginza.
Take the elevated back to Yokohama and reach the boat by 5 p.m.
Play a little poker after dinner and go to bed early. *[As noted previously, the firebombing of Tokyo by 300 B-29s on March 9–10, 1945, left enormous destruction. Although by 1949 some reconstruction had taken place in Tokyo, much rubble could still be seen.]*

Aboard SS Joplin Victory, Saturday, February 12, 1949—
Ship lifts anchor and leaves Yokohama at 6 a.m. I get up for
breakfast at 8 a.m. but feel very bad and lay down again. From this
[time] until and including Tuesday February 15, 1949, stay in bed
and get up animal-like only from time to time to get an orange or
an apple. Physically very weak and psychologically downhearted,
wishing for the voyage to be over. Soon after Yokohama the boat
runs into storm which lasts more than two days and pushes the
ship around a lot, as it is practically empty. Cracking and subsequent leaking of one oil tank also brings added worries and fuss.
Advance clocks 30 minutes.

**Aboard the SS Joplin Victory, Wednesday, February 16,
1949**—Weather fine and feeling a little better. Get up for lunch
and dinner and do some writing in the evening. Hope to God
that weather will remain fine and trip smooth. Advance clocks 30
minutes.

**Aboard the SS Joplin Victory, Thursday, February 17,
1949**—Weather still fine, thank God. Feeling not too bad. Do lots
of reading. Pass Date Line at 13:30 hrs. and so will have another
Thursday tomorrow. Advance clocks 30 minutes. Play poker after
dinner.

Aboard the SS Joplin Victory, Friday, February 18, 1949—
Weather fine. Feeling quite good. Have emergency drill after
lunch. After dinner talk with crew and read. (The ship is an ideal
setting for a detective story. 8 passengers: 4 Americans, 1 Russian,
1 Russian Jew, 1 Austrian Jew and 1 German Jew.) Advance clocks
60 mins.

**Aboard the SS Joplin Victory, Saturday, February 19,
1949**—Sleep late. Sea very choppy. Rain and gale in the morning
but slowly clearing up during the afternoon. Feeling quite good.
After dinner play rummy. Advance clocks 1 hour.

**Aboard the SS Joplin Victory, Sunday, February 20,
1949**—Sleep very late. Shave in the afternoon. Sea very choppy

with great swell all day. Strong wind, and rain at night. Play poker after dinner. Advance clocks 1/2 hour.

Aboard the SS Joplin Victory, Monday, February 21, 1949— Up all night because of rough seas. Arise and have breakfast and then lay down until afternoon. Get up for dinner. After that play a little poker, read, and go to sleep early. Advance clocks 60 minutes. Sea still rough.

Aboard the SS Joplin Victory, Tuesday, February 22, 1949—Get up late after wonderful night's sleep. Prepare my clothes after lunch and read a bit. Big farewell dinner in the evening. After that get-together of passengers but I do not participate much, as I want to watch the entry into San Francisco sober. Weather report says heavy fog in S.F. Bay. After 9 p.m. we run into heavy fog and make spine tingling entry into port through the Golden Gate which is hardly visible at all. Drop anchor about midnight and go to bed, read until 2:30 p.m. Before falling asleep go on deck again and find to my surprise that the fog has lifted. Catch my first glimpse of San Francisco lights. Another passenger standing next to me puts his hand on my arm and says, "Fred, we're home."

San Francisco, Wednesday, February 23, 1949—Boat docks at Pier 45 at 8 a.m. Capt. McBride of the Pacific Star East Lines receives me, assists me through Customs and Immigration, and brings me in his car to Charlie's office.

As his ten-year sojourn in China came to an end, Fred Marcus was once again a refugee. But this time he was not greeted by chanting workmen. There were no rickshaws or whistles of Sikh policemen, no odors of garbage or whiffs of opium. This time, there was true hope for a young man in search of peace and freedom and wholeness. At last, he would be in charge of his own future in a country that he had loved and admired from afar. Indeed, he was truly home.

Epilogue:
Return to the Past

Written by Fred Marcus in October 1983

It was as if we had never been there! More than 20,000 people vanished without a trace!

This was my immediate reaction as Audrey and I stood at the entrance to the former Shanghai ghetto. (In my hands was the old Shanghai map that was reprinted last year in the *Hongkew Chronicle*. This helped us greatly in our exploration by foot and by car of what was once my home for almost ten years.)

I had told the driver to park on Ward Road, just across from the Ward Road Jail, which served as our landmark. (Crowds of people surged toward the huge gate as several police busses carried prisoners from their trials to their incarceration.) On our side of the street, I searched in vain for vestiges of the Ward Road Heim, a first residence for so many of us. It was an exercise in futility and, darting in and out of lanes and entrances, I became more and more frustrated. It seemed impossible that the old brick buildings should have disappeared or been hidden away behind other structures.

When we came to the Chusan Road, things looked a little more familiar, although today this one block thoroughfare is an outdoor street market with vendors' stalls filling the entire block. (Prior to emerging on Wayside Road, we took pictures of buildings where friends and relatives of mine had lived. But I still felt uncertain that we were in the right place.) It all looked so different, so run-down, so ramshackle, so overcrowded. Only the Wayside Theatre and the Broadway Cinema offered assurance that indeed this was the old neighborhood. I pointed to the roof garden of the Wayside Theatre, "Up there I had my first dates and spent many a pleasant summer evening dancing under the stars."

We returned to the car and drove along Ward Road. Again I marveled how much the area seemed to have changed. With the help of the map—there was not a single English sign—I finally found Baikal Road, and we stopped so that our interpreter could ask directions of an elderly man. Then we came upon a big iron gate. Our driver honked, the gate opened, and we drove into a small, charming park surrounded by a wall. Two women, who seemed to be the caretakers, spoke to our interpreter who translated for us: "They say there are still a few tombs here." My heart began to pound. We followed the two women past playing children and old men doing their Tai Chi exercises to the wall at the far end of the little park. I kept searching for tombstones—no sign. But then they pointed to three large white stone slabs flat in the ground. The inscriptions had disappeared or been removed, but by their size I knew I had found the Baikal Road Cemetery. Yes, I had found it. *[Unfortunately, despite two attempts to do so, in 1983 and again in 1996, Fred was never able to find the Columbia Road Cemetery where his father was buried.]*

We headed straight for the place where I had worked and lived until my day of departure, the Cathay Hotel—now Peace Hotel. We entered the lobby and my heart sank. What was once the art deco bar with its subdued lighting had been changed into a conglomeration of gift shops and souvenir stalls. The reception office wall had been broken through to enlarge the office, and the area was filled by a milling multitude. We fled down the hall to the Tower elevators and I felt reassured by the clock face floor indicators above the doors. They at least moved in their accustomed rounds. We ascended to the Tower nightclub and its surrounding public rooms. Though faded, they still reflected their former glory. We walked down the stairs to a guestroom door. Gloom and grime. But signs of refurbishing, too, as whole rooms were being torn apart and redone.

We left the hotel and found the synagogue on the Museum Road, now a printing shop. I located my favorite neighborhood movie house on the banks of the Soochow Creek. Crossing the bridge, I remembered Japanese soldiers hassling young Chinese women at night about their vaccinations. I pointed out the Post Office, the General Post Office, and Broadway Mansions to Audrey.

We came to Tiendong Road and I found the house in which I had lived with my Dad after we left the Heim *[in 2006, the house was no longer there, and the location was a construction site]*. I still have a photo of it. The house and the memories were still there, and I felt close to my father, who eventually died in Shanghai. I shivered in the morning drizzle, for the sun had not yet come out. "Let's head for Broadway Mansions," I said, "I think we can get some coffee there."

Along the way, we found a little girl playing in the street. Out came the Polaroid camera. By the time the first picture developed in my hand, the child's brother and mother and aunt and cousins and grandmother had appeared. And by the time the second picture emerged, we were surrounded by a good natured, rapidly increasing crowd. Everyone was pointing to the tips of their noses, asking to have their picture taken, too. At last, I returned the camera to its case and we began to make our way out of the crowd. *"Nahkuning"* (foreigners), I heard one onlooker say to another. *"Meikuning"*—Americans," I responded instantly, for I wanted our country to get credit for the friendly cultural exchange which had just taken place!

The ambience at Broadway Mansions was similar to that of the Cathay Hotel. Electronic games, pinball machines, and neon signs graced the lobby. In the bar, we ordered what turned out to be the best coffee we had in over three weeks in the People's Republic.

After a few minutes, I said, "I think I am going to have a good cry."

"I've been waiting for it," responded Audrey.

I was glad the place was so dark. And then I began to process the overwhelming feelings that my first return to this city of refuge had triggered. The fear and loneliness, the anxiety and anger so carefully repressed in the past began to emerge into my consciousness. And I realized that the high point of the entire trip had just occurred. It was the moment when, in that Chinese crowd, I responded intuitively with *"Meikuning."* When I was last in Shanghai, I was a stateless refugee, without an address, without a sense of belonging, and feeling like a driven leaf upon the face of the earth. On this day, to stand on that street and call out "I am an American!" was a wonderful and momentous experience, one that made my whole life's journey worthwhile.

Postscript:
The American Years

When he stepped onto the dock at San Francisco in 1949, Fred Marcus left his refugee experience behind him. He was filled with great determination to make good as a citizen of a country with which he could fully identify.

Fred's first job was as a receptionist at the Huntington Hotel in San Francisco, and eventually he was promoted to Assistant Manager. Nevertheless, Jewish education remained foremost in his mind, and he worked part-time as director of education in a number of area religious schools. In 1964, one of these schools, Temple Emanu-El in San Jose, wooed him away from the hotel business to become their full-time Jewish educator. Remarkably, at the same time, he earned an undergraduate college degree, and then a Masters Degree in Jewish Education from the Rhea Hirsch School of Education at Hebrew Union College-Jewish Institute of Religion in Los Angeles. In 1980, his talents, perseverance, and hard work were fully recognized by his colleagues, and he was elected President of the National Association of Temple Educators. Throughout, Fred devoted his free time to giving frequent talks to school children, teachers, and church and synagogue groups about growing up in Nazi Germany and his refugee experience in Shanghai. He never encouraged hatred, but rather urged reconciliation. At the same time, he encouraged his listeners never to forget the Holocaust.

Fred's marriage to Lucille Rosenbloom—with whom he had a daughter, Vivian, and a son, David—ended in divorce. Happily, his second marriage to Jewish educator Audrey Friedman Marcus in 1974 was a union marked by deep love and enduring friendship. He became as devoted a father to Audrey's children as he was to his own, and later an affectionate and caring grandfather to their nine grandchildren. A tenth grandchild was born a year after Fred's death.

After retiring from Jewish education in 1981, Fred began a new career as a travel consultant in Denver, Colorado. He and Audrey led groups on many trips and together visited 103 countries. They went frequently to Germany and twice to Shanghai, enabling Fred to reconnect with the experiences of his youth. For the next 20 years, he became an inspiring and beloved teacher of adults at Temple Sinai. In 2002, on a final trip to Germany, he suffered a fourth heart attack and died in a Bavarian hospital. A few days before his death, he murmured: "I feel like a prisoner in Germany for a second time."

In a heartrending eulogy at Fred's funeral, his grandson Josh Fixler, then 17 years old, said:

> He taught me that there is no greater joy in life than learning and no greater gift in life than teaching. My grandfather studied every day. He continually read about his world, studying current events, art, and history. He didn't stop there. He taught everyone he could. He taught me that those who can, do, and those who want to do more, teach. He shared with us his knowledge and experience in a way that pushed and inspired us all. He taught with a passion and enthusiasm that lit up rooms and minds, and people of all ages are better people because of his lessons.
>
> When I learn, I will remember him . . .
>
> When I teach, I will remember him . . .

Bibliography

Agel, Jerome, and Eugene Boe. *Deliverance in Shanghai*. New York: Dembner Books, 1983.

All about Shanghai: Shanghai and Environs. Shanghai: University Press, 1944–45.

Armbrüster, Georg; Michael Kohlstruck; and Sonja Mühlberger. *Exil Shanghai 1938–1947: Jüdisches Leben in der Emigration*. Teetz, Germany: Hentrich & Hentrich, 2000. (Includes CD with list of refugees)

Bacon, Ursula. *Shanghai Diary*. Milwaukee, Wis.: M Press, 2004.

Beevor, Antony, and Luba Vinogradova, eds. and trans. *A Writer at War: Vassily Grossman with the Red Army 1941–1945*. New York: Pantheon Books, 2005.

Ben-Eliezer, Judith. *Shanghai Lost, Jerusalem Regained*. Jerusalem: Steinmatzky, 1985.

Bird, George E. *Hangchow Holidays: Where to Go and What to See*. Shanghai: Millington: 1948.

Boatner, Mark M., III. *The Biographical Dictionary of World War II*. Novato, Calif.: Presidio Press, 1996.

Bradley, James. *Flyboys: A True Story of Courage*. New York: Little Brown, 2006.

Brailovsky, David. *A Covenant in Shanghai*. San Jose: Calif.: iUniverse, 2000.

Caldwell, Bo. *The Distant Land of My Father*. New York: Harcourt, 2001.

Candlin, Enid Saunders. *Breach in the Wall: A Memoir of the Old China*. New York: Paragon House, 1987.

Chang, Jung, and Jon Halliday. *Mao: The Unknown Story*. New York: Alfred A. Knopf, 2005.

Cohen, Joseph. "The Chronology of the Jews of Shanghai from 1832 to the Present Day." Available at: http://jewsofchina.org/JewsOfChina/communities/chronology_item.asp?cid=1049&iid=12962.

Cohn, Hans. *Risen from the Ashes: Tales of a Musical Messenger*. Lanham, Maryland: Hamilton Books, 2006.

Cope, Elisabeth W. "Displaced Europeans in Shanghai." *Far Eastern Survey*, Vol. 17, No. 23 (December 8, 1948), pp. 274–276.

Cornwall, Claudia. *Letter from Vienna: A Daughter Uncovers Her Family's Jewish Past*. Vancouver: Douglas & McIntyre, 1995. (Grades 10–12)

Crow, Carl. *Handbook for China (including Hong Kong) With Ten Maps and Plans*. Hong Kong: Kelley & Walsh, 1933.

Dicker, Herman. *Wanderers and Settlers in the Far East: A Century of Jewish Life in China and Japan*. New York: Twayne, 1962.

Dien, Albert E., ed. *Occasional Papers of the Sino-Judaic Institute, Vol. II*. Menlo Park, Calif.: Sinao-Judaic Institute, 1996.

Dong, Stella. *Shanghai 1842–1949: The Rise and Fall of a Decadent City*. New York: William Morrow, 2000.

Edoin, Hoito. *The Night Tokyo Burned.* New York: St. Martin's Press, 1987.

Eisfelder, Horst "Peter." *Chinese Exile: My Years in Shanghai and Nanking.* Bergenfield, N.J.: Avotaynu, 2004.

Emigranten Addressbuch. Shanghai: The New Star, 1939. (Republished by Old China Hand Press, Hong Kong, 1995.)

Falbaum, Berl, compiler and editor. *Shanghai Remembered: Stories of Jews Who Escaped to Shanghai from Nazi Europe.* Royal Oak, Mich.: Momentum Books, 2005.

Finnane, Antonia. *Far from Where? Jewish Journeys from Shanghai to Australia.* Victoria, Australia: Melbourne University Press, 1999.

Flying Tigers' Guide to Shanghai. Shanghai: Flying Tigers, 1945. www.earenshaw.com/shanghai-ed-india/tales/t-tigers.htm.

Friedrichs, Theodore. *Berlin Shanghai New York.* Nashville, Tenn.: Cold Tree Press, 2007.

Ganther, Heinz. *Drei Jahre: Immigration in Shanghai.* Shanghai: Modern Times Publishing House, 1942.

Ginsbourg, Anna. *Shanghai: City of Refuge.* Shanghai: The China Weekly Review, 1940.

Goldstein, Jonathan, ed. *The Jews of China: Volumes I and II.* Armonk, N.Y.: M. E. Sharpe, 2000.

Grebenshikoff, I. Betty. *Once My Name Was Sarah.* Ventnor, N.J.: Original Seven, 1993.

Gross, Miriam. *An Oral History of the Shanghai Jewish Community: A Thesis Presented to The Division of History and Social Sciences, Reed College.* May 1991. Unpublished.

Guang, Pan, editor and compiler. *The Jews in China.* China Intercontinental Press, 2001.

———, Editor in Chief. *The Jews in Shanghai.* Shanghai: Shanghai Pictorial Publishing House, 1995.

Headley, Hennelore Heinemann. *Blond China Doll: A Shanghai Interlude 1939–1953.* St. Catharines, Ontario: Blond China Doll Enterprises, 2004.

Henriot, Christian. *Prostitution and Sexuality in Shanghai: A Social History, 1849–1949.* Cambridge, U.K.: Cambridge University Press, 2001.

Heppner, Ernest G. *Shanghai Refuge: A Memoir of the World War II Jewish Ghetto.* Lincoln, Neb.: University of Nebraska Press, 1993.

Hertzman, Elchonon Yosef. *Escape to Shanghai.* Chaim U. Lipschitz, trans. New York: Maznaim Publishing, 1981.

Hillis, Lory. *Japan's Military Masters: The Army in Japan's Military Life.* New York: Viking Press, 1943.

Hochstadt, Steve. *Shanghai-Geschichten: Die Jüdische Flucht nach China.* Teetz, Germany: Hentrich & Hentrich, 2007.

Jackson, Beverley. *Shanghai Girl Gets All Dressed Up.* Berkeley, Calif.: Ten Speed Press, 2005.

Jackson, Stanley. *The Sassoons.* New York: E.P. Dutton, 1963.

Jacob, Ellis. *The Shanghai I Knew: A Foreign Native in Pre-Revolutionary China.* Margate, N.J.: ComteQ Publishing, 2007.

Johnston, Tess. *Frenchtown Shanghai: Western Architecture in Shanghai's Old French Conces-sion.* Hong Kong: Old China Hand Press, 2000.

———. *A Last Look: Western Architecture in China's Old Summer Resorts.* Hong Kong: Old China Hand Press, 1993. (Photos by Deke Ehr)

———. *Near to Heaven: Western Architecture in China's Old Summer Resorts.* Hong Kong: Old China Hand Press, 1994. (Photos by Deke Ehr)

Kaplan, Vivian Jeanette. *Ten Green Bottles: Vienna To Shanghai—Journey of Fear and Hope.* Toronto: Robin Brass Studio, 2002.

Kipen, Israel. *A Life to Live.* Burwood, Victoria, Australia: Chandos Publishing, 1989.

Kluge Scheel, Erna. *The Strength to Persevere.* Long Beach, N.C.: Self-published, 1988.

Kohn, Peter. *Rachel's Chance.* Hawthorn, Australia: Hudson, 1987.

Kranzler, David. *Japanese, Nazis & Jews: The Jewish Refugee Community of Shanghai, 1938–1945.* New York: KTAV Publishing House, 1971.

———. *Jewish Refugee Community of Shanghai 1938–1949.* Monograph Series XLVI. Sankt Augustin, Germany: Monumenta Serica Institute and China Zentrum, 2000.

Krasno, Rena. *Strangers Always: A Jewish Family in Wartime Shanghai.* Berkeley, Calif.: Pacific View Press, 1992.

———. *That Last Glorious Summer 1939: Shanghai Japan.* Hong Kong: Old China Hand Press, 2001.

Laqueur, Walter. *The Holocaust Encyclopedia.* New Haven and London: Yale University Press, 2001.

Leslie, Donald Daniel. *Jews and Judaism in Traditional China: A Comprehensive Bibli-ography.* Monumenta Serica Monograph Series 44. Sankt Augustin, Germany: Monumenta Serica Institute, 1998.

———. *The Survival of the Chinese Jews.* Leiden: E. J. Brill, 1972.

Liberman, Yaakov. *My China: Jewish Life in the Orient 1900–1950.* Berkeley, Calif.: Judah L. Magnes Museum; Jerusalem: Gefen, 1998.

Lipschutz, Chaim U. *The Shanghai Connection.* New York: Maznaim, 1988.

Malek, Roman, ed. *From Kaifeng . . . to Shanghai: Jews in China.* Monumenta Serica Monograph Series XLVI. Sankt Augustin, Germany: Monumenta Serica Institute and China Zentrum, 2000.

Markarian, Yervand. *Kavkaz.* Seal Beach, Calif.: Self-published, 1996. (Available from amazon.com)

Messmer, Matthias. *China: Schauplätze West–Östlicher Begegnungen.* Wien, Köln, Weimar: Böhlau Verlag, 2007.

Meyer, Maisie. *From the Rivers of Babylon to the Whangpoo: A Century of Sephardic Jewish Life in Shanghai.* Washington, D.C.: University Press of America, 2003.

Mühlberger, Sonja. *Geboren in Shanghai als Kind von Emigranten: Leben und Überleben im Ghetto von Hongkew (1938–1947).* Teetz, Berlin, Germany: Hentrich & Hen-trich, 2006.

North, Oliver, with Joe Musser. *War Stories II: Heroism in the Pacific*. Washington, D.C.: Regnery, 2004.

Pan Ling. *In Search of Old Shanghai*. Hong Kong: Joint Publishing (HK), 1982.

Patent, Gregory. *Shanghai Passage*. New York: Clarion Books, 1990. (Grades 4–7)

Piccigallo, Philip R. *The Japanese on Trial: Allied War Crimes Operations in the East, 1945–1951*. Austin, Tex.: University of Texas Press, 1979.

Pollack, Michael. *Mandarins, Jews and Missionaries*. New York: Weatherhill, 1988.

Powell, John B. *My Twenty-five Years in China*. New York: Macmillan, 1945.

Ristaino, Marcia Reynders. *Port of Last Resort: The Diaspora Communities of Shanghai*. Stanford, Calif.: Stanford University Press, 2004.

Ross, James R. *Escape to Shanghai: A Jewish Community in China*. New York: The Free Press, 1994.

Roth, Cecil, and Geoffrey Wigoder. *The New Standard Jewish Encyclopedia*. New York: Doubleday, 1970.

Rubin, Evelyn Pike. *Ghetto Shanghai*. New York: Shengold, 1993.

Ruby, Lois. *Shanghai Shadows*. New York: Holiday House, 2006. (Grades 6–9)

Sakamoto, Pamela Rotner. *Japanese Diplomats and Jewish Refugees: A World War II Dilemma*. Westport, Ct.: Praeger, 1998.

Sergeant, Harriet. *Shanghai*. London: John Murray, 1991.

Spunt, Georges. *A Place in Time*. New York: G.P. Putnam's Sons, 1958.

Staff of the *Mainichi Daily News*. *Fifty Years of Light and Dark: The Hirohita Era*. Tokyo: The Mainichi Newspapers, 1975.

The Story of a Haven: The Jews in Shanghai. Catalogue Listing, The Jewish Museum of Australia, 26 Alma Road, St. Kilda 3182, Australia.

Thorbecke, Ellen. *Shanghai*. Shanghai: North China Daily News & Herald, n.d.

Tobias, Sigmund. *Strange Haven: A Jewish Childhood in Wartime Shanghai*. Urbana, Ill.: University of Illinois Press, 1999.

Tokayer, Marvin, and Mary Swartz. *The Fugu Plan: The Untold Story of the Japanese and the Jews during World War II*. New York: Paddington, 1979.

Tubabao Russian Refugee Camp: Philippines 1949–1951. Sydney, Australia: Russian Historical Society in Australia, November 1999.

Unschuld, Paul U. *Ärtze aus Deutschland und Oesterreich in der Emigration in Shanghai, zwischen 1934 und 1945. From Kaifeng . . . to Shanghai: Jews in China*. Monumenta Serica Monograph Series XLVI. Sankt Augustin, Germany: Monumenta Serica Institute and China Zentrum, 2000.

Wakeman, Frederic Jr. *The Shanghai Badlands: Wartime Terrorism and Urban Crime, 1937–1941*. Cambridge, U.K.: Cambridge University Press, 2002.

Warhaftig, Zorach. *Refugee and Survivor: Rescue Efforts during the Holocaust*. Jerusalem: Yad Vashem, 1988. (Grade 12)

Wasserstein, Bernard. *Secret War in Shanghai*. Boston, Mass.: Houghton Mifflin, 1999.

Wheal, Elizabeth-Anne; Stephan Pope; and James Taylor. *Encyclopedia of the Second World War*. New York: Castle, 1969.

White, Theodore H. *China: The Roots of Madness.* New York: Bantam, 1968.

Yehezkel-Shaked, Ezra. *Jews, Opium and the Kimono: The Story of the Jews in the Far-East.* Jerusalem: Rubin Mass, 2003.

Newspapers

North China Daily News. Shanghai, November 28, 1941.

Our Life (Nasha Jhizn, Russian, *Unser Leben,* Yiddish*).* Shanghai, 1944.

Gelbe Post Ostasiatische Halbmonatschrift. Shanghai, 1939.

Shanghai Jewish Chronicle. Shanghai, 1943.

Films

Another Time ... Another Moses. 25 min. n.d. Oakton Community College, 1600 Golf Rd., Des Plaines, IL 60016.

Empire of the Sun. 154 min. 1987. Available at video stores.

Escape to the Rising Sun. 95 min. 1990. National Jewish Center for Jewish Film, www.brandeis.edu/jewishfilm.

Exil Shanghai. 4 hrs., 35 min. 1996. Ulrike Ottinger Filmproduktion, Fichtestrasse 34, 10967 Berlin, Germany, office@ulrikeottinger.com.

The Last Refuge: The Story of Jewish Refugees in Shanghai. 50 min. 2004. Ergo: Jewish Video Catalog, 877-539-4748, info@jewishvideo.com.

Legendary Sin Cities: Shanghai. 2005. 90 min. Toronto: Paradigm Pictures Corporation, 416-927-7404, or www.amazon.com.

The Lost Children of Berlin. 1997. 50 min. USC Shoah Foundation. Institute for Visual History and Education. View at www.jewishtelevision.com or obtain while available from amazon.com.

A Place to Save Your Life. 52 min. Filmakers Library, 212-808-4980, info@filmakers.com.

Port of Last Resort. 79 min. 1998. National Center for Jewish Film, Brandeis University, www.brandeis.edu/jewishfilm.

Round Eyes in the Middle Kingdom. 52 min. 1996–97. First Run Features/Icarus Films, New York, N.Y., www. frif.com/new79/round_eye.html.

Shanghai Ghetto. 95 min. 2002. Rebel Films, ww.shanghaighetto.com.

Miscellaneous

Diaries of Fred Marcus, translated from German by Rena Krasno, 1944–1949.

Diaries and material collected by Rena Krasno in Shanghai, 1931–1945.

Hoover Institution Archives China Collection:

    Rena Krasno Collection

    Ben Levaco Collection

    Sino-Judaic Institute Collection

    George Spunt Collection

"Jews of Shanghai." Audiotape of report by Susan Stamberg on *All Things Considered* on National Public Radio, September 17 and 18, 1990. New York Public

Library, Dorot Jewish Division.

Letters dated May 11, 1947 and June 6, 1947 from Fred Marcus to Henry Meyer in California.

Marcus, Fred. Unpublished autobiography, 1986.

Oral Histories: Abraham and Ruth Zalcgendler; Henry Politzer; Howard Levin; Kurt Pollack, Max Kopstein, and Gerhardt Heiman; W. Michael Blumenthal. Audiotapes of interviews conducted in 1989 by Susan Stamberg for "Jews of Shanghai." New York Public Library, Dorot Jewish Division.

Personal Papers of D. B. Rabinovich, Honorary Secretary of Shanghai Ashkenazi Jewish Community.

Index